A HISTORY OF THE NORMAN KINGS (1066-1125)
with the *Historia Novella* or history of his own times (1126-1142)

translated by John Sharp

edited by Joseph Stevenson

Reprinted in facsimile 2000
LLANERCH PUBLISHERS
Felinfach.

Note: a facsimile of the title
page of the first edition from
which this work has been taken,
is included for the information
of the reader.

THE CHURCH HISTORIANS
OF ENGLAND.

VOL. III.—PART I.

<small>CONTAINING</small>

THE HISTORY OF THE KINGS OF ENGLAND,
AND OF HIS OWN TIMES,
BY WILLIAM OF MALMESBURY,

TRANSLATED (A.D. 1815) FROM THE LATIN BY THE REV. JOHN SHARPE, B.A.
RECTOR OF CASTLE EATON, WILTSHIRE.

REVISED AND ADAPTED
TO THE TEXT OF THE ENGLISH HISTORICAL SOCIETY, (A.D. 1840,)
WITH NOTES,

BY THE REV. JOSEPH STEVENSON, M.A.
OF UNIVERSITY COLLEGE, DURHAM:
VICAR OF LEIGHTON BUZZARD.

 Seeleys,
FLEET STREET AND HANOVER STREET.
MDCCCLIV.

PREFACE TO WILLIAM OF MALMESBURY.

§ 1. ALTHOUGH universal suffrage[1] has assigned the highest rank amongst the English Historians to William of Malmesbury, yet there are few of our writers concerning whose personal history we have such scanty information. The particulars respecting him which have descended to our times, are, for the most part, gleaned from his own writings, and these notices are fragmentary and unimportant. We learn, indeed, from himself, that one of his parents was of Norman[2] descent, the other of English; but as to their names, residence, and position in society, we know nothing. We are equally ignorant as to the time and place of his birth; but if we may venture to adopt a statement advanced by some biographers,[3] we shall rank him among the natives of the county of Somerset. The love of knowledge which was so conspicuous in his later years, exhibited itself at an early period of his life, and he has preserved an account[4] of the occupations and the studies of his boyhood in a passage of sufficient importance to be inserted entire.

§ 2. "A long period has elapsed since, as well through the care of my parents as by my own industry, I became familiar with books. This pleasure possessed me from my childhood; this source of delight has grown with my years; indeed, I was so instructed by my father, that had I turned aside from these to other pursuits, I should have considered it as jeopardy to my soul, and discredit to my character. Mindful, therefore, of the adage, 'Covet what is necessary,' I constrained my early age to desire eagerly that which it was disgraceful not to desire. I gave, indeed, my attention to various branches of literature, but in different degrees. Logic, for instance, which gives arms to eloquence, I contented myself with barely hearing; medicine, which ministers to the health of the body, I studied with somewhat more of attention; but having

---

[1] Saville, speaking of the historians contained in the volume which he edited, thus expresses himself—"Inter quos cum et narrationis fide et judicii maturitate principem locum teneat Guilielmus Malmesburiensis, homo, ut erant illa tempora, literate doctus, qui septigentorum plus minus annorum res tanta fide ac diligentiâ pertexuit, ut e nostris prope solus historici munus explêsse videatur, hunc . . . e tenebris eruendum . . . curavi." So also Baronius, A.D. 1027, § 2, (classing him, unfortunately, with Ingulfus,) . . . "qui sicut cœteris antiquitate, ita et veritate cum auctoritate præstantes, res Anglorum sunt prosecuti." The Magdeburg Centuriators, sec. xii. cap. 109, are equally laudatory.

[2] See Preface to Book III. p. 217, and another passage to the same effect, p. 216.

[3] Cave, Hist. Litter. ii. 215; Oudin, Comment. de Scripp. Eccl. ii. 1088; Wharton, Angl. Sacr. ii. pref. § 1.

[4] See p. 82.

scrupulously examined the several branches of ethics, I bow down to its majesty, because it spontaneously unveils itself to those who study it, and directs their minds to moral practice ; history more especially, which, by a certain agreeable recapitulation of past events, excites its readers, by example, to frame their lives to the pursuit of good, or to aversion from evil. When, therefore, at my own personal expense, I had procured some historians of foreign nations, I proceeded, during my domestic leisure, to inquire if anything concerning our own country could be found worthy of handing down to posterity. Hence it arose that, not content with the writings of ancient times, I began myself to compose ; not, indeed, in order to display my learning, which is comparatively nothing, but to bring to light events lying concealed in the confused mass of antiquity. In consequence, rejecting vague opinions, I have studiously sought for chronicles, far and near, though I confess I have scarcely profited anything by this industry ; for, perusing them all, I still remain poor in information, though I carried out my researches as long as I could find anything to read."

§ 3. The period to which this extract relates,—the period of anarchy which followed upon the Norman invasion, was one which made the seclusion of a cloister the only safe refuge for a youth of such a disposition as that described above : and we need feel no surprise at discovering the future historian of England an inmate of the Benedictine establishment of Malmesbury. Here, while he devoted himself to the discharge of his more immediate duties, he found leisure for the prosecution of his self-imposed studies. These were directed partly to theology, but chiefly to history, general, local, and biographical ; and the list of his writings preserved by Tanner, Cave, and others, evinces the zeal and the industry of his pen.[1]

§ 4. Of these, the most important is the narrative contained in the present volume, which may be divided into two portions,—" The History of the Kings of England," and its continuation, " The History of his Own Times." The second of these was probably one of the latest works upon which Malmesbury was employed, and he appears to have occupied himself in revising, correcting, and improving it as long as he lived. The former division, " The History of the Kings of England," embraces a chronicle from the earliest period of our authentic history, (for the critical bias of his mind induced Malmesbury to reject the British traditions,) to the year one thou-

---

[1] Scarcely any additional information is to be gathered respecting our historian, save the facts that he filled the office of Librarian in his own monastery (see p. 381) ; that in this capacity he was employed in collecting books, and visited Canterbury, Bury St. Edmunds, and other places, for this purpose, (Hardy, preface, p. vii., quoting Gale, iii. 298, 376) ; that he was appointed the precentor to the monks of Malmesbury, (Leland, ap. Tanner, Bibl. p. 359,) and might have succeeded to the dignity of abbot in the same wealthy establishment, had not he resigned his claims in favour of his competitor, abbot John, who was elected in A.D. 1140, and died in the same year. This last circumstance rests upon the authority of an extract made by Leland, (ap. Tanner, p. 359,) who quotes for it the Itinerarium of Malmesbury, a work now unfortunately lost. Trifling, in one sense, as these facts are, they are valuable in another ; for they tend to throw some light upon the occupations and character of the individual respecting whom we are interested.

sand one hundred and twenty, shortly after which date it appears to have been finished.   So far, however, from regarding the work as perfect, he requests[1] that such of his readers as possessed information with which he was unacquainted, would communicate their knowledge to him while he was yet alive, in order that such events might appear at least in the margin of his history, as did not occur in the body of the text itself.   This appeal seems to have led to numerous alterations, some few of which are important, while the greater number merely affect the style, in the polishing of which Malmesbury has proved himself exceedingly solicitous.

§ 5. The " Historia Novella," or as I have ventured to paraphrase the title, " The History of his Own Times," embraces that period of English history which intervened between the death of Henry the First (A. D. 1135) and the year one thousand one hundred and forty-two.   It ends in a manner somewhat abrupt, which leads to the inference that it does not fully represent the latest intentions of the author, and that a more extended narrative was in contemplation, if not in active progress, when his labours were interrupted by death ;[2] and at the same time the variations which occur in the different copies—variations which have evidently proceeded from the hand of the author[3]—prove that upon this portion of his work, also, Malmesbury's busy pen was employed, until the latest moment, in minute alterations and corrections.

§ 6. Malmesbury was sufficiently well acquainted with the remains of classical antiquity to understand the distinction between a chronicle and a history;[4] and he aimed at the production of a work which should be honoured with the latter designation.   This ambition has been attended with results which we cannot but regret, for it has induced him to pass by, as trivial and undignified, many circumstances, to us of exceeding value, and with which he must have been acquainted ; circumstances which probably would have found a place in the pages of the less aspiring chronicler.   More than this, his proposed imitation of classical antiquity has too often given an artificial and constrained tone to his narrative of events which occurred within the range of his own observation.   We have to lament—what was to him a cause of self-gratulation—that he has so liberally " seasoned his crude materials with Roman salt." What between his theory and his mode of working it out, we are too often defrauded of information with which we should have been thankful to have been made acquainted, and the result is frequently disappointment and regret.

§ 7. All this, however, is said without the remotest wish to detract from the acknowledged merits of our author as an historian. Taking him at his own stand-point, and judging of his work according to his own abstract estimate of perfection, we cannot but assign to it a high grade of intrinsic excellence.   He is cautious

[1] See p. 83.
[2] When Malmesbury died is uncertain.   The " Historia Novella " must have been written between A.D. 1142, with which year it concludes, and 1147, in which year the earl died. Dugd. Monast. i. 155 ; Baron. i. 535.
[3] Several of the more important of these are pointed out in the notes to this edition.   [4] See pp. 4, 5.

how he accepts evidence, calm in the judgment which he pronounces upon disputed questions, and dispassionate when he arbitrates between conflicting interests. His prejudices are generally subservient to his reason. His honest and manly independence of sentiment secures him against the temptation of lending himself either to advocate the theories of a class, or to excuse the errors of an individual, how closely soever he may have been identified with the interests of one, or the passions of the other.[1]

§ 8. The work contained in this volume professes to supply the blank which its writer had observed in our national annals, between the death of its sole historian Beda and his own time. The earlier books are founded upon works still extant, Beda, the Saxon Chronicle, Ethelwerd, Asser, and some few others. Malmesbury sometimes refers to materials of a more ephemeral character, such as popular songs and traditions;[2] but it is only in a few instances, and those of no great importance, that he makes any substantive addition to our stock of historical knowledge during the Saxon dominion. As it advances nearer his own times, his narrative increases in importance, and his history of the Norman kings is of the highest value.

§ 9. Two editions only of this work are extant. In the year one thousand five hundred and ninety-six the learned Sir Henry Saville included it in the volume to which he gave the title, " Rerum Anglicarum Scriptores post Bedam præcipui," which was reprinted at Frankfort in the year one thousand six hundred and one. For all critical purposes Saville's edition is valueless. He has adopted as the basis of his text a family of manuscripts—for the edition is apparently an eclectic one—of secondary authority, and he has inserted into it various additions and alterations, which, from the absence of any mark of distinction, tend only to perplex and confuse the reader.

§ 10. In this unsatisfactory state the text was suffered to continue until the year one thousand eight hundred and forty, when an edition[3] appeared under the auspices of the English Historical Society, and of which the preparation was entrusted to Mr. Hardy, of the Record Office in the Tower. Of this edition it is enough to say, that it is worthy of the editor whose name it bears. The text is reconstructed upon a careful examination of more than seventeen manuscripts, the chief variations of which are recorded; the chronology (respecting which Malmesbury is generally careless, and frequently erroneous) is settled; and a valuable body of notes has been appended. The execution of the whole is such as to leave little to be desired; and the chief merit of the present edition is, that it represents, in a more popularized form, the results of Mr. Hardy's labours.

§ 11. The manuscripts upon which the text of this edition,

---

[1] See pp. 5, 42, 83, 341, 380, 381, 404, 408, &c.
[2] See pp. 122, 130, 262.
[3] " Willelmi Malmesbiriensis monachi Gesta Regum Anglorum, atque Historia Novella; ad fidem codicum manuscriptorum recensuit Thomas Duffus Hardy. Londini, sumptibus Societatis, 1840."

published by the English Historical Society, is based, are as follows:—

A. 1. The Harleian MS. 261, in the British Museum. It is a folio volume, written upon vellum, formerly belonging to the cathedral church of Rochester,[1] to the library in the cloister of which it had been given by Alexander the precentor.

A. 2. The Cottonian MS. Claudius C. ix., in the British Museum; in folio, written upon vellum, in the thirteenth century.

A. 3. A manuscript in the collection of Sir Thomas Phillipps, No. 2777.

C. 1. The Royal MS. 13 B. xix., in the British Museum, written on vellum, in folio, early in the thirteenth century. In the year 1650 it belonged to John Theyer.

C. 2. The Harleian MS. 447, in the British Museum, in folio, written upon vellum, in the thirteenth century, formerly belonging to the monastery of Bury St. Edmunds.[2]

D. 1. The Royal MS. 13 D. v., in the British Museum, a manuscript written upon vellum, of a large folio size, formerly belonging to the monastery of St. Albans.[3]

D. 2. The Royal MS. 13 B. xvii., in the British Museum, a transcript of the seventeenth century, in folio, upon paper, formerly belonging to the collections of the lords Arundel and Lumley.

E. 1. The Royal MS. 13 D. xi., upon vellum, in folio, written in the twelfth century, formerly belonging to the monastery of Margan.[4]

E. 2. A manuscript in the possession of Sir Thomas Phillipps, No. 8239.

F. A manuscript in the library of All Souls College, at Oxford, No. 33, written upon vellum, in folio, towards the end of the twelfth century, by one Ivo.[5]

G. The Laud MS. 548, in the Bodleian Library, written towards the end of the twelfth century, upon vellum, in small folio.

---

[1] It contains two memoranda respecting its former history. The first states it to be the "Liber de claustro Roffensi, Alexandri p'cē;" the second, "Liber S. Andreæ Apostoli de Rouecestria." No list of the precentors of Rochester being extant, we are unable to fix the date of the gift.

[2] "Liber Sancti Ædmundi regis et martyris, C. 49."

[3] At fol. 37 b, occurs the following memorandum—"Hic est liber qui per quorumdam negligentiam fuerat deperditus; sed per industriam venerabilis nostri in Christo patris et domini, domini Johannis abbatis sexti, huic monasterio erat restitutus, et assignatus librariæ conventus." This is apparently the John de Hartford, whose election to the abbot's dignity, in the year 1235, was attended with so much difficulty, and which is detailed with so much minuteness · by M. Paris, in his Vitæ Abbatum S. Albani, p. 136, seq.

[4] At the end occurs the following inscription—"Liber monachorum S. Mariæ de Margan." At the bottom of the last page, in a hand later than that of the text, we read—"Hic deficit prosecutio historiæ, quæ promittitur in volumine sequenti."

[5] It ends in the middle of § 445.* The transcriber's name is indicated in the following lines, which follow in the MS.:—

"Scripserit hunc librum quis, lector forte requiret;
Exacuat sensus, et metra legat, cito discet.
Illius nomen tria componunt elementa,
In numeris quorum primum satis indicat unum,
Ponunt et leges numeri pro quinque secundum,
Si Græcus scribat postremo colligo finem."

It was formerly known by the references Laud F. 37, and is No. 1377 in Bernard's General Catalogue.

H. The Hatton MS. 54, in the Bodleian Library [formerly 47], written in quarto, upon vellum, in the fourteenth century. It formerly belonged to John de Whytefeld,[1] monk of Rochester.

K. The Bodley MS. 712, [formerly Sup. Art. D. 20, and Arch. F. 20, No. 2619 in Bernard's General Catalogue,] apparently once the property of Roger Saville, but written for Robert de Wiville, bishop of Salisbury, (A.D. 1330—1375,) whose arms occur more than once in this fine manuscript.

L. 1. The Arundel MS. 35, in the British Museum, written in folio, upon vellum, in the twelfth century, ending, imperfectly, in the middle of § 411, the manuscript being imperfect.

L. 2. The MS. 14, in Trinity College Library, at Cambridge, written upon vellum, in the thirteenth century.

M. The Arundel MS. 161, in the British Museum, in folio, upon vellum, of the thirteenth century ; an exact transcript of the Royal MS. 13 D. v. [*D.*] described above.

Hardy states that, in addition to these manuscripts, several other copies preserved at Oxford, at Cambridge, in the British Museum, and in the library of Sir Thomas Phillipps, were consulted by him in the formation of his text ; but that, as they appear to have been taken from some exemplar of one or other of the MS. above-mentioned, he did not think it necessary to refer to them.

§ 12. The manuscript which has been adopted by the editor of the edition issued by the English Historical Society, is that furnished by the Royal MS. 13 D. ii., mentioned above [*E.*] Preference was given to the text contained in that magnificent copy for several reasons. Not only is there a strong antecedent prejudice in its favour, from the circumstance of it having formerly belonged to the abbey of Margan, founded by Robert[2] earl of Gloucester, the nobleman to whom Malmesbury dedicates this work— but further, a careful examination and comparison with other manuscripts, proved as well the general accuracy of the text, as also that it contained the latest corrections of the author.

§ 13. It has already been remarked (§ 4) that Malmesbury employed himself in the improvement of his History long after the first edition of it (if we may be allowed the term) had been put into circulation ; and so assiduously was the system persevered in, that it is not easy to find two copies (with the exception of the Royal MS. 13 D. v. and Arundel 161) the readings of which exactly correspond. These variations, it is true, sink into comparative insignificance, in consequence of the existence of the Margan copy (§ 12), which represents the latest corrections of the author ; still they are not without their interest, and it would be instructive could we succeed in establishing the sequence of these different revisions of the text. Hardy (preface, p. xxii.) believes " that traces may be found of at least four distinct classes of copies of the ' Gesta Regum Anglorum,' and two of the ' Historia Novella.'

---

[1] " Liber Johannis de Whytefeld, monachi de Rouccestria."
[2] See Dugd. Monast. i. 477.

We have to regret that he has not furnished us with the reasons which led him to this conclusion, or stated under which of these four heads he would have respectively classed the many manuscripts which he has collated for his Various Readings; and this the more especially as he had investigated [1] the matter with much patience, and his intimate acquaintance with the various copies of our author (the result of his accurate collation of their several texts) would have invested his remarks with great authority.

§ 14. It is from this text, then, that the translation is made which is contained in our series of Ecclesiastical Historians. It is fundamentally the English version published in the year one thousand eight hundred and fifteen, by the Rev. John Sharpe—the merits of which have been long and generally recognised—but so corrected and extended as to represent the improved text published by Mr. Hardy in one thousand eight hundred and forty. The notes of that later edition have been freely used in the preparation of this; and much of the value of my labours (such as it is) arises from this circumstance. I have not hesitated, however, to make such omissions, alterations and additions, as to me appeared necessary, for the sake of securing uniformity with the rest of our series; and in so doing I have made myself responsible for the whole.

The Proprietors of this series of English Church Historians beg to offer their thanks to the Rev. John Sharpe, B.A., Rector of Castle Eaton, Wiltshire, and to Thomas Duffus Hardy, Esq., Assistant Keeper of Her Majesty's Records, for permission to make free use of their respective editions of William of Malmesbury.

---

[1] He writes thus, Preface, p. ix.—"An examination of every point connected with the subject has been made; but with anything beyond the mere result it seems unnecessary to burthen these remarks. That Malmesbury, after he had published his work, was in the constant habit of correcting it, is beyond doubt."

J. S.

Leighton Buzzard,
   19th September, 1854.

PREFACE TO BOOK III.

INCITED by different motives, both Normans and English have written of king William : the former have praised him to excess, alike extolling to the utmost his good and his bad actions ; while the latter, out of national hatred, have laden their conqueror with undeserved reproach. For my part, as the blood of each people flows in my veins, I shall steer a middle course; where I am certified of his good deeds, I shall openly proclaim them ; his bad conduct I shall touch upon lightly and sparingly, though not so as to conceal it; so that neither shall my narrative be condemned as false, nor will I brand that man with ignominious censure, almost the whole of whose actions may reasonably be excused, if not commended. Wherefore I shall willingly and carefully relate such particulars of him as may be matter of incitement to the indolent, of example to the enterprising, useful to the present age, and pleasing to posterity. But I shall spend little time in relating such things as are of service to no one, and which produce disgust in the reader, as well as ill-will to the author. There are always people, more than sufficient, ready to detract from the actions of the noble: my course of proceeding will be, to extenuate evil, as much as can be done consistently with the sacrifice of truth, and not to bestow excessive commendation even on good actions. For this moderation all true judges will, I imagine, esteem me neither timid nor unskilful. And this rule, too, my history will regard equally, with respect both to William and his two sons; that nothing shall be dwelt on too fondly, nothing untrue be admitted. The elder of these did little worthy of praise, if we except the early part of his reign ; gaining, throughout the whole of his life, the favour of the military at the expense of the people. The second, more obedient to his father than to his brother, possessed his spirit, unsubdued either by prosperity or adversity : on regarding his warlike expeditions, it is matter of doubt whether he was more cautious or more bold ; on contemplating their event, whether he was more fortunate or unsuccessful. There will be a time, however, when the reader may judge for himself. I am now about to begin my third volume ; and I think I have said enough to make him attentive, and disposed to be instructed ; his own feelings will persuade him to be candid.

THE THIRD BOOK OF WILLIAM OF MALMESBURY'S HISTORY OF THE KINGS OF ENGLAND.

BOOK III.

Of the Arrival of the Normans in England.

§ 229. ROBERT,[1] second son of Richard the Second, after he had, with great glory, held the duchy of Normandy for seven years, resolved on a pilgrimage to Jerusalem. He had at that time a son, seven

---

[1] Robert I. See § 178.

years of age, born of a concubine, whose beauty he had accidentally beheld, as she was dancing, and had become so smitten with it as to form a connexion with her; after which he loved her exclusively, and, for some time, regarded her as his wife. He had by her this boy, named after his great-great-grandfather, William, whose future glory was portended to his mother by a dream, wherein she imagined her intestines were stretched out, and extended over the whole of Normandy and England; and at the very moment, also, when the infant burst into life and touched the ground, he filled both hands with the rushes strewed upon the floor, firmly grasping what he had taken up. This prodigy was joyfully witnessed by the women gossiping on the occasion; and the midwife hailed the propitious omen, declaring that the boy would be a king.

§ 230. Every provision being made for the expedition to Jerusalem,[1] the chiefs were summoned to a council at Fescamp, where, at his father's command, all swore fidelity to William: earl Gilbert was appointed his guardian,[2] and the protection of the earl was assigned to Henry, king of France.[3] While Robert was prosecuting his journey, the Normans, each in his several station, united in common in defence of their country, and regarded their infant lord with great affection. This fidelity continued till the report of Robert's death,[4] which universally gaining ground, their affection changed with his fortune; and then they began severally to fortify their towns, to build castles, to carry in provisions, and to seek the earliest opportunities of revolting from the child.[5] In the meantime, however,—doubtless by the special aid of God, who had destined him to the sovereignty of such an extended empire,—he grew up uninjured; while Gilbert, almost alone, defended by arms what was just and right; the rest being occupied by the designs of their respective parties. But Gilbert being at this time killed by his cousin Radulph,[6] fire and slaughter raged on all sides. The country, formerly most flourishing, was now torn with intestine broils, and divided at the pleasure of the plunderers; so that it was justly entitled to complain, "Woe to the land whose king is a child!"[7] William, however, as soon as his age permitted, receiving the badge of knighthood from the king of France, inspirited the inhabitants to hope for quiet. The sower of dissension was one Guy, a Burgundian[8] on

---

[1] Robert's expedition to Jerusalem was in 1035. (Bouq. xi. 420.)

[2] Ordericus Vitalis tells us that young William was placed under the care of his relative Alan, earl of Brittany; but Malmesbury here alludes to Gilbert earl of Ou. See Guil. Gemet. vi. 2, p. 649, ed. Camd.

[3] Henry I. succeeded to the throne of France in 1031.

[4] He died at Nice in Bithynia on his return from Palestine. A narrative of his expedition may be seen in Michaud's History of the Crusades, i. 27, 28, ed. 1852.   [5] See Guil. Pict. pp. 179, 180.

[6] "Gilbert, earl of Ou (son of earl Godfrey), the sagacious and courageous guardian of his lord, the boy William, was, one morning, while riding and talking with his compeer, Wascelin de Pont Erchenfred, and suspecting no danger, slain, together with Fulko Fitz Geroh. This crime was committed at the treacherous instigation of Ralph de Waco, son of the archbishop Robert, by the cruel hands of Odo le Gros and Robert Fitz Geroh."—(William of Jumiéges, vi. 2.)

[7] Eccles. x. 16.

[8] This Guy,-count of Brienne and Vernon, was the son of Raynald, carl of Burgundy, by Alice, daughter of Richard II. duke of Normandy. See Brady's Hist. Engl. i. 186.

his father's side, and grandson to Richard the Second by his daughter. William and Guy had passed their childhood together, and were at that time equally approaching to manhood. Mutual intercourse had produced an intimacy between them which had ripened into friendship. Moreover, thinking, as they were related, that he ought to deny him nothing, he had given him the castles of Brienne and Vernon. The Burgundian,[1] unmindful of this, estranged himself from the earl, feigning sufficient cause of offence to colour his conduct. It would be tedious and useless to relate what actions were performed on either side, what castles were taken; for his perfidy had found abettors in Nigell viscount of Coutances, Ralph viscount of Bayeux,[2] and Haimo Dentatus,[3] grandfather of Robert, who was the occupier of many estates in England in our time. With these persons, this most daring plunderer, allured by vain expectation of succeeding to the earldom, was devastating the whole of Normandy. A sense of duty, however, compelled the guardian-king to succour the desperate circumstances of his ward. Remembering, therefore, the kindness of his father, and that he had, by his influence, exalted him to the kingdom, he rushed on the revolters at Valdes Dunes :[4] many thousands of them were there slain, many drowned in the river Orne by its rapidity, while, being hard pressed, they spurred their horses to ford the current. Guy, escaping with difficulty, betook himself to Brienne; but driven thence by William, and unable to endure this disgrace, he retired, of his own accord, to Burgundy, his native soil. Here, too, his unquiet spirit found no rest; for being expelled thence by his brother William,[5] earl of that province, against whom he had conceived designs, it appears not what fate befel him. Nigell and Ralph were admitted to fealty; Haimo fell in the field of battle, whose remarkable daring is signalized in having unhorsed the king himself; in consequence of which he was slain by the surrounding guards; and in admiration of his valour, honourably buried at the king's command. King Henry received a compensation for this favour, when a Norman lord actively assisted him against Geoffrey Martel, at Herle-Moulin, which is a fortress in the country of Anjou; for William had now attained his manly vigour; an object of dread even to his elders, and though alone, a match for numbers. Unattended he would rush on danger; and when unaccompanied, or with only a few followers, charge into the thickest ranks of the enemy. By this expedition he gained a reputation for admirable bravery, as well as the sincerest regard of the king; so that, with parental affection, he would often admonish him not to hold life in contempt, by encountering danger so precipitately; a life which was the ornament of the French, the safeguard of the Normans, and an example to both.

§ 231. At that time Geoffrey was earl of Anjou, who had

[1] See Guil. Pict. pp. 179, 180.   [2] MS. Baiocensem.
[3] He was lord of Torigni in Normandy, and probably ancestor of the family of Duredent, or Duerden, settled in England.
[4] The editors of the collection of French Historians (Bouq. xi. 178) are unable to identify this locality ; but they fix the date of the battle as having occurred in 1047.   [5] William the First, duke of Burgundy, called Le Grand.

boastingly taken the surname of Martel,[1] as he seemed, by a certain kind of felicity, to beat down all his opponents. Finally, he had made captive, in open battle, his liege lord the earl of Poictou,[2] and loading him with chains, had compelled him to accept dishonourable terms of peace : namely, that he should yield up Bourdeaux and the neighbouring cities, and pay an annual tribute for the rest. But he, as it is thought, through the injuries of his confinement and want of food, was, after three days, released from eternal ignominy by a timely death.[3] Martel then, that his effrontery might be complete, married the stepmother of the deceased ; taking his brothers under his protection until they should be capable of governing the principality. Next entering the territories of Theobald, earl of Blois, he laid siege to the city of Tours ;[4] and while he was hastening to the succour of his subjects, made him participate in their afflictions; for being taken and shut up in prison, he ceded the city from himself and his heirs for ever. Who shall dare cry shame on this man's cowardice, who, for the enjoyment of a little longer life, defrauded his successors for ever of the dominion of so great a city? for although we are too apt to be severe judges of others, yet we must know that we should, possibly in like manner, consult our own safety if we were ever to be placed in similar circumstances. In this manner, Martel, insolent from the accession of so much power, obtained possession of the castle of Alençon, even from the earl of Normandy, its inhabitants being faithlessly disposed. Irritated at this outrage, William retaliated, and invested Danfront,[5] which at that time belonged to the earl of Anjou. Geoffrey, immediately, excited by the complaints of the besieged, hastily rushed forward with a countless force. Hearing of his approach, William sent Roger Montgomery[6] and William Fitz-Osbern[7] to reconnoitre. They, from the activity of youth, proceeding many miles in a short time, espied Martel on horseback, and apprised him of the dauntless boldness of their lord. Martel immediately began to rage, to threaten mightily what he would do, and said that he would come thither the next day, and show to the

[1] Geoffrey II. son of Fulco III. earl of Anjou, whom he succeeded A.D. 1040.

[2] William IV. earl of Poitiers, 1029—1038. See L'Art de Vérifier les Dates, ii. 355.

[3] The earl of Poitiers, having endured a captivity of about three years and a half, was redeemed by his wife Eustachie; but he survived his deliverance only three days.

[4] In the year 1044, Geoffrey Martel took captive earl Theobald of Tours, and made him surrender the city of Tours. See the Chron. S. Mich, in Peric. Maris. ; and also Chron. Andegave. apud Labbeum, Nov. Bibl. Libr. MSS. i. 257.

[5] See note in Bouquet, xi. 178.

[6] He was the son of Hugh de Montgomery and Jocelina his wife, daughter of Turolf of Pont-Audomare, by Weva, sister to Gunnora, great-grandmother to the Conqueror. He led the centre of the army at the battle of Hastings, and was afterwards governor of Normandy. William the Conqueror gave him the earldoms of Arundel and Shrewsbury. See more of him in Sir Henry Ellis's Introduction to Domesday, i. 479.

[7] William Fitz-Osbern de Crepon, dapifer of Normandy; he was related to the Conqueror, by whom, after the Conquest, he was created earl of Hereford. In the Domesday Book this nobleman is described as " Comes Willelmus." The particulars of his death, which happened abroad in the year 1071, are related by Ordericus Vitalis, p. 536, and by Malmesbury, § 256.

world at large how much an Angevin could excel a Norman in battle; at the same time, with unparalleled insolence, describing the colour of his horse, and the devices on the arms he meant to use. The Norman nobles, with equal vanity relating the same of William, returned and stimulated their party to the conflict. I have described these things minutely for the purpose of displaying the arrogance of Martel. On this occasion, however, he manifested none of his customary magnanimity, retreating without coming to battle; on hearing which, the inhabitants of Alençon surrendered, stipulating for personal safety; and afterwards those of Danfront also listed under the more fortunate standard.[1]

§ 232. In succeeding years, William, earl of Arques,[2] his illegitimate uncle, who had always been faithless and a turncoat from his first entrance on the duchy, rebelled against him; for, even during the siege of Danfront, he had unexpectedly stolen away, and had communicated to many persons his secret designs. In consequence of this, William had committed the custody of his castle to some persons whom he had erroneously deemed faithful; but the earl, with his usual skill in deception, had seduced even these people to his party by giving them much, and promising them more. Thus possessed of the fortress, he declared war against his lord. William, with his customary alacrity, contrary to the advice of his friends, laid siege to Arques, declaring publicly that the miscreants would not dare attempt anything if they came into his sight. Nor was his assertion false; for more than three hundred soldiers, who had gone out to plunder and forage, the instant they beheld him, though almost unattended, fled back into their fortifications. Being inclined to settle this business without bloodshed, he fortified a castle in front of Arques, and turned to matters of hostile operation which required deeper attention, because he was aware that the king of France, who had already become adverse to him, from some unknown cause, was hastening to the succour of the besieged; for with very laudable forbearance, though he certainly appeared to have the juster cause, yet he was reluctant to engage[3] with that person to whom he was bound both by oath and by obligation. He left some of his nobility, however, to repress the impetuosity of the king, who, falling into an ambush laid by their contrivance, had most deservedly to lament the loss of Isembard, earl of Ponthieu, who was killed in his sight, and Hugo Pardulf, who was taken prisoner. Not long after, in consequence of his misadventure, retiring to his beloved France, the earl of Arques, wasted with hunger and worn to a skeleton, consented to surrender, and was preserved life and limb, an example of clemency and a proof of perseverance. During the interval of this siege, the

---

[1] On this transaction compare the narrative of Guil. Pictav. p. 181.

[2] William, comte d'Arques, was son of Richard II. duke of Normandy, by his third wife, Papia. See William of Jumiéges, vii. 20, as to the rebellion mentioned by Malmesbury; and Guil. Pictav: pp. 182, 183.

[3] Upon these words the editors of the Rec. des Hist. de France remark, " For William, before he engaged in war with king Henry, ought to have renounced his homage and fealty; a thing which he might well have done on account of the king's bad behaviour."

people of the fortress called Moulin becoming disaffected, at the instigation of one Walter, went over to the king's side. An active party of soldiers was placed there under the command of Guy, brother of the earl of Poictou, who diligently attended for some time to his military duties; but on hearing the report of the victory at Arques, he stole away into France, and contributed by this means considerably to the glory of the duke.

§ 233. King Henry, however, did not give indulgence to inactivity : but, muttering that his armies had been a laughing-stock to William, immediately collected all his forces, and dividing them into two bodies, he overran the whole of Normandy.[1] He himself headed all the military power which came from that part of Celtic Gaul which lies between the rivers Garonne and Seine; and gave his brother Odo[2] the command over such as came from that part of Belgic Gaul which is situated between the Rhine and the Seine. In like manner William divided his army with all the skill he possessed, approaching by degrees the camp of the king, which was pitched in the neighbourhood of Evreux, in such a manner as neither to come to close engagement, nor yet suffer the province to be devastated in his presence. His generals were Robert, earl of Auch, Hugo de Gournay, Hugo de Montfort, and William Crispin, who opposed Odo at a town called Mortemer.[3] Nor did the other, relying on the numerous army which he commanded, at all delay coming to action; yet making only slight resistance at the beginning, and afterwards being unable to withstand the attack of the Normans, he retreated, and was himself the first to fly: and there, while Guy, earl of Ponthieu, was anxiously endeavouring to revenge his brother, he was made captive, and felt, together with many others of surpassing affluence and rank, the weight of that hand which was so fatal to his family. When William was informed of this success by messengers, he took care that it should be proclaimed in the dead of night near the king's tent; on hearing which he retired, after some days spent in Normandy, into France; and soon after, ambassadors passing between them, it was concluded by treaty that the king's partizans should be set at liberty, and that the earl should become legally possessed of all that had been, or should hereafter be, taken from Martel.

§ 234. It would be both tedious and useless to relate their perpetual contentions, or how William always came off conqueror. What shall we say besides, when, through magnanimity, despising the custom of modern times, he never condescended to attack him suddenly, or without acquainting him of the day. Moreover, I pass by the circumstance of king Henry's again violating his friendship; his entering Normandy,[4] and proceeding through the district of Hiesmes[5] to the river Dive, boasting that the sea was the sole obstacle to his farther progress. But William now perceiving him-

---

[1] Here again Guil. Pictav. should be consulted, pp. 187, 188.   [2] See § 187.
[3] The famous battle of Mortemer is fixed in the year 1054 by the interpolator of William of Jumiéges.
[4] King Henry entered Normandy for the third time in the year 1058.
[5] Per Pagum Oxionensem. Orig.

self reduced to extremities by the king's perfidy, at length bran-
dished the arms of conscious valour, and defeated the royal forces
which were beyond the river,—for part of them hearing of his
arrival had passed over some little time before,—with such entire
loss, that henceforth France feared nothing so much as to irritate
the ferocity of the Normans. The death of Henry[1] soon following,
and, shortly after, that of Martel,[2] put an end to these broils. The
dying king entrusted the care of his son Philip, at that time extremely young, to Baldwin earl of Flanders. He was a man equally
celebrated for fidelity and wisdom ; in the full possession of bodily
strength, and also ennobled by a marriage with the king's sister :
his daughter Matilda, a woman who was a singular mirror of
prudence in our time, and the perfection of virtue, had been already
married to William. Hence it arose, that being mediator between
his ward, and his son-in-law, Baldwin restrained, by his wholesome
counsels, the feuds of the chiefs, and of the people.

§ 235. But since mention has been so often made of Martel, I
shall briefly trace the genealogy of the earls of Anjou,[3] as far as the
knowledge of my informant reaches, apologizing as usual for the
digression. Fulco the elder,[4] presiding over that country for many
years, even to advanced age, performed many great and prudent
actions. There is only one thing for which I have heard him
branded : for, having induced Herbert earl of Maine to come to
Saintes, under the promise of yielding him that city, he caused him,
in the midst of their conversation, to be surrounded by his attendants, and compelled him to submit to his own conditions : in other
respects he was of irreproachable integrity. In his latter days, he
ceded his principality to Geoffrey his son,[5] so often mentioned.
Geoffrey conducted himself with excessive barbarity to the inhabitants, and with equal haughtiness even to the person who had
conferred this honour upon him : on which account, being ordered
by his father to lay down the government and ensigns of authority,
he was arrogant enough to take up arms against him. The blood
of the old man, though grown cold and languid, yet boiled with
indignation ; and in the course of a few days, by adopting wiser
counsels, he so brought down the proud spirit of his son, that after
carrying his saddle on his back[6] for some miles, he cast himself with

[1] King Henry died on the 4th of August, A.D. 1060.
[2] Geoffrey Martel died on the 14th of November, 1060. "In the same year
(1060), on the nativity of St. John, died king Henry; and my uncle Geoffrey died
peacefully on the third day after the feast of St. Martin." Ex Historiæ Andega-
vensis fragmento, auctore Fulcone, comite Andegavensi ; apud Acherium, Spici-
leg. iii. 233.
[3] For an account of the earls of Anjou, consult the Gesta Consulum Andega-
vensium, auctore Monacho Benedictino Majoris Monasterii, in the third volume of
the Spicilegium of D'Achery, iii.
[4] Fulco III. called Nerra, or Le Noir, and Le Jerosolymitain, and also Le
Palmier. He succeeded his father Geoffrey I. in the year 987.
[5] Geoffrey II., surnamed Martel.
[6] To carry a saddle was a punishment of extreme ignominy for certain crimes.
See another instance in William of Jumiéges, Du Chesne, p. 259. Ducange, in
voce "Sella," very justly supposes the disgrace to arise from the offender acknowledging himself a brute, and putting himself entirely in the power of the person
he had offended.

his burthen at his father's feet.   He, fired once more with his ancient courage, rising up and spurning the prostrate youth with his foot, exclaimed, "You are conquered at last! you are conquered!" repeating his words several times.   The suppliant had still spirit enough to make this admirable reply, " I am conquered by you alone, because you are my father; by others I am utterly invincible."   With this speech his irritated mind was mollified, and having consoled the mortification of his son by paternal affection, he restored him to the principality, with admonitions to conduct himself more wisely: telling him that the prosperity and tranquillity of the inhabitants of the district were creditable to him abroad, as well as advantageous at home.   In the same year the old man, having discharged all secular concerns, and making provision for his soul, proceeded to Jerusalem, where compelling two servants by an oath to do whatever he commanded, he was by them publicly dragged, naked, in the sight of the Turks, to the Holy Sepulchre. One of them twisted a rope about his neck, the other with a rod scourged his bare back, whilst he cried out, "Lord, receive the wretched Fulco, thy perfidious, thy deserter: regard my repentant soul, O Lord Jesus Christ."   His prayer was not then granted; but, peacefully returning home, he died[1] some few years after.   The precipitate boldness of his son Geoffrey has been amply displayed in the preceding pages.   He dying,[2] bequeathed his inheritance to Geoffrey, his sister's son,[3] but his worldly wisdom he could not leave him: for being a youth of simple manners, and more accustomed to pray in church than to handle arms, he excited the contempt of the people of that country, who knew not how to live in quiet.   In consequence, the whole district becoming exposed to plunderers, Fulco, his brother, of his own accord, seized on the duchy.   Fulco was called Rechin,[4] from his perpetual growling at the simplicity of his brother, whom he finally despoiled of his dignity, and kept in continual custody: he had a wife,[5] who, being enticed by the lust of an higher title, deserted him and married Philip king of France; who so desperately loved her, regardless of the adage,

> "Majesty and love
> But ill accord, nor share the selfsame seat,"

that he patiently suffered himself to be completely governed by her, though he was at the same time desirous of ruling over every other person.   Lastly, merely through regard for her, he suffered himself for some years to be pointed at like an idiot, and to be excommunicated[6] from the whole Christian world.   The

[1] Fulco III. died at Metz on the 21st of June 1040.
[2] Geoffrey Martel died without issue by any of his three wives.
[3] Geoffrey III called Le Barbu. He was the son of Geoffrey Ferreol, comte de Château-Landon, and Ermengarde, daughter of Fulco le Noir.
[4] Fulco IV. also called Le Querelleur.
[5] Her name was Betrade. Fulco married her in the year 1089, during the lives of his second and third wives, whom he repudiated.
   This occurred A. D. 1094. See Pagi ad an. § xi.; and the sentence of excommunication was confirmed by the council of Clermont, in November 1095. See Bernoldi Chron. p. 464.

sons of Fulco were Geoffrey and Fulco. Geoffrey obtaining the hereditary surname of Martel, ennobled it by his exertions; procuring such peace and tranquillity in those parts, as no one ever had seen, or will see in future. On this account being killed by the treachery of his people, he forfeited the credit of his consummate worth. Fulco succeeding to the government, is yet living;[1] and as I shall perhaps have occasion to speak of him in the times of king Henry, I will now proceed to relate what remains concerning William.

§ 236. When, after much labour, he had quelled all civil dissension, he meditated an exploit of greater fame, and determined to recover those countries anciently attached to Normandy,[2] though now disunited by long custom. I allude to the counties of Maine and Brittany; of which Mans, long since burnt by Martel and deprived of its sovereign Hugh, had lately experienced some little respite under Herbert the son of Hugh; who, with a view to greater security against the earl of Anjou, had submitted, and sworn fidelity to William; besides, he had solicited his daughter in marriage, and had been betrothed to her, though he died by disease ere she was marriageable. He left William his heir, adjuring his subjects to admit no other; telling them they might have, if they chose, a mild and honourable lord; but, should they not, a most determined assertor of his right. On his decease, the inhabitants of Maine rather inclined to Walter of Mantes, who had married Hugh's sister; but at length, being brought to their senses by many heavy losses, they acknowledged William. This was the time, when Harold was unwillingly carried to Normandy by an unpropitious gale; whom, as is before mentioned,[3] William took with him in his expedition to Brittany, to make proof of his prowess, and, at the same time, with the deeper design of showing to him his military equipment, that he might perceive how far preferable was the Norman sword to the English battle-axe. Alan, at that time, earl of Brittany, flourishing in youth, and of transcendent strength, had overcome his uncle Eudo, and performed many famous actions; and so far from fearing William, had even voluntarily irritated him. But he, laying claim to Brittany as his hereditary territory, because Charles had given it with his daughter, Gisla, to Rollo, shortly acted in such wise, that Alan came suppliantly to him, and surrendered himself and his possessions. And since I shall have but little to say of Brittany hereafter, I will here briefly insert an extraordinary occurrence, which happened about that time in the city of Nantes.

§ 237. There were in that city two clerks, priests, though not yet of legal age, which office they had obtained from the bishop of

---

[1] From this passage it is clear that Fulco IV. was still the reigning earl of Anjou, which therefore proves that Malmesbury had finished this work before 1129, in which year Geoffrey le Bel, better known as Geoffrey Plantagenet, son of Fulco, became earl of Anjou.

[2] " In the year 991, the Bretons who inhabited the town of Gaul, rising against the Normans, to whom they were subjected, were subdued by William Long-espée." Ex libello Hugonis Floriacensis Monachi, ap. Bouquet, xi. 181, note ▪.

[3] See § 228.

that p ace, more by entreaty than desert; the pitiable death of one
of whom, at length taught the survivor how near they had before
been to the brink of hell. As to their knowledge of literature, they
were so instructed, that they wanted little of perfection; from their
earliest infancy, they had in such wise vied in offices of friendship,
that according to the expression of the comic writer,[1] "To serve
each other they would not only stir hand and foot, but even risk
the loss of life itself." Wherefore, one day, when they found their
minds more than usually free from outward cares, they spoke their
sentiments, in a secret place, to the following effect :—"That for
many years they had given their attention sometimes to literature,
and sometimes to worldly gain; nor had they satisfied their minds,
which had been occupied rather in wrong, than proper pursuits;
that in the meanwhile that bitter day was insensibly approaching,
which would burst the bond of union which was indissoluble while
life remained; wherefore they should provide in time, that the
friendship which united them while living should accompany him
who died first to the place of the dead." They agreed, therefore,
that whoever of the two should first depart, should certainly appear
to the survivor, whether waking or sleeping, if possible within
thirty days, to inform him that, according to the Platonic tenet,
death does not extinguish the spirit, but sends it back again, as it
were from prison, to God its Author : but if this did not take place,
then they must agree with the sect of the Epicureans, who hold
that the soul, liberated from the body, vanishes into air, or mingles
with the wind. Mutually plighting their faith, they repeated their
oath in their daily conversation.

A short time elapsed, and behold a sudden and a violent death
deprived one of them of mortal existence. The other remained,
and seriously revolving the promise of his friend, and constantly
expecting his presence, during thirty days, found his hopes disappointed. At the expiration of this time, when, despairing of seeing
him, he had occupied his leisure in other business, the deceased,
with that pale countenance which dying persons assume, suddenly
stood before him, when he was awake, and busied on some matter.
The dead first addressing the living man, who was silent :—"Do
you know me?" said he; "I do," replied the other; "nor am I
so much disturbed at your unusual presence, as I wonder at your
continued absence." But when he had excused the tardiness of
his appearance, he said, "At length, having overcome every impediment, I am present; which presence, if you please, my friend,
will be advantageous to you, but to me totally unprofitable; for I
am doomed, by a sentence which has been pronounced and
ratified, to eternal punishment." When the living man promised
to give all his property to monasteries, and to the poor, and
to spend days and nights in fasting and prayer, for the release of
the defunct; he replied, "What I have said is fixed; for the judgments of God, by which I am plunged in the sulphureous whirlpool of hell, are without repentance. There I shall be tossed for
my crimes, 'as long as the pole whirls round the stars, or ocean

[1] Terent. Andr. iv. 1.

beats the shores ;' the rigour of this irreversible sentence remains for ever, devising lasting and innumerable kinds of punishment, although the whole world should seek for availing remedies ! And that you may experience some little of my numberless pains, here," said he, stretching out his hand, dripping with a corrupted ulcer, " is one of the very smallest of them ; does it appear trifling to you ?" When the other replied that it did appear so, bending his fingers into the palm, he threw three drops of the purulent matter upon him ; two of which touching his temples, and one his forehead, they penetrated the skin and flesh, as if with a burning cautery, and made holes of the size of a nut. Acknowledging the acuteness of the pain by the cry he uttered, " This," said the dead man, " will be a strong proof to you, as long as you live, of my pains ; and, unless you neglect it, a singular warning for your own salvation. Wherefore, while you have the power, while wrath is suspended over your head, while God's lingering mercy waits for you, change your habit, change your disposition, become a monk at Rennes, in the monastery of St. Melanius." When the living man was unwilling to agree to these words, the other, sternly glancing at him, " If you doubt, wretched man," said he, " turn and read these letters ;" and with these words, he stretched out his hand, inscribed with black characters, in which Satan, and all the company of infernals sent their thanks, from hell, to the whole ecclesiastical body; as well for denying themselves no single pleasure, as for sending, through neglect of their preaching, more of their subject souls to hell, than any former age had ever witnessed. With these words the shade of the speaker vanished ; and the hearer, distributing his whole property to the church and to the poor, went to the monastery of St. Melanius; admonishing all, who heard or saw him, of his sudden conversion, and extraordinary intercourse, so that they exclaimed, " This is a change of the right hand of the most High."

§ 238. I feel no regret at having inserted this for the benefit of my readers ; now I shall return to William. For since I have briefly, but I hope not uselessly, gone over the transactions in which he was engaged when only earl of Normandy, for thirty years, the order of time now requires a change in the narrative ; that I may, as far as my inquiries have discovered, detect that is false, and declare the truth relating to his regal government.

When king Edward died, England, fluctuating with doubtful favour, was uncertain to which ruler she should commit herself ; to Harold, William, or Edgar ; for the king had recommended him also to the nobility, as nearest to the sovereignty in point of birth ; concealing his better judgment from the tenderness of his disposition. Wherefore, as I have said above, the English were distracted in their choice, although all of them openly wished well to Harold. He, indeed, when once dignified with the diadem, thought nothing of the covenant betwixt himself and William ; but he said that he was absolved from his oath, because his daughter, to whom he had been betrothed, had died ere she was marriageable. For this man, though possessing numberless good qualities, is reported to have been careless about abstaining from breach of trust, if he might, by any device whatever, elude the reasonings of men on this matter ; moreover, he supposed that the threats of William would never be put into execution, because the latter was occupied in wars with neighbouring princes, and so he and his subjects gave full indulgence to their fancied security ; and indeed, had he not heard that the king of Norway was approaching, he would neither have condescended to collect troops, nor to array them. William, in the meantime, began mildly to address him by messengers, to expostulate on the broken covenant, to mingle threats with entreaties, and to warn him, that ere a year expired, he would claim his due by the sword, and that he would come to that very place where Harold supposed he had firmer footing than himself. Harold again rejoined what I have related,[1] concerning the nuptials of his daughter, and added that he had been presumptuous on the subject of the kingdom, in having confirmed to him by oath another's right, without the universal consent and edict of the council, and of the people ; again, that a rash oath ought to be broken ; for if the oath, or vow, which a maiden, under her father's roof, made concerning her person, without the knowledge of her parents, were adjudged invalid ; how much more invalid must that oath be, which he had made concerning the whole kingdom, when he was himself only a subject under the king's authority, and compelled by the necessity of the time, and without the knowledge of the nation :[2] besides it was an unjust request to ask him to resign a government which he had assumed by the universal kindness of his fellow subjects ; a thing which would neither be agreeable to the people nor safe for the military.

In this way, confounded either by true or plausible arguments, the messengers returned without success. The earl, however, made every necessary preparation for war during the whole of that year ; retained his own soldiers with increased pay, and invited those of others ; ordered his ranks and battalions in such wise, that the soldiers should be tall and stout ; that the commanders and standard-bearers, in addition to their military science, should be looked up to for their wisdom and age ; insomuch, that each of them, whether seen in the field or elsewhere, might be taken for a prince rather than a leader. The bishops and abbots of those days vied so much in piety, and the nobility in princely liberality, that it is wonderful,[3] how within so very few years nearly all the attri-

---

[1] See § 228.

[2] These words seem to imply that the Great Council of the kingdom had never agreed to any settlement of the crown on the duke ; and without such sanction no oath made by Harold in favour of William would have been binding.

[3] Some MSS. (A. G. H. L.) read, "That it is wonderful within a period of less than sixty years, how either order should have become so unfruitful in goodness as to take up a confederate war against justice; the former, through lust of ecclesiastical promotion, embracing wrong in preference to right and equity; and the latter, casting off shame, seeking every occasion for begging money as for their daily pay. But at that time, &c." The expression of "not less than sixty years" in the above passage enables us to approximate to the date of the first completion of the Gesta Regum ; but it would seem that a less definite expression, as appears by the text, was adopted ; probably when the author revised his work at some later period.

butes of either order should have become so changed : the former, in some things more sluggish, but in general more liberal ; and the latter more prudent in every thing but more penurious ; yet both, in defending their country, valiant in battle, prudent in counsel ; prompt to advance their own fortune, and depress that of their enemies. But at that time the energy of William, seconded by the providence of God, already anticipated the invasion of England ; and that no rashness might stain his just cause, he sent to the pope, formerly Anslem, bishop of Lucca, but who had assumed the name of Alexander,[1] alleging the justice of the war he meditated with all the eloquence of which he was master. Harold omitted to do this, either because he was proud by nature, or else distrusted his cause ; or because he feared that his messengers would be obstructed by William and his partisans, who beset every port. The pope duly examining the pretensions of both parties, delivered a standard to William, as an auspicious presage of the kingdom ; on receiving which he summoned an assembly of his nobles at Lillebon, for the purpose of ascertaining their sentiments on this attempt. And when he had encouraged, by splendid promises, all who approved his design, he ordered them to prepare shipping, in proportion to the extent of their possessions. Thus they departed at that time, and in the month of August reassembled in a body at St. Valery, for so that port is called by its new name.[2] Collecting, therefore, ships from every quarter, they awaited the propitious gale which was to carry them to the place of their destination. When this delayed blowing for several days, the common soldiers, as is generally the case, began to mutter in their tents, that the man must be mad, who wished to subjugate a foreign country; that, God opposed him, for He withheld the wind ; that, his father purposed a similar attempt, and was in like manner frustrated ; that, it was the fate of that family to aspire to things beyond their reach, and find that God was their adversary. In consequence of these things, which were enough to enervate the force of the brave, being publicly noised abroad, the duke held, a council with his chiefs, and ordered the body of St. Valery to be brought forth, and to be exposed to the open air, for the purpose of imploring a wind. No delay now interposed, but the wished-for gale filled their sails. A joyful shout then arising, summoned every one to the ships. The earl himself first launching[3] from the continent into the deep, awaited the rest, at anchor nearly in mid-channel. All then assembled round the crimson sail of the admiral's ship, and, having first dined, they arrived, after a favourable passage, at

[1] Alexander II. He was crowned pope on the 30th of September 1061, and died 21st of April 1073.

[2] There are two places called St. Valeri ; one in Picardy, situate at the mouth of the Somme, and formerly called Leugonaus; the other is a large seaport town situate in Normandy, in the diocese of Rouen, and was formerly called St. Valeri les Plains, but now St. Valeri en Caux. It seems to be the former place to which Malmesbury here refers. "In Pontivo apud S. Walericum in anchoris congrue stare fecit," writes William of Jumiéges ; and yet more definitely the author of the poem upon the battle of Hastings, printed from the Brussels MS. in Petrie's Monumenta, p. 857, line 48.

[3] This was early on the morning of the 27th of September, 1066.

Hastings. As he disembarked he slipped down, but turned the accident to his advantage; a soldier who stood near calling out to him, "You hold England,[1] my lord, its future king." He then restrained his whole army from plundering; warning them that they should now abstain from what must hereafter be their own;[2] and for fifteen successive days he remained so perfectly quiet that he seemed to think of nothing less than of war.

§ 239. In the meantime Harold returned from the battle which he had waged against the Norwegians, happy in his own estimation, at having conquered; but not so in mine, as he had secured the victory by parricide.[3] When the news of the Norman's arrival reached him, reeking as he was from battle, he proceeded to Hastings, though accompanied by very few forces. No doubt the fates urged him on, as he neither summoned his troops, nor had he been willing to do so would he have found many ready to obey his call, so hostile were all to him, as I have before observed,[4] from his having appropriated the northern spoils entirely to himself. He sent out some persons, however, to reconnoitre the number and strength of the enemy: these, being taken within the camp, William ordered to be led amongst the tents, and after feasting them plentifully, to be sent back uninjured to their lord. On their return, Harold inquired what news they brought; when, after relating at full the noble confidence of the general, they gravely added, that almost all his army had the appearance of priests; as they had the whole face with both lips shaven; for the English[5] leave the upper lip unshorn, suffering the hair continually to increase, which Julius Cæsar, in his treatise on the Gallic War,[6] affirms to have been a national custom with the ancient inhabitants of Britain. The king smiled at the simplicity of the relators, observing, with a

---

[1] This was said in allusion to the feudal investiture, or formal act of taking possession of an estate by the delivery of a portion of the soil. This story, however, is rendered a little suspicious by these words being in exact conformity with those of Cæsar when he stumbled and fell at his landing in Africa, "Teneo te, Africa." The silence of William of Poictou, who was the duke's chaplain, and with him at his landing, makes the truth of it still more doubtful.

[2] Whatever may have been the Conqueror's orders to restrain his army from plundering, it is conclusive from the Domesday Survey that they were of no avail. The whole of the country in the neighbourhood of Hastings appears to have been laid waste. Sir Henry Ellis, in the last edition of his General Introduction to Domesday, observes that the destruction occasioned by the Conqueror's army on its first arrival is apparent, more particularly under Hollington, Bexhill, &c. The value of each manor is given as it stood in the reign of the Confessor; afterwards it is said, "vastatum fuit;" and then follows the value at the time of the survey. The situation of those manors evidently shows their devastated state to have been owing to the army marching over it; and this clearly evinces another circumstance relating to the invasion, which is, that William did not land his army at one particular spot,—at Bulverhithe or Hastings, as is supposed,—but at all the several proper places for landing along the coast from Bexhill to Winchelsea.

[3] Malmesbury here seems to refer, though incorrectly, to the death of Harold's brother Tosti, who fell, on the side of the Norwegians, at the battle of Stanford Bridge.

[4] See § 228.

[5] This national distinction between the English and the Normans is carefully observed in the Bayeux Tapestry.

[6] "Capilloque sunt promisso, atque omni parte corporis rasa, præter caput et labrum superius." Lib. v. 14.

pleasant laugh, that they were not priests, but soldiers, strong in arms and invincible in spirit. His brother Gurth,[1] a youth on the verge of manhood, and of knowledge and valour surpassing his years, caught up his words: " Since," said he, " you extol so much the valour of the Norman, I think it ill-advised for you, who are his inferior in strength and desert, to contend with him. Nor can you deny that you are bound to him by oath, either willingly or by compulsion : wherefore you will act wisely, if, yourself withdrawing from this pressing emergency, you allow us to try the issue of a battle; we, who are free from all obligation, shall justly draw the sword in defence of our country. It is to be apprehended if you engage, that you will be either subjected to flight or to death ; whereas, if we only fight, your cause will be safe at all events ; for you will be able both to rally the fugitives and to avenge the dead."

§ 240. His unbridled rashness yielded no placid ear to the words of his adviser, thinking it base, and a reproach to his past life, to turn his back on danger of any kind.; and, with similar impudence, or to speak more favourably, imprudence, he drove away a monk, the messenger of William, not deigning him even a complacent look; imprecating only, that God would decide between him and the earl. He was the bearer of three propositions : either that Harold would relinquish the kingdom, according to his agreement; or hold it of William; or decide the matter by single combat, in the sight of either army. For William[2] claimed the kingdom on the ground that king Edward, by the advice of Stigand the archbishop, and of the earls Godwin and Siward, had granted it to him, and had sent the son and nephew of Godwin to Normandy, as sureties of the grant. If Harold should deny this, he would abide by the judgment of the pope, or by battle: on all which propositions, the messenger being frustrated by the single answer I have related, returned, and communicated to his party fresh spirit for the conflict.

§ 241. The courageous leaders mutually prepared for battle, each according to his national custom. The English, as we have heard, passed the night without sleep, in drinking and singing, and in the morning proceeded without delay towards the enemy; all on foot, armed with battle-axes and covering themselves in front by the junction of their shields, they formed an impenetrable body, which would have secured their safety that day, had not the Normans, by a feigned flight, induced them to open their ranks, till that time, according to their custom, closely compacted. The king himself on foot, stood, with his brothers, near the standard ; in order that while all shared equal danger, none could think of retreating. This standard

---

[1] Gurth, the brother of Harold, was undoubtedly slain at the battle of Hastings; but in the Harleian MS. 3776, fol. 21 b. there is a legend that Gurth escaped alive, and was seen in extreme age by King Henry the Second.

[2] This is from W. Pictaviensis, who puts it in the mouth of the Conqueror, but it is evidently false, for Godwin died A.D. 1053, Siward A.D. 1055, and in 1054 we find Edward the Confessor sending his nephew from Hungary, to make him his successor in the kingdom, who accordingly arrived in A.D. 1057, and died almost immediately after. He could not, therefore, have made the settlement as here asserted. And see Malmesbury's Gesta Pontificum, f. 116 b.

William sent, after the victory, to the pope; it was sumptuously embroidered with gold and precious stones, and represented the form of a man fighting.

§ 242. On the other hand, the Normans passed the whole night in confessing their sins, and received the communion of the Lord's Body in the morning; their infantry, with bows and arrows, formed the vanguard, while their cavalry, divided into wings, were thrown back. The earl, with serene countenance, declaring aloud that God would favour his, as being the righteous side, called for his arms; and presently, when through the hurry of his attendants, he had put on his hauberk the hind part before,[1] he corrected the mistake with a laugh, saying, " The power of my dukedom shall be turned into a kingdom." Then beginning the song of Roland,[2] that the war-like example of that man might stimulate the soldiers; and calling on God for assistance, the battle commenced on both sides, and was fought with great ardour, neither side giving ground during the greater part of the day. Finding this, William gave a signal to his party, that, by a feigned flight, they should retreat. Through this device, the close body of the English, opening for the purpose of cutting down the straggling enemy, brought upon itself swift destruction; for the Normans, facing about, attacked them thus disordered, and compelled them to fly. In this manner, deceived by a stratagem, they met an honourable death in avenging their country; nor indeed were they at all without their own revenge, for by frequently making a stand, they slaughtered their pursuers in heaps. Getting possession of an eminence, they drove down the Normans, when roused with indignation and anxiously striving to gain the higher ground, into the valley beneath, where, easily hurling their javelins and rolling down stones on them as they stood below, they destroyed them to a man. Besides, by a short passage with which they were acquainted, avoiding a deep ditch, they trod under foot such a multitude of their enemies in that place, that they made the hollow level with the plain, by the heaps of carcases. This vicissitude of first one party conquering, and then the other, prevailed as long as the life of Harold continued; but when he fell, from having his brain pierced with an arrow, the flight of the English ceased not until night. The valour of both leaders was here eminently conspicuous.

§ 243. Harold, not merely content with the duty of a general in exhorting others, diligently entered into every soldier-like duty; often would he strike the enemy when coming to close quarters, so that none could approach him with impunity; for immediately the same blow levelled both horse and rider. Wherefore, as I have related, receiving the fatal arrow from a distance, he yielded to death. One of the soldiers with a sword gashed his thigh, as he lay prostrate; for which shameful and cowardly action he was

---

[1] As the armour of that time was of mail, this might easily happen.

[2] What this was is not known, but it is supposed to have been a ballad or romance commemorating the heroic achievements of the Paladin Roland and other peers of Charlemagne, who fell at Roncevault. Rivet (Histoire littéraire de la France, vii. 72,) infers from this passage that *la langue Romane* was in use at that period.

branded with ignominy by William, and expelled from the army.

§ 244. William, too, was equally ready to encourage his soldiers by his voice and by his presence; to be the first to rush forward; to attack the thickest of the foe. Thus everywhere raging, everywhere furious, he lost three chosen horses, which were that day killed under him. The dauntless spirit and vigour of the intrepid general, however, still persisted, though often called back by the kind remonstrance of his body-guard; he still persisted, I say, till approaching night crowned him with complete victory. And no doubt the hand of God so protected him, that the enemy should draw no blood from his person, though they aimed so many javelins at him.

§ 245. This was a fatal day to England, a melancholy havoc of our dear country, in the struggle for the change of its new lords. For it had long since adopted the manners of the Angles, which had been very various, according to the times; for in the first years of their arrival, they were barbarians in their look and manners, warlike in their usages, heathens in their rites; but after embracing the faith of Christ, by degrees, and in process of time, in consequence of the peace which they enjoyed, they regarded arms only in a secondary light, and they gave their whole attention to religion. I say nothing of the poor, the meanness of whose fortune often restrains them from overstepping the bounds of justice; I omit men of ecclesiastical rank, whom sometimes respect for their profession, and sometimes the fear of shame, suffers not to deviate from the true path: I speak of princes, who from the greatness of their power might have full liberty to indulge in pleasure; some of whom in their own country, and others at Rome, changing their habit, obtained an heavenly kingdom, and a saintly intercourse; and many during their whole lives, in outward appearance, devoted themselves to worldly affairs, in order that they might exhaust their treasures on the poor, or divide them amongst monasteries. What shall I say of the multitudes of bishops, hermits, and abbots? Does not the whole island blaze with such numerous reliques of its natives, that you can scarcely pass a village of any consequence but you hear the name of some new saint? And of how many have all notices perished through the want of records? Nevertheless, in process of time, the desire after literature and religion had decayed for several years before the arrival of the Normans. The clergy, contented with a very slight degree of learning, could scarcely stammer out the words of the sacraments; and a person who understood grammar was an object of wonder and astonishment.[1] The monks mocked the rule of their order by fine vestments, and the use of every kind of food. The nobility, given up to luxury and wantonness, went not to church in the morning after the manner

---

[1] See § 123. King Alfred, in his preface to Gregory's Pastoral, states that learning was so decayed in England, that very few priests on this side of the Humber could understand the common service of the church, and he knew none south of the Thames who could turn an ordinary piece of Latin into English. On this point see Maitland's Dark Ages, p. 30, et seq.

of Christians, but merely, in a careless manner, heard matins and masses from a hurrying priest in their chambers, amid the blandishments of their wives. The commonalty, left unprotected, became a prey to the most powerful, who amassed fortunes, by either seizing on their property or by selling their persons into foreign countries; although it is characteristic of this people to be more inclined to revelling than to the accumulation of wealth. There was one custom repugnant to nature, which they adopted; namely to sell their female servants, when pregnant by them, and after they had satisfied their lust, either to public prostitution or foreign slavery. Drinking in parties was an universal practice, in which occupation they passed entire nights as well as days.[1] They consumed their whole substance in mean and despicable houses; unlike the Normans and French, who, in noble and splendid mansions, live with frugality. The vices attendant on drunkenness, which enervate the human mind, followed; hence it arose that when they engaged William, more with rashness and precipitate fury than military skill, they doomed themselves and their country to slavery, by one, and that an easy victory. For nothing is less effective than rashness; and what begins with violence, quickly ceases, or is repelled. In fine, the English[2] at that time wore short garments, reaching to the mid-knee; they had their hair cropped, their beards shaven, their arms laden with golden bracelets, their skin adorned with punctured designs; they were accustomed to eat till they became surfeited, and to drink till they were sick. These latter qualities they imparted to their conquerors; as to the rest, they adopted their manners. I would not, however, have these bad propensities ascribed to the English universally: I know that many of the clergy, at that day, trod the path of sanctity, by a blameless life; I know that many of the laity, of all ranks and conditions, in this nation, were well-pleasing to God. Be injustice far from this account; the accusation does not involve the whole, indiscriminately: but, as in peace, the mercy of God often cherishes the bad and the good together; so, equally, does His severity sometimes include them both in captivity.

§ 246. The Normans,—that I may speak of them also,—were at that time, and are even now, exceedingly particular in their dress and delicate in their food, but not so to excess. They are a race inured to war, and can hardly live without it, fierce in rushing against the enemy, and, where force fails of success, ready to use stratagem, or to corrupt by bribery. As I have said,[3] they live in large edifices with economy, envy their equals, wish to excel their superiors, and plunder their subjects, though they defend them

---

[1] See § 149.

[2] This description of the English must refer to the ancient British, and not to the Saxons. It accords with the notices of them by Cæsar, Diodorus, Pomponius Mela, and Dion Cassius, but more particularly with that by Herodian. (Herodiani Histor.; ed. Irmisch, Lipsiæ, 1789.) The British, that historian writes, go naked as to the greater part of their bodies. Indeed they do not know the use of clothing. They gird with iron their loins and necks, deeming it an ornament, and an evidence of opulence; they puncture their bodies with pictured forms of all kinds of animals, and therefore they wear no clothing, lest they should hide the figures on their bodies.   [3] See § 245.

from others ; they are faithful to their lords, though a slight offence renders them perfidious.   They weigh treachery by its chance of success, and change their sentiments with money.   The politest, however, of all nations, they esteem strangers worthy of equal honour with themselves : they also intermarry with their vassals. They revived, by their arrival, the rule of religion[1] which had everywhere grown lifeless in England.   You might see churches rise in every village, and monasteries in the towns and cities, built after a style unknown before; you might behold the country flourishing with renovated rites; so that each wealthy man accounted that day lost to him, which he had neglected to signalize by some magnificent action.   But having enlarged sufficiently on these points, let us pursue the operations of William.

How William was acknowledged by the English.

§ 247.   When his victory was complete, he caused his dead to be interred with great pomp, granting the enemy the liberty of doing the like, if they thought proper.   He sent the body of Harold to his mother, (who begged it,) unransomed, though she proffered large sums by her messengers.   She buried it, when thus obtained, at Waltham ;[2] a church he had built at his own expense, in honour of the Holy Cross, and which he had filled with canons.   William then, by degrees proceeding, (as became a conqueror,) with his army, not after an hostile but a royal manner, journeyed towards London, the principal city of the kingdom ; and shortly after all the citizens came out to meet him with gratulations.   Crowds poured out of every gate to greet him, instigated by the nobility, and principally by Stigand, archbishop of Canterbury, and Aldred of York.   For, shortly before, Edwin and Morcard, two brothers of great expectation, hearing at London the news of Harold's death, solicited the citizens to raise one of them to the throne; failing, however, in the attempt, they had departed for Northumberland, conjecturing by a surmise of their own that William would never come thither.   The other chiefs would have chosen Edgar, had the bishops supported them ; but, danger and domestic broils closely impending, neither did this take effect.   Thus the English, who, had they been united in one resolution, might have repaired the ruin of their country, introduced a stranger, while they were

[1] Malmesbury here alludes to the monastic rule, in contradistinction to the system of the secular clergy.   Lanfranc, Walkelin and others revived monachism.

[2] There seems to have been a fabulous story current during the twelfth century that Harold escaped from the battle of Hastings.   Giraldus Cambrensis asserts that it was believed Harold had fled from the battle-field pierced with many wounds, and with the loss of his left eye, and that he ended his days piously and virtuously as an anchorite at Chester.   Both Knighton and Brompton quote this story.   W. Pictaviensis says that William refused the body to his mother, who offered its weight in gold for it, ordering it to be buried on the sea-coast. In the Harleian MS. 3776, before referred to, Gurth, Harold's brother, is said to have escaped alive: he is represented in his interview with Henry the Second to have spoken mysteriously respecting Harold, and to have declared that the body of that prince was not at Waltham.   Sir Henry Ellis, quoting this MS. justly observes that the whole was, probably, the fabrication of one of the secular canons, who were ejected at the re-foundation of Waltham abbey in 1177.

unwilling to choose a native, to govern them. Being now decidedly hailed king, he was crowned on Christmas day by archbishop Aldred ;[1] for he was careful not to accept this office from Stigand, as he was not canonically an archbishop.

Summary of William's military Transactions in England.

§ 248. Of the various wars which he carried on, this is a summary. Favoured by God's assistance, he easily reduced the city of Exeter,[2] when in a state of rebellion ; for part of the wall fell down accidentally, and made an opening for him. Indeed he had attacked it with the more ferocity, asserting that those irreverent men would be deserted by God's favour, because one of them, standing upon the wall, had bared his posteriors, and had broken wind, in contempt of the Normans. He almost annihilated the city of York,[3] that sole remaining shelter for rebellion, destroying its citizens with sword and famine. For there Malcolm, king of the Scots, with his party, there Edgar, and Marcher, and Weldeof, with the English and Danes, often brooded over the nest of tyranny; there they frequently killed his generals ; whose deaths were I severally to commemorate, perhaps I should not be out of order, though I might risk the peril of creating disgust ; while I should be not easily pardoned as an historian, if I were led astray by the falsities of my authorities.

How William took York, and laid waste the whole Province.

§ 249. Malcolm willingly received all the English fugitives, affording to each every protection in his power, but more especially to Edgar, whose sister he had married out of regard to her noble descent. On his behalf he infested the adjacent provinces of England with plunder and fire ; not that he supposed by so doing he could be of any service to him with respect to the kingdom, but merely to annoy William, who was incensed that his territories were subject to Scottish incursions. In consequence, William, collecting a body of foot and horse, repaired to the northern parts of the island, and first of all received into subjection the metropolitan city, which the English, Danes, and Scots obstinately defended ; its

---

[1] A full account of William's coronation will be found in the Chronicle of William of Poictou, the Conqueror's chaplain, of which a translation will be given in the present series of Chronicles.

[2] It may be observed that, with the exception of the MS. used by Savile, all the MSS. agree in reading Exeter ; but Matthew Paris, who has followed Malmesbury, seems to have written Oxford instead of Exeter ; the best MSS. of Matthew Paris (MS. Reg. 14, C. vii. and MS. Cott. Nero, D. v.) reading Oxford. Upon a passage in the Domesday Survey describing Oxford as containing four hundred and seventy-eight houses which were so desolated that they could not pay geld, Sir Henry Ellis remarks : "The extraordinary number of houses specified as desolated at Oxford requires explanation. If the passage is correct, Matthew Paris, who here copies Malmesbury, probably gives us the cause of it, under the year 1067, when William the Conqueror subdued Oxford, in his way to York. Matt. Par. sub ann. 1067. The siege of Exeter in 1067 is also mentioned by Simeon of Durham, col. 197 ; Hoveden, col. 258 ; Ralph de Diceto, col. 482 ; Florence of Worcester, fol. Francof. 1601, p. 635 ; and by Ordericus Vitalis, p. 510.

[3] The destruction of York took place in 1068.

citizens being wasted with continued want. He destroyed also in a great and severe battle a considerable number of the enemy, who had come to the succour of the besieged; though the victory was not bloodless on his side, as he lost many of his people. He then ordered both the towns and fields of the whole district to be laid waste;[1] the fruits and grain to be destroyed by fire or by water, more especially on the coast, as well on account of his recent displeasure, as because a rumour had gone abroad, that Cnut, king of Denmark, the son of Swane, was approaching with his forces. The reason of such a command was, that the plundering pirate should find no booty on the coast to carry off with him, if he designed to depart again directly; or should be compelled to provide against want, if he thought proper to stay. Thus the resources of a province, once flourishing, and the nurse of tyrants, were cut off by fire, slaughter, and devastation; the ground, for more than sixty miles, totally uncultivated and unproductive, remains bare even to the present day. Should any stranger now see it, he laments over the once magnificent cities! the towers threatening heaven itself with their loftiness; the fields abundant in pasturage and watered with rivers: and, if any ancient inhabitant remains, he knows it no longer.

Account of Malcolm, King of the Scots.

§ 250. Malcolm surrendered himself, without coming to an engagement, and for the whole of William's time passed his life under treaties, uncertain, and frequently broken. But when in the reign of William, the son of William, he was attacked in a similar manner, he diverted the king from pursuing him by a false oath. Soon after he was slain, together with his son,[2] by Robert Mowbray, earl of Northumberland, while regardless of his faith he was devastating the province with more than usual insolence. For many years he lay buried at Tynemouth: lately he was conveyed by Alexander his son to Dunfermelin, in Scotland.

Account of Edgar.

§ 251. Edgar, having submitted to the king with Stigand and Aldred the archbishops, violated his oath the following year, by going over to the Scot: but after living there some years, and acquiring no present advantage, no future prospects, but merely his

---

[1] Domesday Book bears ample testimony to this statement, and that which closely follows, viz. that the resources of this once flourishing province were cut off by fire, slaughter, and devastation; and that the ground for more than sixty miles, totally uncultivated and unproductive, remained bare to that very day. The land which had belonged to Edwin and Morcar in Yorkshire almost everywhere in the Survey is stated to be *wasta;* and in Amunderness, after the enumeration of no fewer than sixty-two places, the possessions in which amounted to one hundred and seventy carucates, it is said, " Omnes hæ villæ jacent ad Prestune et iii. ecclesiæ. Ex his xvi. a paucis incoluntur, sed quot sint habitantes ignoratur. Reliqua sunt wasta." Moreover *wasta* is added to numerous places belonging to the archbishop of York, St. John of Beverley, the bishop of Durham, and to those lands which had belonged to Waltheof, Gospatric, Siward, and Merleswain.

[2] Malcolm, with his son Edward, was slain on the 13th of November 1093, by Morael of Bamborough, the steward of the earl of Northumberland. See the Sax. Chron.

daily sustenance, being willing to try the liberality of the Norman, who was at that time beyond sea, he sailed over to him. They relate it to have been extremely agreeable to the king, that England should be thus rid of a fomenter of dissension. Indeed it was his constant practice, under colour of high honour, to carry over to Normandy all the English he suspected, lest any disorders should arise in the kingdom during his absence. Edgar, therefore, was well received, and presented with a considerable largess: and remaining at court for many years, silently sunk into contempt through his indolence, or more mildly speaking, his simplicity. For how great must his simplicity be, who would yield up to the king, for a single horse, the pound of silver, which he received as his daily stipend? In succeeding times he went to Jerusalem with Robert, the son of Godwin, a most valiant knight. This was the time when the Turks besieged king Baldwin, at Rama; who, unable to endure the difficulties of a siege, rushed through the midst of the enemy, by the assistance of Robert alone, who preceded him, and hewed down the Turks, on either hand, with his drawn sword; but while, excited to greater ferocity by his success, he was pressing on with too much eagerness, his sword dropped from his hand, and when stooping down to recover it, he was surrounded by a multitude, and cast into chains. Taken thence to Babylon, as they report, when he refused to deny Christ, he was placed as a mark in the middle of the market-place, and being transfixed with darts, died a martyr. Edgar, having lost his companion, returned and received many gifts from the Greek and German emperors; who, from respect to his noble descent, would also have endeavoured to retain him with them; but he gave up everything through regard to his native soil: for, truly, the love of their country deceives some men to such a degree, that nothing seems pleasant to them, unless they can breathe their native air. Edgar, therefore, deluded by this foolish desire, returned to England: where, as I have before said, after various revolutions of fortune, he now grows old in the country in privacy and quiet.[1]

Account of the Brothers, Edwin and Morcard.

§ 252. Edwin and Morcard were brothers;[2] the sons of Elfgar, the son of Leofric. They had received charge of the county of Northumberland, and jointly preserved it in tranquillity: for, as I

---

[1] It is probable that Edgar resided in Hertfordshire, as in the Domesday Survey he occurs as a tenant in capite in Hertfordshire. (Doms. i. fol. 142 a.) Fordun (lib. v. c. 27—34) has a story of Edgar being cleared from an accusation of treason against William Rufus, by one Godwin, in a duel; whose son Robert is afterwards described as one of Edgar's adherents in Scotland; and the Saxon Chronicle states that in the year 1106 he was one of the prisoners taken at the battle of Tinchebrai, in Normandy. Edgar is stated by Dr. Sayers, in his Disquisitions, 8vo. 1808, p. 296, upon the authority of the Spelman Manuscripts, to have again visited Scotland at a very advanced period of life, and died in that kingdom in the year 1120. If this date can be relied upon, the passage above noted would prove that Malmesbury had written this portion of his history before the close of that year.

[2] They were the brothers-in-law of Harold, he having married their sister Ealdgyth, widow of Griffith, king of Wales.

have before observed,[1] a few days previous to the death of king Edward, the inhabitants of the north had risen in rebellion and expelled Tosti their governor: and, with Harold's approbation, had requested and received one of these brothers as their lord. These circumstances, as we have heard from persons acquainted with the affair, took place against the inclination of the king, who was attached to Tosti; but being languid through disease, and worn down with age, he had become so universally disregarded, that he could not assist his favourite. In consequence, his bodily ailments increasing from the anxiety of his mind, he died shortly after. Harold persisted in his resolution of banishing his brother: wherefore, first tarnishing the triumphs of his family by piratical excursions, he was, as I have above written,[2] afterwards killed with the king of Norway. His body being known by a wart between the shoulders, obtained burial at York. Edwin and Morcard, by Harold's command, then conveyed the spoils of war to London, for he himself was proceeding rapidly to the battle of Hastings; where, falsely presaging, he looked upon the victory as already gained. But, when he was there killed, the brothers, flying to the territories they possessed, disturbed the peace of William for several years; infesting the woods with secret robberies, and never coming to close or open engagement. Often were they taken captive, and as often surrendered themselves, but were again dismissed with impunity, from pity to their youthful elegance, and respect to their nobility. At last, murdered, neither by the force nor craft of their enemies, but by the treachery of their partisans,[3] their fate drew tears from the king, who would even long since have united them in marriage with his relations, and granted them the honour of his friendship, if they would have acceded to terms of peace.

§ 253. Waltheof, an earl of high descent,[4] had become extremely intimate with the new king, who had, heedless of his former offences, attributed them rather to courage than to disloyalty. For Waltheof, singly, had killed many of the Normans in the battle of York; cutting off their heads, one by one, as they entered the gate. He was muscular in the arms, brawny in the chest, tall and robust in his whole person; the son of Siward, a most celebrated earl, whom by a Danish term they called "Digera," which implies Strong. But after the fall of his party, he voluntarily surrendered himself, and was honoured by a marriage with Judith,[5] the king's niece, as well as with his personal friendship. Unable, however, to restrain his evil inclinations, he could not preserve his fidelity. For all his countrymen who had thought proper to resist, being

---

[1] See § 228.   [2] See § 228.

[3] The Saxon Chronicle states that earl Edwin was treacherously slain by his own men in 1071, and that earl Morcar surrendered himself to the king in the same year.

[4] Earl Waltheof, or Wallef, as he is always styled in Domesday Book, was, according to the Saxon Chronicle, beheaded at Winchester on the 31st of May, 1076. The Chronicle of Mailros and Florence of Worcester, however, assign this event to the preceding year.. Further particulars respecting him may be seen in Ingulf and Ordericus Vitalis.

[5] Judith was daughter of count Enguerrand, and Adeliza, sister of the Conqueror. William seems to have been very profuse in his grants to her.

either slain or subdued, he became a party even in the perfidy of Ralph de Waher; but the conspiracy being detected, he was taken, kept in chains for some time, and at last, being beheaded, was buried at Croland; though some assert that he joined the league of treachery more through necessity than inclination. This is the excuse the English make for him, and those, of the greater credit, for the Normans affirm the contrary, to whose decision the Divinity itself appears to assent, showing many and very great miracles at his tomb; for they declare that, during his captivity, he wiped away his transgressions by daily sorrow.

§ 254. On this account perhaps the conduct of the king may reasonably be excused, if he was at any time rather severe against the English; for he scarcely found any one of them faithful. This circumstance so exasperated his ferocious mind, that he deprived the more powerful, first of their wealth, next of their estates, and finally, some of them of their lives. Moreover, he followed the device of Cæsar, who drove out the Germans concealed in the vast forest of Ardennes, whence they harassed his army with perpetual irruptions, not by means of his own countrymen, but by the confederate Gauls; that, while strangers destroyed each other, he might gain a bloodless victory. Thus, I say, William acted towards the English. For, allowing the Normans to be unemployed, he opposed an English army and an English commander to those who, after the first unsuccessful battle, had fled to Denmark and Ireland, and had returned at the end of three years with considerable force; foreseeing that whichever side should conquer, it must be a great advantage to himself. Nor did this device fail him; for both parties of the English, after some conflicts between themselves, without any exertion on his part, left an easy victory for the king; the invaders being driven to Ireland, and those on the king's side purchasing the empty title of conquest, at their own special loss, and that of their general. His name was Ednod,[1] equally celebrated, before the arrival of the Normans, both at home and abroad. He was the father of Herding, who yet survives: a man more accustomed to kindle strife by his malignant tongue, than to brandish arms in the field of battle. Thus having overturned the power of the laity, he made an ordinance, that no monk or clergyman of that nation should be suffered to aspire to any dignity whatever; excessively differing from the gentleness of Cnut, the former king, who restored their honours, unimpaired, to the conquered: whence it came to pass, that at his decease, the natives easily expelled the foreigners and reclaimed their original right. But William, from certain causes, canonically deposed some persons, and in the place of such as might die, appointed diligent men of any nation except English. Unless I am deceived, their inveterate frowardness towards the king required such a measure; since, as I have said before,[2] the Normans are by nature kindly disposed to those strangers who live amongst them.

---

[1] Ednoth was Harold's master of the horse. He was killed in 1068, in opposing the sons of Harold when they came upon their expedition from Ireland.

[2] See § 246.

§ 255. Ralph, whom I mentioned before,[1] was, by the king's gift,, earl of Norfolk and Suffolk; a Breton on his father's side;[2] a man of a disposition foreign to every thing good. This man, in consequence of being betrothed to the king's relation, the daughter of William Fitz-Osberne, conceived a most unjust design, and meditated an attack on the sovereignty.[3] Wherefore, on the very day of his nuptials, whilst splendidly banqueting (for the luxury of the English had now been adopted by the Normans), and when the guests had become intoxicated and heated with wine, he disclosed his intention in a copious harangue. As their reason was entirely clouded by drunkenness, they loudly applauded the orator. Here Roger, earl of Hereford, brother to the wife of Ralph, and here Weldeof, together with many others, conspired the death of the king. Next day, however, when the fumes of the wine had evaporated,. and cooler thoughts influenced the minds of some of the party, the majority, repenting of their conduct, retired from the meeting. One of them, (said to have been Weldeof,) at the recommendation of archbishop Lanfranc, sailing to Normandy, related the matter to the king; concealing merely his own share of the business.[4] The earls, however, persisted in their design, and each incited his dependents to rebel : but God opposed them, and brought all their machinations to nought. For immediately, the king's officers, who had been left in charge, on discovering the affair, reduced Ralph to such distress, that seizing a vessel at Norwich, he put out to sea : his wife, stipulating for personal safety, and delivering up the castle, followed her husband. Roger being thrown into chains by the king,· visited, or rather inhabited, a prison, during the remainder of his life; a young man of abominable treachery, and by no means imitating his father's conduct.

§ 256. His father,[5] indeed, William Fitz-Osbern, might have been compared, nay, I know not if he might not even have been preferred, to the very best of princes. By his advice, William had first been inspirited to invade, and next, assisted by his valour, to keep possession of England. The energy of his mind was seconded by the almost boundless liberality of his hand : hence it arose, that by the multitude of soldiers, to whom he gave extravagant pay, he repelled the rapacity of the enemy, and ensured the favour of the people.   In consequence, by this boundless profusion, he incurred the king s severe displeasure ; because he had improvidently exhausted his treasures.   The regulations which he established in his county of Hereford, remain in full force at the present day ; that is to say, that no knight[6] should be fined more than seven shillings for whatever offence : whereas, in other provinces, for a very small fault in transgressing the commands of their lord, they pay twenty

[1] See § 253.   [2] See the Saxon Chronicle, A. D. 1075.
[3] The history of this conspiracy derives some illustrations from the correspondence of Lanfranc and the narrative of Ordericus Vitalis.
[4] Compare, here, the statement of the Saxon Chronicle.
[5] William Fitz-Osbern was only the father-in-law of Ralph de Guader.
[6] There is considerable difficulty in distinguishing exactly the various meanings of the term "miles." Sometimes it is, in its legitimate sense, a soldier generally; sometimes it implies a horseman, and frequently it is to be taken in its modern acceptation for a knight; the latter appears to be the meaning here.

or twenty-five. Fortune, however, closed these happy successes by a dishonourable termination, when the supporter of so great a government, the counsellor of England and Normandy, went into Flanders, through fond regard for a woman, and there died by the hands of his enemies. For the elder Baldwin, of whom I have before spoken, the father of Matilda, had two sons ; Robert, who, marrying the countess of Frisia while his father yet lived, acquired the surname of Le Frison: and Baldwin, who, after his father, presided some years over Flanders, and died prematurely, leaving two children, Arnulf and Baldwin, by his wife Richilda, surviving, the guardianship of whom he had entrusted to Philip king of France, (whose aunt was his mother,[1]) and to William Fitz-Osberne. William readily undertook this office, that he might increase his dignity by an union with Richilda : but she, through female pride, aspiring to things beyond her sex, and exacting fresh tributes from the people, excited them to rebellion ; wherefore despatching a messenger to Robert Le Frison, entreating him to accept the government of the country, they adjured all fidelity to Arnulf, who was already called earl. Nor indeed were there wanting persons to espouse the party of the ward : so that, for a long time, Flanders was disturbed by intestine commotion. Fitz-Osbern, who was deeply in love with the lady, could not endure this, but entered Flanders with a body of troops; and, being immediately well received by the persons whom he came to defend, after some days, he rode securely from castle to castle, in a hasty manner with few attendants. On the other hand, Le Frison, who was acquainted with this piece of folly, entrapped him unawares by a secret ambush, and killed him, fighting bravely but to no purpose, together with his nephew Arnulf.

§ 257. Thus possessed of Flanders, he often irritated king William, by plundering Normandy. His daughter married Cnut, king of the Danes, whose son Charles now rules in Flanders.[2] He made peace with king Philip, giving him his daughter-in-law in marriage, by whom he had Lewis,[3] who at present reigns in France; but not long after, being heartily tired of the match, because his queen was extremely corpulent, he divorced her, and, in defiance of law and equity, married the wife of the earl of Anjou. Robert, safe by his affinity with these princes, encountered nothing to distress him during his government; though Baldwin, the brother of Arnulf, who had an earldom in the province of Hainault and in the castle of Valenciennes, by William's assistance made many attempts for that purpose. Three years before his death, when he was now hoary-headed, he went to Jerusalem, as a means of obtaining

---

[1] "Robert (king of the Franks) begat Henry, who reigned twenty-nine years; Henry begat Philip, who was a child at the death of his father, Henry the king of the Franks, and whose guardian was Baldwin, earl of Flanders; for he (i.e. Baldwin) had married his (i e. Philip's) aunt, the sister of king Henry." Lib. de Castro Ambasiæ, ap. Acherium, iii. p. 272. Bouquet, xi. 186.

[2] Charles, called the Good. He was the son of Cnut IV., king of Denmark, and Adele, daughter of Robert le Frison. He succeeded Balduin VII. as earl of Flanders (17th June 1119,) and died 2d March 1127.

[3] Louis the Fat, A.D. 1108—1137.

pardon for his sins : and on his return, he renounced the world, calmly awaiting his dissolution with Christian earnestness. His son was that Robert so universally famed in the expedition into Asia, which, in our times, Europe undertook against the Turks ; but through some mischance, after his return home, he tarnished that noble exploit, being mortally wounded [1] in a tournament, as they call it. Nor did a happier fate attend his son Baldwin, who voluntarily harassing the forces of Henry king of England, in Normandy, paid dearly for his youthful temerity : for, being struck on the head with a pole, and deceived by the professions of several physicians, he lost his life ; the principality devolving on Charles, of whom we have spoken before.

§. 258. King William, conducting himself with mildness towards the obedient, but with severity to the rebellious, possessed the whole of England in tranquillity, holding all the Welsh tributary to him. At this time, too, beyond sea, being never unemployed, he nearly annihilated the county of Maine, leading thither an expedition composed of English,[2] who though they had been easily conquered in their own, yet always appeared invincible in a foreign country. He lost multitudes of his men at Dol,[3] a town of Brittany, whither, irritated by some broil, he had led a military force. He constantly found Philip king of France, the daughter of whose aunt he had married, unfaithful to him ; because he was envious of the great glory of a man who was vassal both to his father and to himself. But William did not the less actively resist his attempts, although his first-born son, Robert, through foolish counsel, assisted him in opposition to his father : whence it happened, that in an attack at Gerborai, the son became personally engaged with his father, wounded him, and killed his horse ;[4] William, the second son, departed with a hurt also, and many of the king's party were slain. In all other respects, during the whole of his life, he was so fortunate, that foreign and distant nations feared nothing so much as his name. He had subdued the inhabitants so completely to his will, that, without any opposition, he first caused an account to be taken of every person ; he compiled a register of the rent of every estate throughout England ;[5] and made all freemen, of every description, take the oath of fidelity to him. Cnut,[6] king of the Danes, who was most highly elevated, both by his affinity to Robert

---

[1] He died in the year 1111.

[2] " A. D. 1073. This year led king William an army of English and French over sea, and won the district of Maine." Sax. Chron.

[3] " King William now went over sea, and led his army to Brittany, and beset the castle of Dol; but the Bretons defended it, until the king came from France ; whereupon king William departed thence, having lost there both men and horses, and many of his treasures." (Sax. Chron. A. D. 1076.) This event is more correctly attributed by Florence and others to the preceding year.

[4] " A.D. 1079. This year Robert fought with his father without Normandy, by a castle called Gerborai, and wounded him in the hand ; and the horse that he sat upon was killed under him." Sax. Chron.

[5] Malmesbury here alludes to that noble and invaluable record, Domesday Book, which was printed at the expense of the nation in the year 1783, and has been since so learnedly and ably explained and commented upon by Sir Henry Ellis, principal librarian of the British Museum. Two vols. 8vo. 1833.

[6] Cnut IV. A. D. 1080 —1086.

le Frison and by his own power, alone menaced his dignity;
a rumour being generally prevalent that he would invade England,
as a country belonging to him from his relationship to the ancient
Cnut; and indeed he would have effected it, had not God counteracted
his boldness by an unfavourable wind. But this circumstance
reminds me that I should briefly trace the genealogy of the Danish
kings, who succeeded after our Cnut, adding, at the same time,
somewhat concerning the Norwegians.

§ 259. As it has been before observed, Harold succeeded him[1]
in England, Hardecnut and his sons in Denmark: for Magnus the
son of Olaf, whom I have mentioned in the history of Cnut,[2] as
having been killed by his subjects, had recovered Norway, which
Cnut had subdued. Harold dying in England, Hardecnut held
both kingdoms for a short time.[3] On his decease, Edward the
Simple succeeded, who, satisfied with his paternal kingdom, despised a foreign empire as burthensome and barbarous. One Swane,
doubtless a most exalted character, was then made king of the
Danes. When his government had prospered for several years,
Magnus, king of the Norwegians,[4] with the consent of some of the
Danes, expelled him by force, and subjected the land to his own
will. Swane, thus expelled, went to the king of Sweden, and collecting by his assistance the Swedes, Vandals, and Goths, he returned
to regain the kingdom; but through the exertions of the Danes,
who were attached to the government of Magnus, he experienced
a repetition of his former ill-fortune. This was a great and memorable battle among those barbarous people: on no other occasion
did the Danes ever experience severer conflict or happier success.
Indeed, to this very time they keep unbroken the vow by which
they had bound themselves before the contest, that they would
consecrate to future ages the vigil of St. Lawrence, (for on that day
the battle was fought,) by fasting and alms; and then also Swane
fled, but soon after, on the death of Magnus, he received his kingdom entire.

§ 260. To Magnus, in Norway, succeeded one Swane, surnamed
Herdhand, not elevated by royal descent, but by his boldness and
cunning; to him Olaf, the uncle of Magnus, whom they call a saint;
to Olaf, Harold Havagre, the brother of Olaf, who had formerly,
when a young man, served under the emperor of Constantinople,
and who, when at his command he was exposed to a lion, for having
ravished a woman of quality, strangled the huge beast by the bare
strength of his arms. He was slain in England, by Harold the son
of Godwin.[5] His sons, Olaf and Magnus, divided the kingdom of
their father; but Magnus dying prematurely, Olaf seized the whole.
To him succeeded his son Magnus, who was lately miserably slain
in Ireland, on which he had rashly made a descent. They relate
that the last mentioned Magnus, the son of Harold, was, after the

---

[1] Cnut died, according to Suenon, the Danish historian, on the 12th of Nov.
1036; but see § 187.   [2] See § 181.   [3] See § 188.
[4] Magnus, king of Norway, succeeded Hardacnut in 1042, but in the following
year Sweyn attempted to deprive him of the kingdom of Denmark. Upon the
death of Magnus, in 1047, Sweyn obtained the kingdom.
[5] See § 228.

death of his father, compassionately sent home by Harold, king of England; and that in return for this kindness, he humanely treated Harold, the son of Harold, when he came to him after William's victory; that he took him with him in an expedition he made to England, in the time of William the younger, when he conquered the Orkney and Mevanian Isles[1], and meeting with Hugh earl of Chester, and Hugh earl of Shrewsbury, put the first to flight, and the second to death. The. sons of the last Magnus, Hasten and Siward, yet reign conjointly, having divided the empire; the latter, a seemly and spirited youth, shortly since went to Jerusalem, by the route of England, performing many famous exploits against the Saracens; more especially in the siege of Sidon, whose inhabitants raged furiously against the Christians, through their connexion with the Turks.

§ 261. But Swane, as I have related, on his restoration to the sovereignty of the Danes, being impatient of quiet, sent his son Cnut twice into England; first with three hundred, and then with two hundred ships. His associate in the former expedition was Osbern, the brother of Swane, in the latter, Hacco; but, being each of them bribed, they frustrated the young man's designs, and returned home without effecting their purpose. In consequence, becoming highly disgraced by king Swane for bartering their fidelity for money, they were driven into banishment. Swane, when near his end, bound all the inhabitants by oath, that, as he had fourteen sons, they should confer the kingdom on each of them in succession, as long as his issue remained. On his decease his son Harold succeeded for three years; to him Cnut, whom his father had formerly sent into England. Remembering his original failure, he prepared, as we have heard, more than a thousand vessels against England;[2] his father-in-law, Robert le Frison, the possessor of six hundred more, supporting him; but being detained for almost two years by the adverseness of the wind, he changed his design, affirming that it must be by the determination of God that he could not put to sea; but afterwards, misled by the suggestions of some persons who attributed the failure of their passage to the conjura-tions of certain old women, he sentenced the chiefs whose wives were accused of this transgression to an intolerable fine; cast his brother Olaf, the principal of the suspected faction, into chains, and sent him into exile to his father-in-law. The barbarians, in conse-quence, resenting this attack upon their liberty, killed[3] him while in church, clinging to the altar, and promising reparation. They say that many miracles were shown from heaven at that place; because he was a man strictly observant of fasting and almsgiving, and pur-sued the transgressors of the divine laws more rigorously than those who offended against himself; from which circumstance he was consecrated a martyr by the pope of Rome. After him, the mur-derers, that they might atone for their crime by some degree of

---

[1] Man and Anglesey.

[2] Cnut's meditated invasion may be referred to the year 1085.

[3] Cnut was murdered in the church of Odensee on the 10th of July 1086. Vide Johnston's Antiq. Celto-Scand. p. 228.

good, redeemed Olaf from captivity, for ten thousand marks of
silver. After ignobly reigning during eight years, he left the government to his brother Henry, who, living virtuously for twenty-nine
years,[1] went to Jerusalem, and breathed his last at sea. Nicholas,
the fifth in the sovereignty, still survives.[2]

§ 262. The king of Denmark then, as I have said, was the only
obstacle to William's uninterrupted enjoyment : on whose account
he enlisted such an immense multitude of stipendiary soldiers out
of every province on this side the mountains, that their numbers
oppressed the kingdom : but he, with his usual magnanimity, not
regarding the expense, had engaged even Hugh the Great, brother
to the king of France, with his bands to serve in his army. He was
accustomed to stimulate and incite his own valour, by the remem-
brance of Robert Guiscard ;[3] saying it was disgraceful to yield in
courage to him whom he surpassed in rank. For Robert, born of
middling parentage[4] in Normandy, that is, neither very low nor
very high, had gone, a few years before William's arrival in England, with fifteen knights, into Apulia, to remedy the narrowness
of his own circumstances, by entering into the service of that
inactive people. Not many years elapsed, ere, by the stupendous
assistance of God, he reduced the whole country under his power :
for where his strength failed, his ingenuity was alert : first receiving
the towns, and after the cities, into confederacy with him. Thus he
became so successful, as to make himself duke of Apulia and Calabria ; his brother Richard, prince of Capua; and his other brother,
Roger, earl of Sicily. At last, giving Apulia to his son Roger, he
crossed the Adriatic with his other son Boamund, and taking
Durazzo,[5] was immediately proceeding against Alexis, emperor of
Constantinople, when a messenger from pope Hildebrand stopped
him in the heat of his career. For Henry, emperor of Germany,
son of that Henry[6] we have before mentioned,[7] being incensed
against the pope, for having excommunicated him on account of
the ecclesiastical investitures, led an army against Rome; besieged
it ;[8] expelled Hildebrand, and introduced Guibert of Ravenna.
Guiscard learning this by the letter of the expelled pope, left his
son Boamund, with the army, to follow up his designs, and returned
to Apulia ; where quickly collecting together a body of Apulians

---

[1] Eric I. after a reign of seven years only, died, on his way to the Holy Land,
at Cyprus, on the 11th of July, 1103.

[2] Nicolas succeeded his brother, after an inter-regnum of two years, A.D. 1105;
and was murdered on the 25th of June, 1135.

[3] The birth, character, and first actions of. Robert Guiscard may be found in
Jeffrey Malaterra (lib. i. cap. 3, 4, 11, 16, 17, 18, 38, 39, 40); William Apulus (lib.
ii. pp. 260—362); William of Jumiéges (lib. xi. c. 30, pp. 663, 664 ; edit. Camden);
and Anna Comnena (Alexiad, lib. i. pp. 23—27 ; lib. vi. p. 165), with the anno-
tations of Ducange (notes in Alexiad, pp. 230—232, 320), who has swept all the
French and Latin chronicles for supplemental intelligence. Gibbon, Dec. Rom.
Emp., vii. 217.

[4] The pedigree of Robert Guiscard is variously deduced from the peasants and
dukes of Normandy. His genuine descent may be ascribed to the second or
middle order of private nobility. He sprang from a race of "valvassors" or
"bannerets," of the diocese of Coutances in Lower Normandy.

[5] Durazzo was taken on the 8th of February 1082.

[6] Henry IV.   [7] See § 189.

[8] Rome was besieged by Henry in the years 1081 and 1084.

and Normans, he proceeded to Rome. Nor did Henry wait for a messenger to announce his approach; but, affrighted at the bare report, he fled with his pretended pope. Rome, freed from intruders, received its lawful sovereign ; but soon after again lost him by similar violence. Then, too, Alexis, learning that Robert was called home by the urgency of his affairs, and hoping to put a finishing hand to the war, rushed against Boamund, who commanded the troops which had been left. The Norman youth, however, observant of his native spirit, though far inferior in number, put to flight, by dint of military skill, the undisciplined Greeks and the other collected nations. At the same time, too, the Venetians, a people habituated to the sea, attacking Guiscard, who having settled the object of his voyage, was now sailing back, met with a similar calamity : part were drowned or killed, and the rest put to flight. He, continuing his intended expedition, induced many cities, subject to Alexis, to second his views. The emperor removed by crime the man whom he was unable to subdue by arms : falsely promising his wife an imperial match: by her artifices, he drank poison,[1] which she had prepared, and died; deserving, had God so pleased, a nobler death : unconquerable by the sword of an enemy, yet falling a victim to domestic treachery. He was buried at Venusium in Apulia,[2] having the following epitaph :—

> " Here Guiscard lies, the terror of the world,
> Who from the Capitol Rome's sovereign hurl'd.
> No band collected could Alexis free,
> Flight only : Venice, neither flight nor sea."

§ 263. And since mention has been made of Hildebrand,[3] I shall relate some anecdotes of him, which I have not heard trivially, but from the sober relation of a person who would swear that he had learned them from the mouth of Hugh abbot of Clugny; whom I admire and commend to notice, from the consideration, that he used to declare the secret thoughts of others, by the prophetic intuition of his mind. Alexander, an able pope, seeing the energetic bent of his disposition, had made him chancellor[4] of the holy see. In consequence, by virtue of his office, he used to go through the provinces to correct abuses. All ranks of people flocked to him, requiring judgment on various affairs: all secular power was subject to him, as well out of regard to his sanctity, as to his office. It happened, one day, when there was a greater concourse on horseback than usual, that the abbot aforesaid, with his monks, was gently proceeding in the last rank ; and beholding, at a distance, the distinguished honour of this man, that so many earthly rulers

---

[1] The most authentic writers, William of Apulia, lib. v. p. 277; Jeffrey Malaterra, lib. iii. c. 41, p. 589; and Romuald de Salerna (Chron. in Muratori, Script. Rerum Ital. tom. vii.) are ignorant of this accusation. Hoveden, moreover (p. 710, in Script. post Bedam), who follows Malmesbury, adds that Alexis married, crowned, and then burnt alive his female accomplice. See Gibb. Dec. Rom. Emp. vii. 247.

[2] He died 17th of July, 1085, in the isle of Cephalonia, in his tent.

[3] The Lives of Gregory VII. are either legends or invectives, and his miraculous or magical performances are alike incredible to a modern reader.

[4] He was first archdeacon, and afterwards chancellor. See Baronii Annal. x. 289.

awaited his nod, he was revolving in his mind sentiments to the following effect : " By what dispensation of God was this fellow, of diminutive stature and obscure parentage, surrounded by a retinue of so many rich men. Doubtless, from having such a crowd of attendants, he was vainglorious, and conceived loftier notions than were becoming." Scarcely, as I have said, had he imagined this in his heart, when the archdeacon, turning back his horse, and spurring him, cried out, from a distance, beckoning the abbot, " You," said he, " you have imagined falsely ; wrongly deeming me guilty of a thing, of which I am innocent altogether : for I neither impute this as glory to myself, if glory that can be called which vanishes quickly, nor do I wish it to be so imputed by others, but to the blessed apostles, to whose servant it is exhibited." Reddening with shame, and not daring to deny a tittle, he replied only, " My lord, I pray thee, how couldest thou know the secret thought of my heart, which I have communicated to no one ?" " All that inward sentiment of yours," said he, " was brought from your mouth to my ears, as though by a pipe."

§ 264. Again, entering a country church, in the same province, they prostrated themselves before the altar side by side. When they had continued their supplications for a long period, the archdeacon looked on the abbot with an angry countenance. After they had prayed some time longer, he went out, and asking the reason of his displeasure, received this answer, " If you love me, do not again attack me with an injury of this kind: my Lord Jesus Christ, beautiful beyond the sons of men, was visibly present to my entreaties, listening to what I said, and kindly looking assent ; but, · attracted by the earnestness of your prayer, He left me, and turned to you : I think you will not deny it to be a species of injury, to take from a friend the Author of his salvation. Moreover, you are to know, that mortality of mankind, and destruction, hang over this place ; and the token by which I formed such a conclusion was, by seeing the angel of the Lord standing upon the altar, with a naked sword, and waving it to and fro : I possess a more manifest proof of the impending ruin, from the thick cloudy air, which, as you see, already envelopes that province. Let us make haste to escape, then, lest we perish with the rest." Having said this, they entered an inn for refreshment ; but as soon as food was placed before them, the lamentations of the household took away their famished appetites : for first one, and then another, and presently many of the family suddenly lost their lives by some unseen disaster. The contagion then spreading to the adjoining houses, they mounted their mules, and departed ; fear adding wings to their flight.

Account of a Bishop who obtained his See by Simony.

§ 265. Hildebrand had presided for the pope, at a council in Gaul, where many bishops, being degraded for having formerly acquired their churches by simony, gave place to better men. There was one, to whom a suspicion of this apostasy attached, but he could neither be convicted by any witnesses, nor confuted by any argument: when it was supposed he must be completely foiled, still, like the slippery snake, he eluded detection ; so skilled was he in speaking, that he baffled all. Then said the archdeacon, " Let the oracle of God be resorted to, let man's eloquence cease ; we know for certain that episcopal grace is the gift of the Holy Spirit, and that whosoever purchases a bishopric, supposes the gift of the Holy Ghost may be procured by money. Before us then, who are assembled by the will of the Holy Ghost, let him say, " Glory be to the Father, and to the Son, and to the Holy Ghost," and if he shall speak it articulately, and without hesitation, it will be manifest to me that he has obtained his office, not by purchase, but legally." He willingly accepted the condition, supposing nothing less than any difficulty in these words ; and indeed he perfectly uttered, "Glory be to the Father, and to the Son," but he hesitated at the " Holy Ghost." A clamour arose on all sides, but he was never able, by any exertion, either at that time or for the remainder of his life, to name the Holy Spirit. The abbot so often mentioned was a witness of this miracle : who taking the deprived bishop with him into different places, often laughed at the issue of the experiment. Any person doubting the certainty of this relation, must be confuted by all Europe, which is aware that the numbers of the Clugniac order were increased by this abbot.

§ 266. On the death of Alexander, therefore, Hildebrand, called Gregory the Seventh,[1] succeeded. He openly asserted, what others had whispered ; excommunicating those persons who, having been elected, should receive the investiture of their churches by the ring and staff, through the hands of a layman. On this account, Henry, emperor of Germany, being incensed that one elected without his concurrence should so far presume, expelled him from Rome, as I observed, after the expiration of eleven years, and brought in Guibert. Not long after, the pope being seized with that fatal disease, which he had no doubt would be mortal, was requested by the cardinals to appoint his successor; referring him to the example of St. Peter, who, in the church's earliest infancy, had, while yet living, nominated Clement. He refused to follow this example, because it had anciently been forbidden by councils : he would advise, however, that if they wished a person powerful in worldly matters, they should choose Desiderius, abbot of Cassino, who would quell the violence of Guibert successfully, and opportunely, by a military force ; but, if they wanted a religious and eloquent man, they should elect Odo bishop of Ostia. Thus died a man highly acceptable with God, though perhaps rather too austere towards man. Indeed it is affirmed, that in the beginning of the first commotion between him and the emperor, he would not admit him within his doors, though bare-footed, and carrying[2] sheers and scourges ; despising a man guilty of sacrilege, and of incest with

---

[1] Elected pope 22d of April, 1073, and died 25th May, 1085.
[2] This seems intended to denote his absolute submission and willingness to undergo any kind of penance which might be enjoined him. Sometimes excommunicated persons wore a halter about their necks; sometimes they were shorn or scourged prior to receiving absolution. V. Basnage, Pref. in Canisium, p. 69, 70.

his own sister. The emperor, thus excluded, departed, vowing that this repulse should be the death of many a man. And immediately doing all the injury he was able to the Roman see, he excited thereby the favourers of the pope, on every side, to throw off their allegiance to himself; for one Rodulph, revolting at the command of the pope, who had sent him a crown in the name of the apostles, he was immersed on all sides in the tumults of war. But Henry, ever superior to ill-fortune, at length subdued him, and the rest of the faithless rebels. At last, driven from his power, not by a foreign attack, but the domestic hatred of his son, he died miserably. To Hildebrand succeeded Desiderius, called Victor, who, at his first mass, fell down dead, though from what mischance is unknown; the cup, if it be possible to credit such a thing, being poisoned. The election then fell upon Odo, a Frenchman by birth; first arch-deacon of Rheims, then prior of Clugny, afterwards bishop of Ostia, lastly pope, by the name of Urban.

§ 267. Thus far I shall be pardoned for having wandered abroad, as from the mention of William's transactions some things occurred which I thought it improper to omit; now the reader, who is so inclined, shall learn the more common habits of his life, and his domestic manners. Above all, then, he was humble to the servants of God; affable to the obedient; inexorable to the rebellious. He attended the offices of the Christian religion as much as a layman was able; so that he daily was present at mass, and heard vespers and matins. He built one monastery in England, and another in Normandy; that at Caen [1] first, which he dedicated to St. Stephen, and endowed with suitable estates, and most magnificent presents. There he appointed Lanfranc, afterwards archbishop of Canterbury, abbot; a man worthy to be compared to the ancients, in knowledge, and in religion: of whom it may be truly said, "Cato the third is descended from heaven;" so much had an heavenly savour tinctured his heart and tongue; so much was the whole western world excited to the knowledge of the liberal arts by his learning; and so earnestly did the monastic profession labour in the work of religion, either from his example or authority. No sinister means profited a bishop in those days; nor could an abbot procure advancement by purchase: he who had the best report for undeviating sanctity, was most honoured and most esteemed both by the king and by the archbishop. William built the other monastery near Hastings, dedicated to St. Martin, which was also called Battle,[2] because there the principal church stands on the very spot, where, as they report, Harold was found in the thickest heaps of the slain. When little more than a boy, yet gifted with the wisdom of age, he removed his uncle Malger from the archbishopric of Rouen. He was a man not ordinarily learned, but,

---

[1] The abbey of St. Stephen's, Caen, is stated to have been completed in 1064, but when it was dedicated is not accurately known; some fix the dedication in 1073, others in 1081, and Ordericus Vitalis in 1077. There was, however, a foundation charter granted subsequently to 1066, for in it William styles himself king.

[2] Although William the Conqueror founded and endowed Battle Abbey, yet the church, according to Florence, was not dedicated till 1094, when William Rufus stopped at Hastings on his way to Normandy.

through his high birth, forgetful of his profession, he gave too much attention to hunting and hawking; and consumed the treasures of the church in a splendid mode of living: this being much bruited about, he never, during his whole life-time, obtained the pall, the holy see refusing the distinction of that honour to a man who neglected his sacred office. Wherefore being frequently cited, his nephew reprehending his offences; but he, still conducting himself in the same manner, was, from the urgency of the case, ultimately degraded. Some report that there was a secret reason for his being deprived: that Matilda, whom William had married, was very nearly related to him: that Malger, in consequence, through zeal for the Christian faith, could not endure that they should riot in the bed of consanguinity; and that he hurled the weapon of excommunication against his nephew and his consort: that, when the anger of the young man was roused by the complaints of his wife, an occasion was sought out, through which the persecutor of their crime might be driven from his see: but that afterwards, in riper years, for the expiation of their offence, he built the monastery to St. Stephen at Caen; and she also one, in the same town, to the Holy Trinity;[1] each of them choosing the inmates according to their own sex.

§ 268. To Malger succeeded Maurilius, a monk of Fescamp; he was commendable for many virtues, but principally for his abstinence. After a holy and well-spent life, when he came, by the call of God, to his end, bereft of vital breath, he lay, as it were, dead for almost half a day: nevertheless, when preparation was made to carry him into the church, recovering his breath, he melted the by-standers to tears of joy, and comforted them, when lost in amazement, with this address :—" Let your minds be attentive while you hear the last words of your pastor. I have died a natural death, but I am come back to relate to you what I have seen; yet shall I not continue with you long, because it delights me to sleep in the Lord. The conductors of my spirit were adorned with every elegance, both of countenance and attire; the gentleness of their speech accorded with the splendour of their garments; so much so, that I could wish for nothing more than the attentions of such men. Delighted, therefore, with their soothing approbation, I went, as it appeared to me, towards the East. A seat in Paradise was promised me, which I was shortly to enter. In a moment, passing over Europe and entering Asia, we came to Jerusalem; where, having worshipped the saints, we proceeded to Jordan; the residents on either bank joining company with my conductors, made a joyful party. I was now hastening to pass over the river, through longing desire to see what was beyond it, when my companions informed me that God had commanded, that I must first be terrified by the sight of the demons, in order that the venial sins which I had not wiped out by confession, might be expiated, by the

---

[1] The convent of the Holy Trinity was founded by Matilda in 1066, and its church dedicated on the 18th of June in that year. Duke William, on the same day, presenting at the altar his infant daughter Cecilia, devoted her to the service of God in this monastery, where she became the second abbess.

dread of terrific forms. As soon as this was said, there came opposite to me such a multitude of devils, brandishing pointed weapons,
and breathing out fire, that the plain appeared like steel, and the
air like flame. I was so dreadfully alarmed at them, that had the
earth clave asunder, or the heaven opened, I should not have known
where to have betaken myself for safety. Thus panic-stricken, and
doubting where to go, I suddenly recovered my life, though instan-
taneously about to lose it again, that by this relation I might be
serviceable to your salvation, unless you neglect it;" and almost as
soon as he had so said, he breathed out his soul. His body, then
buried underground, in the church of St. Mary, is now, by divine
miracle, as they report, raised up more than three feet above the earth.

§ 269. Moreover, William, following up the design he had formerly begun in Normandy, permitted Stigand, the wicked and false
archbishop, to be deposed by the Roman cardinals and by Ermen-
fred bishop of Sion. Walkelin succeeded him at Winchester, whose
good works, surpassing fame, will resist the power of oblivion as
long as the episcopal see shall there continue; in Kent succeeded
Lanfranc, of whom I have before spoken, who was, by the gift of
God, as resplendent in England,

> " As Lucifer, who bids the stars retire,
> Day's rosy harbinger with purple fire;"

so much did the monastic germ sprout by his care, so strongly
grew the pontifical power while he survived. The king was but the
servant of his advice, in such wise that he deemed it proper to
concede whatever Lanfranc asserted ought to be done. At his instigation, also, was abolished the infamous custom of those ill-disposed
people who used to sell their slaves into Ireland. The credit of
this action I know not exactly whether to attribute to Lanfranc or
to Wulstan bishop of Worcester; who would scarcely have induced
the king, reluctant from the profit it produced him, to this measure,
had not Lanfranc recommended it, and Wulstan, powerful from his
sanctity of character, enjoined it by episcopal authority : Wulstan,
than whom none could be more just, nor could any in our time
equal him in the power of miracles, or the gift of prophecy; of
which I purpose hereafter to relate some particulars, should it meet
his most holy approbation.

§ 270. But since the die of fortune is subject to uncertain
casts, many calamities happened during those times. There was a
disgraceful contention[1] between the abbot of Glastonbury and his
monks; so that after altercation they came to blows. The monks
being driven into the church, bewailed their miseries at the holy altar;
but the soldiers, rushing in, slew two of them, wounded fourteen,
and drove away the rest: nay, the rage of the military even bristled
the crucifix with arrows. The abbot, rendered infamous by such a
criminal outrage, was driven into exile for the whole of the king's
life; but, upon his decease, he was restored to his honours; a sum

---

[1] This disgraceful contention happened in the year 1083. It seems to have
arisen from the abbot (Thurstan) attempting to introduce a new style of chant,
brought from Fescamp, instead of the Gregorian, to which the monks had been
accustomed.

of money being paid to such as interceded for him, for the expiation of his transgression.

§ 271. Again, a cruel and ignominious end overtook Walker,[1] bishop of Durham, whom the Northumbrians, a people ever ripe for rebellion, throwing off all respect for his holy orders, put to death, after having severely insulted him. A considerable number of Lorrainers were killed there also; for the bishop was of that country. The cause of the murder was this: the bishop, independently of his see, was governor of the whole country:[2] over public business he had set his relation Gilbert, and over domestic, the canon Leobin; both men of diligence in their respective employments, but rash. The bishop endured their want of moderation in this respect, out of regard to their activity; and, as he had placed them in office, treated them with great kindness: for our nature ever indulges itself, and favourably regards its own kind works. This Leobin caused Liulf, a servant so dearly beloved by St. Cuthbert that the saint himself used to appear to him, even when waking, and direct his decisions; him, I say, he caused to be killed by Gilbert; smitten with envy at his holding the higher place in the prelate's esteem for his knowledge and equity in legal determinations. Walker, terrified with this intelligence, offered the furious family of the deceased the result of a legal inquiry,[3] affirming that Leobin would be the cause of his death and of that of his friends. When the matter came to a trial, this ferocious race of people were not to be soothed by reasons of any kind; on the contrary, they threw the whole blame on the bishop, because they had seen both the murderers familiarly entertained in his court after the death of Liulf. Hence arose clamour and indignation, and Gilbert, as he was, of his own accord, going out of the church where he had been sitting with the bishop, that he might, at his personal peril, save the life of his master, was impiously slain. The bishop, while making overtures of peace before the gates, next glutted the rage of the people with his blood: the fomenter of the crime, too, Leobin, was half-burnt, as he would not quit the church till it was set on fire, and when he rushed out, he was received on a thousand spears. This had been predicted by Edgitha, relict of king Edward; for when she had formerly seen Walker, with his milk-white hair, rosy countenance, and extraordinary stature, conducted to Winchester to be consecrated: "We have here," said she, "a noble martyr:" being led to form such a presage, by reflecting on the mutinous disposition of that people. To him succeeded William abbot of St. Carilef,[4] who established monks at Durham.

[1] Bishop Walcher was murdered on the 1st of May, 1080.

[2] The bishops of Durham were palatinate lords, and had in the county of Durham "regalem potestatem in omnibus" as fully as the king had in his palace. Bract. iii. 8, § 4.

[3] Walcher offered to purge himself, by oath, from all participation in the murder. See Florence of Worcester, A.D. 1080.

[4] William de S. Karilepho, consecrated bishop of Durham January 3d, 1082, held the office of chief justice of England under William the Conqueror. He was driven from his see for a considerable time by William Rufus, and died January 6th, 1095.

§ 272. Moreover, the year before the king's death, there was a mortality both among men and cattle, and severe tempests, accompanied with such thunder and lightning as no person before had ever seen or heard. And in the year he died, a contagious fever destroyed more than half the people; indeed the attack of the disease killed many, and then, from the unseasonableness of the weather, a famine following, it spread universally and cut off those whom the fever had spared.

§ 273. In addition to his other virtues, he, more especially in early youth, was observant of chastity; insomuch, that it was very commonly reported that he was impotent: marrying, however, at the recommendation of the nobility, he conducted himself, during many years, in such wise, as never to be suspected of any criminal intercourse. He had many children by Matilda, who, obedient to her husband and fruitful in issue, excited his mind to the tenderest regard for her; although there are not wanting persons who prate about his having renounced his former chastity; and that, after he had acceded to the royal dignity, he was connected with the daughter of a certain priest, whom the queen caused to be removed by being hamstrung by one of her servants; on which account he was exiled, and Matilda was scourged to death with a bridle. But I esteem it folly to believe this of so great a king; though I decidedly assert that a slight disagreement arose between them, in latter times, on account of their son Robert, whom his mother was said to have supplied with military forces out of her revenues. Nevertheless, he proved that his conjugal affection was not in the least diminished by this circumstance; as he buried her with great magnificence on her death, four years before his own; and, weeping most profusely for many days, showed how keenly he felt her loss: moreover, from that time, if we give credit to report, he refrained from every gratification. The queen was buried at Caen, in the monastery of the Holy Trinity.[1] The same proof of regard was evident in the care he took of the funeral of queen Edgitha;[2] who, having been entombed, by his directions, near her husband at Westminster, has a tomb richly wrought with gold and silver.

§ 274. His sons were Robert, Richard, William, and Henry. The two last reigned after him successively in England: Robert, irritated that Normandy was refused him during his father's lifetime, went indignantly into Italy, that by marrying the daughter of Boniface the marquis, he might procure assistance in those parts to oppose the king; but failing of this connection, he excited Philip king of France against his father: wherefore, disappointed of his paternal blessing and inheritance, at his father's death, he missed England, retaining with difficulty the duchy of Normandy; and pawning[3] even this, at the expiration of nine years, to his brother William, he joined the expedition into Asia, with the other

---

[1] Matilda died 2d of November, 1083. She bequeathed to this monastery her crown, sceptre, and ornaments of state. A copy of her will may be seen in the Essais Historiques, by the Abbé de la Rue, ii. 437.

[2] The queen of Edward the Confessor. See the Saxon Chronicle, A.D. 1075.

[3] Robert mortgaged Normandy to his brother in 1096 for the trifling sum of ten thousand marks.

Christians. From thence, at the end of four years, he returned with credit for his military exploits; and without difficulty sat himself down in Normandy,[1] because, his brother William being recently dead, king Henry, unsettled on account of his fresh-acquired power, deemed it enough to retain England under his command; but, as I must speak of this in another place, I will here pursue the relation I had begun concerning the sons of William the Great.

§ 275. Richard afforded his noble father hopes of his future greatness; he was a noble youth and of an aspiring disposition, considering his age; but an untimely death quickly withered the bud of this promising flower. They relate, that while hunting deer in the New Forest, he contracted a disorder from a stream of foul air.[2] This is the place which William, his father, desolating the towns and destroying the churches for more than thirty miles, had turned into a forest and haunt for wild beasts. [3]Here he willingly passed his time, here he delighted to follow the chase, I will not say for days, but even months together. Here, too, many accidents befel the royal race, which the recent recollection of the inhabitants supplies to inquirers; for in this very forest, William his son, and his grandson Richard, son of Robert, earl of Normandy, by the severe judgment of God, met their deaths, one by a wound in the breast by an arrow, the other by a wound in the neck; or as some say, from being suspended by the jaws on the branch of a tree, as his horse passed beneath it.

§ 276. His daughters were five; first, Cecilia,[4] abbess of Caen, who still survives; the second, Constantia, married to Alan Fergant earl of Brittany, excited the inhabitants by the severity of her justice to administer a poisonous potion to her; the third, Adela, the wife of Stephen earl of Blois, a lady celebrated for secular industry, lately took the veil at Marcigny. The names of the two others have escaped me:[5] one of these, as we have said,[6] was be-

---

[1] "During the harvest time of this year (1100) came the earl Robert home into Normandy; and he was there joyfully received by all his people." Sax. Chron.

[2] Some historians relate that he died from the wounds he received from the goring of a stag's horns about three years before his father's decease. Malmesbury's account, however, is probably the truest. Richard was buried at Winchester, and his epitaph styles him Beorniæ dux. Sanderson's Geneal. Hist. fol. 1707.

[3] Some MSS. instead of this read, "A dreadful spectacle indeed, that, where before had existed human intercourse and the worship of God, there deer and goats, and other animals of that kind, should now range unrestrained; and not allowed to be taken by the people at large. Hence it is truly asserted that in this very forest &c." (as in the text.)

[4] Balderic, abbot of Bourgueil, in verses dedicated "To Cecilia, daughter of the king of England," mentions a sister whom Cecilia had taken with her into the monastery; he thus writes:—
"Audivi quandam te detinuisse sororem,
Cujus fama meas aliquando perculit aures.
Nomen it elapsum, vidisse tamen reminiscor."
Note in Bouq. xi. 189.

[5] The names of William the Conqueror's five daughters, as given by Ordericus Vitalis (lib. iv. 512), were Agatha, Constantia, Adeliza, Adela, and Cecilia. William of Jumiéges (vi. 31) states that Adeliza was betrothed to Harold. Later historians speak of Margaret and Elianor; the former as being betrothed to Harold, the other to Alfonso VI. king of Leon. See Tyrrel, Hist. Engl. ii. 61; and Lyttleton's Hist. of Henry II. i. 356.

[6] See § 228.

trothed to Harold, and died ere she was marriageable; the other was affianced, by messengers, to Alphonso, king of Gallicia, but obtained from God a virgin-death. A hard substance, which proved the frequency of her prayers, was found upon her knees after her decease.

§ 277. Honouring the memory of his father, by every practicable method, in the latter part of his life, he caused his bones, formerly interred at Nicea, to be taken up by means of a person sent for that purpose, in order to convey them elsewhere; who successfully returning, stopped in Apulia, on hearing of the death of William, and there buried this illustrious man's remains. He treated his mother, who, before the death of his father, had married one Herlewin de Conte-ville, a man of moderate wealth, with singular indulgence as long as she lived. William's brothers by this match were Robert,[1] a man of heavy sluggish disposition, whom he made earl of Moriton; and Odo,[2] whom, while he was earl, he made bishop of Baieux; and when king, created him earl of Kent. Being of quicker talents than the other, he was governor of all England, under the king, after the death of William Fitz-Osbern. He had wonderful skill in accumulating treasure, possessed extreme craft in dissembling, so that, though absent, yet, stuffing the scrips of the pilgrims with letters and money, he had nearly purchased the Roman papacy from the citizens. But when, through the rumour of his intended journey, soldiers eagerly flocked to him from all parts of the kingdom, the king, taking offence, threw him into confinement, saying that he did not seize the bishop of Baieux, but the earl of Kent. His partisans being intimidated by threats, discovered such quantities of gold that the heap of precious metal would surpass the belief of the present age; and at last many sacks full of wrought gold were also taken out of the rivers, which he had secretly buried in certain places. When released, at the death of his brother, he joined Robert's party, as he was averse to his nephew William; but then, too, matters turning out unfavourably, he was banished England, and went over to his nephew and his bishopric in Normandy. Afterwards, proceeding with him on his enterprise to Jerusalem, he died at Antioch while it was besieged by the Christians.

§ 278. King William kindly admitted foreigners to his friendship, bestowed honours on them without distinction, and was attentive to almsgiving; he gave many possessions in England to foreign churches, and scarcely did his own munificence, or that of his nobility, leave any monastery unnoticed, more especially in Normandy, so that their poverty was mitigated by the riches of England. Thus, in his time, the monastic flock increased on every side, monasteries arose, ancient in their rule, but modern in building; but at this I fancy I hear some persons mutter that it would

---

[1] Robert, soon after the Conquest, was advanced to the earldom of Cornwall, and had extensive possessions in almost every county conferred upon him by his uterine brother. He died in 1091.

[2] Odo became bishop of Baieux in 1049, and was made earl of Kent in 1067; he died at Palermo on his way to the Holy Land in 1097.

have been better that the old should have been preserved in their original state, than that new ones should have been erected from their plunder.

§ 279. He was of moderate stature, extraordinary corpulence, and fierce countenance; his forehead was bare of hair; he was of such great strength of arm that it was often matter of surprise that no one was able to draw his bow, which he himself could bend when his horse was at full gallop; he was majestic, whether sitting or standing, although the protuberance of his belly deformed the dignity of his appearance; of excellent health, so that he was never confined with any dangerous disorder, except at the last; so addicted was he to the pleasures of the chase, that, as I have before said, ejecting the inhabitants, he let a space of many miles grow desolate, that, when at liberty from other avocations, he might there pursue his pleasures.   He gave sumptuous and splendid entertainments at the principal festivals; passing, during the years he could conveniently remain in England, Christmas at Gloucester, Easter at Winchester, and Pentecost at Westminster.   At these times a royal edict summoned thither all the principal persons of every order, that the ambassadors from foreign nations might admire the splendour of the assemblage, and the costliness of the banquets.   Nor was he at any time more affable or indulgent; in order that the visitants might proclaim universally that his generosity kept pace with his riches.   This mode of banqueting was constantly observed by his first successor; the second omitted it.

§ 280. The only thing for which he can deservedly be blamed is his hoarding of money, which he sought all opportunities of scraping together, provided he could allege that they were honourable and not unbecoming the royal dignity: but he will readily be excused, because a new government cannot be administered without large revenues.   I have here no excuse whatever to offer, unless it be, as one has said, that " Of necessity he must fear many whom many fear."   For through dread of his enemies he used to drain the country of money, with which he might retard, or repel their attacks; very often, as it happens in human affairs, where strength failed, purchasing the forbearance of his enemies with gold.   This disgraceful calamity is still prevalent, and every day increases; so that, both towns and churches are subjected to contributions; nor is this done with firm-kept faith on the part of the imposers, but whoever offers the higher bribe carries off the prize, all former agreements being disregarded.

§ 281. Residing in his latter days in Normandy, when enmity had arisen between him and the king of France, he for a short period was confined to the house; Philip, scoffing at this forbearance, is reported to have said, " The king of England is lying-in at Rouen, and keeps his bed, like a woman after her delivery;" jesting on his belly, which he had been reducing by medicine.   Cruelly hurt at this sarcasm, he replied, " When I go to mass, after my confinement, I will make him an offering of an hundred thousand candles."[1]   He swore this, " by the Resurrection and the splendour

[1] The Romish ritual directs the woman to kneel, with a lighted taper in her

of God;" for he was wont purposely to swear such oaths as, by the very opening of his mouth, would strike terror into the minds of his hearers.

§ 282. Not long after, in the end of the month of August, when the corn was ripe in the fields, the clusters on the vines, and the orchards laden with fruit in full abundance, collecting an army, he entered France in an hostile manner, trampling down, and laying everything waste; nothing could assuage his irritated mind, so determined was he to revenge this injurious taunt at the expense of multitudes. At last he set fire to the city of Mantes, where the church of St. Mary was burnt, together with a recluse who did not think it justifiable to quit her cell even under such an emergency; and the whole property of the citizens was destroyed. Exhilarated by this success, while furiously commanding his people to add fuel to the conflagration, he approached too near the flames, and contracted a disorder from the violence of the fire and the intenseness of the autumnal heat. Some say that his horse leaping over a dangerous ditch, ruptured his rider, for his belly projected over the front of the saddle. Injured by this accident he sounded a retreat, and returning to Rouen, as the malady increased he took to his bed. His physicians, when consulted, affirmed, from an inspection of his urine, that his decease was inevitable. On hearing this he filled the house with his lamentations, because death had suddenly seized him before he could effect that reformation of life which he had for a long time meditated. Recovering his fortitude, however, he performed the duties of a Christian in confession and by receiving the communion. Reluctantly, and by compulsion, he bestowed Normandy on Robert, to William he gave England, while Henry received his maternal possessions.[1] He ordered all his prisoners to be released and pardoned, his treasures to be brought forth and distributed to the churches; he gave also a certain sum of money to repair the church which had been lately burnt. Thus rightly ordering all things, he departed on the eighth of the ides of September, in the twenty-first year of his reign, the fifty-second of his duchy, the fifty-ninth of his age, and in the year of our Lord one thousand and eighty-seven. This was the same year in which Cnut, king of Denmark, as we have before related,[2] was killed; and in which the Spanish Saracens raging against the Christians, were shortly compelled to retire to their own territories by Alfonso, king of Gallicia, unwillingly evacuating even the cities they had formerly occupied.

§ 283. The body, embalmed after royal custom, was brought down the river Seine to Caen, and there consigned to the earth, a large assembly of the clergy attending, but few of the laity. Here

hand, at the church door, where she is sprinkled with holy water, and afterwards conducted into the church. The practice seems connected with the festival of the Purification. V. Durand. Rationale, vii. 7.

[1] But according to Ordericus Vitalis, William only gave to Henry five thousand pounds of silver.

[2] See § 261. Malmesbury here follows the Saxon Chronicle, which refers the death of Cnut to 1087; but this event should be attributed to the preceding year. L'Art de Vérifier les Dates, ii. 85.

might be seen the wretchedness of earthly vicissitude; for that
man, who was formerly the glory of all Europe, and more powerful
than any of his predecessors, could not find a place for his last
rest without contention : for a certain knight,[1] to whose patrimony
the place belonged, loudly exclaiming at the robbery, forbade his
burial; saying, that the ground was his own by paternal right, and
that the king had no claim to rest in a place which he had forcibly
invaded. Whereupon, at the desire of Henry, (the only one of
his sons who was present,) an hundred pounds of silver were paid to
this brawler, and quieted his audacious claim : for at that time
Robert, his elder born, was in France, carrying on a war against
his own country; William had sailed for England ere the king had
well breathed his last, thinking it more advantageous to look to
his future benefit than to be present at the funeral of his father.
Moreover, neither slow nor sparing in spending money, he brought
forth from its secret hoard all that treasure which had been accu-
mulated at Winchester, during a reign of so many years : to the
monasteries he gave a piece of gold, to each parish church five
shillings in silver, to each county an hundred pounds, to be divided
to each poor man severally. He also very splendidly adorned the
tomb of his father, with a large mass of gold and silver and the
refulgence of precious stones.

§ 284. At this time lived Berengar, the heresiarch of Tours, who
denied that the bread and wine, when placed on the altar and consecrated by the priest, were, as the holy church affirms, the real
and substantial Body of the Lord. Already was the whole of Gaul
infected with this his doctrine, disseminated by means of poor
scholars, whom he allured by daily hire. On this account pope
Leo, of holiest memory, alarmed for the catholic faith, calling a
council against him at Vercelli, dispersed the darkness of this misty
error by the effulgence of evangelical testimony: but when, after
his death, the poison of heresy again burst forth from the bosoms
of some worthless people where it had long been nurtured, Hildebrand, in councils, when he was archdeacon, at Tours, and afterwards, when pope, at Rome, compelled him, after being convicted,
to the abjuration of his opinion; which matters any person desirous
of seeing will find recorded in their proper place. Archbishop
Lanfranc[2] and Guimund, the most eloquent man of our times, first
monk of St. Leufrid, in Normandy, afterwards bishop of Aversa in
Apulia, confuted him, but principally and most forcibly the latter.
And, indeed, though Berengar disgraced the earlier part of his life
by defending certain heresies, yet he came so much to his senses in
riper age, that without hesitation he was by some esteemed a saint;
admired for innumerable good qualities, but especially for his humility
and alms-giving; shewing himself master of his large possessions
by dispersing, not their slave by hoarding and worshipping, them.
He was so guarded with respect to female beauty, that he would

[1] His name is reported to have been Asselin Fitz-Arthur.
[2] "Lanfranc," says Sigebert, "wrote epistolary invectives against Berengar of
Tours, refuting his writings concerning the Body and Blood of our Lord. Lanfranc, says the same writer, wrote panegyrics on and chronicled the triumphs and
deeds of William, earl of Normandy." Bouquet, xi. 191, note.

never suffer a woman to appear before him, lest he should seem to enjoy that beauty with his eye which he did not desire in his heart. He was used neither to despise the poor nor flatter the rich: to live by nature's rule, "and having food and raiment," in the language of the apostle, "therewith to be content." In consequence, Hildebert,[1] bishop of Mans, an excellent poet, highly commends him; whose words I have purposely inserted, that I may shew this celebrated bishop's regard to his master; and at the same time his opinion will serve for an example to posterity, how he thought a man ought to live, although, perhaps from the strength of his affection, he may have exceeded the bounds of just commendation.

> " The fame, the world allows his due,
> Shall Berengar, when dead, pursue ;
> Whom, placed on faith's exalted height
> The fifth day ravish'd with fell spite :
> Sad was that day, and fatal too,
> Where grief and loss united grew,
> Wherein the church's hope and pride,
> The law, with its supporter, died.
> What sages taught or poets sung,
> Bowed to his wit and honey'd tongue.
> Then holier wisdom's path he trod,
> And filled his heart and lips with God.
> His soul, his voice, his actions proved
> The great Creator's praise he loved.
> So good, so wise, his growing fame
> Shall soar above the greatest name :
> Whose rank preserved his honours gain'd,
> Preferr'd the poor to rich ; maintain'd
> The sternest justice. Wealth's wide power
> Ne'er gave to sloth, or waste, an hour,
> Nor could repeated honours, high,
> Seduce him from humility ;
> Who ne'er on money set his mind,
> But grieved he could no object find
> Where he might give ; and help'd the poor
> Till poverty assail'd his door,
> His life by nature's laws to guide,
> His mind from vice, his lips from pride,
> Still was his care ; to false, the true
> Prefer, and nothing senseless do ;
> Evil to none, but good impart,
> And banish lucre, hand and heart.
> Whose dress was coarse, and temperance just,
> Awaited appetite's keen gust ;
> Was chastity's perpetual guest,
> Nor let rank lust disturb his rest.
> When nature formed him, 'See,' said she,
> 'While others fade, one born for me.'
> Ere justice sought her place of rest
> On high, he lock'd her in his breast.
> A saint from boyhood, whose great name
> Surpasses his exceeding fame,
> Which, though the wide world it may fill,
> Shall never reach his merit still.
> Pious and grave, so humble yet,
> That envy ne'er could him beset ;
> For envy weeps, whom still before
> She hated, prone now to adore ;
> First for his life, but now his fate
> She moans, laments his frail estate.

---

[1] S. Hildeberti Opera, p. 1323, ed. fol. Par. 1708.

> Man truly wise and truly blest !
> Thy soul and body both at rest,
> May I, when dead, abide with you,
> And share the self-same portion too."

§ 285. You may perceive in these verses that the bishop exceeded the just measure of praise, but eloquence is apt to recommend itself in such wise; thus a brilliant style proceeds in graceful strain; thus

> " Bewitching eloquence sheds purple flowers."

But though Berengar himself changed his sentiments, yet was he unable to convert all whom he had infected throughout the world, so dreadful a thing it is to seduce others from what is right, either by example or by word; as perhaps, in consequence, you must bear the sins of others after having atoned for your own. Fulbert, bishop of Chartres, whom Mary, the mother of our Lord, was seen to cure when sick, by the milk of her breasts,[1] is said to have predicted this; for when, lying in the last extremity, he was visited by many persons, and the house was scarcely large enough to hold the company, he darted his eye through the throng, and endeavoured to drive away Berengar with all the force he had remaining, protesting that an immense devil stood near him, and attempted to seduce many persons to follow him by beckoning with his hand and whispering some enticement. Moreover, Berengar himself, when about to expire on the day of the Epiphany, sadly sighing at the recollection of the wretched people whom, when a very young man, in the heat of error, he had infected with his opinions, exclaimed, " To-day, in the day of his manifestation, my Lord Jesus Christ will appear to me, either to glorify me, as I hope, for my repentance, or to punish me, as I fear, for the heresy I have propagated among others."

§ 286. We indeed believe that, after the benediction of the priest, those mysteries become the very Body and Blood of the Saviour, induced to such an opinion by the authority of the ancient church and by many miracles recently manifested; such as that which St. Gregory exhibited at Rome and such as Paschasius relates to have taken place in Germany, that the priest Plegild visibly touched the form of a boy upon the altar, and that after kissing him he partook of him, turned into the similitude of bread, after the custom of the church : which, they relate, Berengar used arrogantly to cavil at, and to say that it was the treacherous covenant of a scoundrel, to destroy with his teeth him whom he had kissed with his mouth. Such, too, is that concerning the Jewish boy, who by chance running playfully into a church, with a Christian of the same age, saw a child torn to pieces on the altar and severally divided to the people; which, when with childish innocence he related as truth to his parents, they placed him in a furnace, where the fire was burning and the door closed : whence, after many hours, he was snatched by the Christians, without injury to his person, clothes, or hair; and being asked how he could escape the devouring flames, he replied, " That beautiful woman whom I saw sitting in the chair, whose Son was divided among the people, always stood at my right

[1] See § 186.

hand in the furnace, keeping off the threatening flames and fiery
volumes with her garments."

The Discovery of the Body of Walwen.

§ 287. At that time, in a province of Wales, called Ros, was
found the sepulchre of Walwen, the noble nephew of Arthur: he
reigned, a most renowned knight, in that part of Britain which is
still named Walweitha, but was driven from his kingdom by the
brother and nephew of Hengist, of whom I have spoken in my first
book, though not without first making them pay dearly for his expulsion.   He deservedly shared with his uncle the praise of re-
tarding, for many years, the calamity of his falling country.   The
sepulchre of Arthur is no where to be seen, whence ancient ballads
fable that he is still to come.   But the tomb of the other, as I have
suggested, was found in the time of king William on the sea coast,
fourteen feet long: there, as some relate, he was wounded by his
enemies and suffered shipwreck, others say he was killed by his
subjects at a public entertainment.   The truth consequently is
doubtful; though neither of these men was inferior to the reputation they have acquired.

§ 288. This, too, was the period in which Germany, for fifty
years, bewailed the pitiable, and almost fatal government of Henry,
of whom I have spoken in the history of William.   He was neither
unlearned nor indolent; but so singled out by fate for every person
to attack, that whoever took up arms against him, seemed, to himself, to be acting for the good of religion.   He had two sons, Conrad
and Henry; the first, not violating the rights of nature towards his
father,[1] having subjugated Italy, died at Arezzo, a city of Tuscany:
the other, in his early age, attacking his father, when he was somewhat at rest from external molestation, compelled him to retire
from the empire, and when he died, shortly after, honoured him
with an imperial funeral.   He still survives, obstinately adhering to
those very sentiments, on account of which he thought himself jus-
tified in persecuting his father; for he grants the investiture of
churches by the staff and ring, and looks upon the pope as not
legally elected without his concurrence; although Calixtus, who now
presides over the papal see,[2] has greatly restrained this man's inor-
dinate ambition: but let the reader wait my farther relation of these
matters in their proper order.

§ 289. Moreover, pope Hildebrand dying, as I have said, and
Urban being elected by the cardinals, the emperor persisted in his
intention of preferring Guibert, of proclaiming him pope, and of
bringing him to Rome, by the expulsion of the other.   The army,
however, of the marchioness Matilda,[3] a woman who, forgetful of

---

[1] That is, though he rebelled against his father, yet he never, like Henry, laid
violent hands on him.

[2] Calixtus became pope on the 1st of February, 1119, and died on the 12th of
13th of December, 1124.

[3] This extraordinary woman, daughter of Boniface, duke of Tuscany, was a
powerful supporter of the Holy See, and at her death bestowed her vast property
on it.

her sex, and comparable to the ancient Amazons, used to lead forth her hardy troops to battle, espoused the juster cause, as it seemed; by her assistance, in succeeding time, Urban obtaining the papal throne, held quiet possession of it for eleven years. After him Paschal was appointed by the Romans, who held Henry's concurrence in contempt. Guibert yet burdened the earth with his existence, the only sower of sedition, who never during his whole life laid aside his obstinacy nor conformed to justice, saying, that the decision of the emperor ought to be observed; not that of the assassins or parchment-mongers of Rome.[1] In consequence, both of them being excommunicated in several councils, they treated the sentence with ridicule. Notwithstanding these circumstances, there were many things praiseworthy in the emperor: he was eloquent, of great abilities, well-read, actively charitable; had many good qualities, both of mind and person; was ever prepared for war, insomuch that he was sixty-two times engaged in battle; was equitable in adjusting differences: and when matters were unsuccessful, he would pour out his griefs to heaven, and wait for redress from thence. Many of his enemies perished by untimely deaths.

Story of the Man who was eaten by Mice.

§ 290. I have heard a person of the utmost veracity relate, that one of his adversaries, a weak and factious man, while reclining at a banquet, was on a sudden so completely surrounded by mice, as to be unable to escape: so great was the number of these little animals, that there could scarcely be imagined more in an whole province. It was in vain that they were attacked with clubs and fragments of the benches which were at hand; and though they were for a long time assailed by all, yet they wreaked their deputed curse on no one else; pursuing him only, with their teeth and with a kind of dreadful squeaking. And although he was carried out to sea about a javelin's cast by the servants, yet he could not by this means escape their violence; for immediately so great a multitude of mice took to the water, that you would have sworn the sea was strewed with chaff. But when they began to gnaw the planks of the ship, and the water, rushing through the chinks, threatened inevitable shipwreck, the servants turned the vessel to the shore. The animals then also swimming close to the ship, landed first. Thus the wretch, set on shore, and soon after entirely gnawed in pieces, satiated the dreadful hunger of the mice.

Another Legend.

§ 291. I deem this the less wonderful, because it is well known, in Asia, that if a leopard bite any person, a party of mice approach directly to discharge their urine on the wounded man; and that a filthy deluge of their water attends his death; but if, by the care

---

[1] This seems a sneer at the sanguinary disposition of the Roman people, and at the bulls of the pope. In a dispute on the credibility of evidence adduced, it is observed that the oral testimony of three bishops was certainly to be preferred "to sheep-skins blackened with ink and loaded with a leaden seal." Edmer. Hist. Novor. p. 65.

of servants driving them off, the destruction can be avoided during nine days, then medical assistance, if called in, may be of service. My informant had seen a person wounded after this manner, who, despairing of safety on shore, proceeded to sea, and lay at anchor; when immediately a multitude of mice swam out, wonderful to relate, in the rinds of pomegranates, the insides of which they had eaten; but they were drowned through the exertions of the sailors; for the Creator of all things has left nothing He has made destitute of sagacity, nor any pest without its remedy.

§ 292. During this emperor's reign flourished Marianus Scotus,[1] first a monk of Fulda, afterwards a recluse at Mentz, who, by renouncing the present life, secured the happiness of that which is to come. During his long continued leisure, he examined the writers on chronology, and discovered the disagreement of the cycles of Dionysius the Little with the Evangelical computation: so reckoning every year from the beginning of the world, he added twenty-two, which were wanting, to the above-mentioned cycles; but he had few or no followers of his opinion. Wherefore I am often led to wonder, why such unhappiness should attach to the learned of our time, that in so great a number of scholars and students, pale with watching, scarcely one can obtain unqualified commendation for knowledge. So much does ancient custom please, and so little encouragement, though deserved, is given to new discoveries, however consistent with truth: all are anxious to grovel in the old track, and everything modern is contemned; and therefore, as patronage alone can foster genius, when that is withheld, every exertion grows languid.

Account of a Miracle which happened in the Monastery of Fulda.

§ 293. But as I have mentioned the monastery of Fulda, I will relate what a reverend man, Walker, prior of Malvern, (whose words if any disbelieve he offends against holiness,) told me had happened there. "Not more than fifteen years have elapsed," said he, "since a contagious disease attacked the abbot of that place, and afterwards destroyed many of the monks. The survivors, at first, began each to fear for himself, and to pray and give alms more abundantly than usual: in process of time, however, for such is the nature of man, their fear gradually subsiding, they began to omit them; the cellarer more especially, who publicly and absurdly exclaimed, that the stock of provision was not adequate to such a consumption; that he had lately hoped for some reduction of expense from so many funerals, but that his hopes were at an end, if the dead consumed what the living could not. It happened on a certain night, when, from some urgent business, he had deferred going to rest for a long time, that having at length despatched every concern, he went towards the dormitory. And now you shall hear a strange circum-

---

[1] Marianus Scotus was born in Ireland A.D. 1028. He was the compiler of a chronicle (first published in 1569) from the commencement of the world to his own time (A.D. 1082), and which formed the basis of that of Florence of Worcester; he appears to have died in the year 1086. Malmesbury's imagined correction of Dionysius is founded in error.

stance : he saw in the chapter-house the abbot, and all who had died that year, sitting in the order they departed ;˙when affrighted and endeavouring to escape, he was detained by force. Being reproved and corrected, after the monastic manner, with a scourge, he heard the abbot speak precisely to the following effect : That it was foolish to look for advantage by another's death, when all were subject to one common fate ; that it was an impious thing, that a monk who had passed his whole life in the service of the church should be grudged the pittance of a single year after his death ; that he himself should die very shortly, but that whatever others might do for him, should redound only to the advantage of those whom he had defrauded ; that he might now go and correct, by his example, those whom he had corrupted by his expressions. He departed, and demonstrated that he had seen nothing imaginary, as well by his recent stripes, as by his death, which shortly followed.

§ 294. In the mean time, while employed on other subjects, both matter and inclination have occurred for the relation of what was determined in William's time, concerning the controversy still existing between the archbishops of Canterbury and York. And that posterity may be fully informed of this business, I will subjoin the opinions of the ancient fathers.

EXTRACTS SHEWING THAT EVERY BISHOP THROUGHOUT BRITAIN
IS SUBJECT TO THE ARCHBISHOP OF CANTERBURY.

Pope Gregory to Augustine, first Archbishop of Canterbury.

§ 295. "Let your jurisdiction not only extend over the bishops you shall have ordained, or such as have been ordained by the bishop of York, but also over all the priests of Britain, by the authority of our Lord Jesus Christ."

Boniface to Justus, Archbishop of Canterbury.

§ 296. "Far be it from every Christian, that anything concerning the city of Canterbury be diminished or changed, in present or future times, which was appointed by our predecessor pope Gregory, however human circumstances may be changed: but more especially by the authority of St. Peter, the prince of the apostles, we command and ordain, that the city of Canterbury shall ever hereafter be esteemed the metropolitan see of all Britain ; and we decree and appoint immutably, that all the provinces of the kingdom of England shall be subject to the metropolitan church of the aforesaid see. And if any one attempt to injure this church, which is more especially under the power and protection of the holy Roman church, or to lessen the jurisdiction conceded to it, may God expunge him from the book of life ; and let him know, that he is bound by the sentence of a curse."

Alexander to William, King of England.

§ 297. "The cause of Alric, formerly called bishop of Chichester, we have entrusted to our brother, bishop Lanfranc, to be

by him diligently reconsidered and determined. We have also commended to him the labour of deciding the dispute which has arisen
between the archbishop of York and the bishop of Dorchester, on
matters belonging to their dioceses; strictly ordering him to
examine this cause most diligently and bring it to a just termination. Besides, we have so fully committed to him the authority
of our personal and pontifical power in considering and settling
causes, that whatever he shall, according to justice, have determined, shall be regarded as firm and indissoluble hereafter, as
though it had been adjudged in our presence."[1]

EVIDENCE THAT THE ARCHBISHOP OF YORK AND HIS SUFFRAGANS ARE SUBJECT TO THE ARCHBISHOP OF CANTERBURY.

A General English Council concerning the Jurisdiction and Primacy of the Church of Canterbury.

§ 298. "In the year of our Lord Jesus Christ's Incarnation one
thousand and seventy-two, of the pontificate of pope Alexander the
eleventh, and of the reign of William, glorious king of England, and
duke of Normandy, the sixth; by the command of the said pope
Alexander, and permission of the same king, in presence of himself,
his bishops, and abbots, the question was agitated concerning the
primacy which Lanfranc, archbishop of Canterbury, claimed in
right of his church over that of York; and concerning the ordination of certain bishops, of which it was not clearly evident to
whom they especially appertained; and at length, after some time
it was proved and shewn by the distinct authority of various
writings, that the church of York ought to be subject to that of
Canterbury, and to be obedient to the appointments of its archbishop, as primate of all England, in all such matters as pertained
to the Christian religion. But the homage of the bishop of Durham, that is of Lindisfarn, and of all the countries beyond the
limits of the bishop of Litchfield, and the great river Humber, to
the farthest boundaries of Scotland, and whatever on this side of
the aforesaid river justly pertains to the diocese of the church of
York, the metropolitan of Canterbury allowed for ever to belong to
the archbishop of York and his successors; in such sort however,
that if the archbishop of Canterbury chose to call a council, where-
ever he deemed fit, the archbishop of York was bound to be
present at his command, with all his suffragan bishops, and be
obedient to his canonical injunctions. And Lanfranc the archbishop
proved from the ancient custom of his predecessors, that the archbishop of York was bound to make profession, even with an oath,
to the archbishop of Canterbury, but through regard to the king,
he dispensed with the oath from Thomas, archbishop of York; and

---

[1] One MS. (L. i.) adds, "The laws of William, occupying almost one folio, are
wanting." Another MS. (A.) contains the laws of the Conqueror, in the same
words as those of the Carta Willelmi of Thorpe's Ancient Laws and Institutes
of England, i. 488 (ed. 8vo.); and also a long section, not found in that work,
treating of the rights, duties, and qualities of a king, several lines being adapted
from Senoca.

received his written profession only: but not thereby forming a precedent for such of his successors as might choose to exact the oath, together with the profession, from Thomas's successors. If the archbishop of Canterbury should die, the archbishop of York shall come to Canterbury; and, with the other bishops of the church aforesaid, duly consecrate the person elected, as his lawful primate. But if the archbishop of York shall die, his successor, accepting the gift of the archbishopric from the king, shall come to Canterbury, or where the archbishop of Canterbury shall appoint, and shall from him receive canonical ordination. To this ordinance consented the king aforesaid, and the archbishops, Lanfranc of Canterbury, and Thomas of York; and Hubert subdeacon of the holy Roman church, and legate of the aforesaid pope Alexander; and the other bishops and abbots present. This cause was first agitated at the festival of Easter in the city of Winchester, in the royal chapel, situated in the castle; afterwards in the royal town called Windsor, where it received its termination, in the presence of the king, the bishops, and abbots of different orders, who were assembled at the king's court on the festival of Pentecost. The signature of William the king: the signature of Matilda the queen. I, Hubert, subdeacon of the holy Roman church, and legate from pope Alexander, have signed. I, Lanfranc, archbishop of Canterbury, have signed. I, Thomas, archbishop of York, have signed. I, William, bishop of London, have assented. I, Herman, bishop of Shireburn, have signed. I, Wulstan, bishop of Worcester, have signed. I, Walter, bishop of Hereford, have assented. I, Giso, bishop of Wells, have assented. I, Remigius, bishop of Dorchester, have signed. I, Walkelin, bishop of Winchester, have signed. I, Herefast, bishop of Helmham, have signed. I, Stigand, bishop of Chichester, have assented. I, Siward, bishop of Rochester, have assented. I, Osbern, bishop of Exeter, have assented. I, Odo, bishop of Baieux, and earl of Kent, have assented. I, Geoffrey, bishop of Coutances, and one of the nobles of England, have assented. I, Scotland, abbot of St. Augustine's monastery, have assented. I, Elfwin, abbot of the monastery of Ramsey, have assented. I, Elnoth, abbot of Glastonbury, have assented. I, Thurstan, abbot of the monastery which is situate in the isle of Ely, have assented. I, Wulnoth, abbot of Chertsey, have assented. I, Elfwin, abbot of Evesham, have assented. I, Frederic, abbot of St. Alban's, have assented. I, Gosfrid, abbot of the monastery of St. Peter, near London, have assented. I, Baldwin, abbot of St. Edmund's monastery, have assented. I, Turold, abbot of Peterborough, have assented. I, Adelelm, abbot of Abingdon, have assented. I, Ruald, abbot of the Newminster at Winchester, have assented."

§ 299. " It becomes every Christian to be subject to Christian laws, and by no means to run counter to those things which have been wholesomely enacted by the holy fathers. For hence arise strifes, dissensions, envyings, contentions, and other things, which plunge the lovers of them into eternal punishment. And the more exalted the rank of any person is, so much the more exact should be his obedience to divine commands : Wherefore I, Thomas, now ordained metropolitan bishop of the church of York, hearing and knowing your authorities, make unlimited profession of canonical obedience, to you, Lanfranc, archbishop of Canterbury, and your successors ; and I promise to observe whatever shall be lawfully and canonically enjoined me, either by you or them. Of this matter I was doubtful, while I was yet about to be ordained by you ; wherefore I promised obedience unconditionally to you, but conditionally to your successors."

§ 300. The archbishop of Canterbury, as I remember to have observed in my first book,[1] originally had subject to him these bishops, London, Winchester, Rochester, Shireburn, Worcester, Hereford, Litchfield, Selsey, Leicester, Helmham, Sidnacester, Dunwich ; in the time of king Edward the Elder were added, Cornwall, Crediton, Wells in West Saxony, and Dorchester in Mercia, as I noticed in my second book.[2] The archbishop of York had all the bishops, on the farther side of the Humber, subject to him ; as Ripon, Hexham, Lindisfarn, Candida Casa, which is now called Whithern, and all the bishops of Scotland and the Orkneys, as the archbishop of Canterbury and those of Ireland and Wales. The bishoprics of Ripon and Hexham have long since perished by hostile ravages ; Leicester, Sidnacester, and Dunwich, by means that I cannot account for ; and, in the time of king Edward the Simple, Cornwall and Crediton were united, and the bishopric translated to Exeter. In king William's time, at this council, it was determined that according to the decrees of the canons the bishops should quit the villages, and fix their abode in the cities of their dioceses ; Lichfield therefore migrated to Chester, which was anciently called the City of Legions, Selsey to Chichester, Helmam first to Thetford, and now, by bishop Herbert, to Norwich ; Shireburn to Salisbury, Dorchester to Lincoln. For Lindisfarn had long before passed to Durham, and, lately, Wells to Bath.

§ 301. In this assembly, Lanfranc, who was yet uninstructed in English matters, inquired of the elder bishops, what was the order of sitting in council, as originally appointed. They, alleging the difficulty of the question, deferred their answer till the next day ; when, carefully calling circumstances to mind, they asserted that they had seen the arrangement as follows : that the archbishop of Canterbury, presiding at the council, should have on the right hand the archbishop of York, and next him the bishop of Winchester ; and on his left the bishop of London ; but should it ever happen that the primate of Canterbury should be unavoidably absent, or should he be dead, the archbishop of York, presiding at the council, should have the bishop of London on his right hand, and of Winchester on his left ; and the rest should take their seats according to the time of their ordination.

§ 302. At that time, too, the claim of the archbishop of York on the sees of Worcester and Dorchester was decided and set at rest ;—(for he said that they ought to be subject to his jurisdiction :)

which, after having pondered for some time in secret, when he proceeded to Rome with Lanfranc to receive their palls from the pope, he brought publicly before the Roman court. Lanfranc, though for the most part unmoved by injury, could not help betraying, by his countenance, his emotion at such a wanton and unheard-of attack, though he for some time refrained from speaking. But pope Alexander, who felt much for Lanfranc's distress, (for he had even condescendingly risen from his seat when he approached, professing that he paid him this mark of respect, not from honour to him as archbishop but regard to his learning,) removed from himself the unpleasant task of deciding, referring the adjudication of it to an English council. In consequence, as I have related, the matter, after deep investigation, came to this termination in the present council; that, as these bishops were on this side of the Humber, they should belong to Canterbury; but all beyond that river, to York.

§ 303. Here the pious simplicity of St. Wulstan, bishop of Worcester, and his noble confidence in God, demand praise and approbation. For when called in question, as well concerning this business, as on his slender attainments in learning, he had retired to consider more carefully what answer he should make, his mind undisturbed by tumult: "Believe me," said he, "we have not yet sung the service for the sixth hour; let us sing the service therefore." And, on his companions suggesting the necessity of first expediting the business they had met upon; that there was ample time for singing, and that the king and the nobility would laugh at them, if they heard of it; "Truly," said he, "let us first do our duty towards God, and afterwards settle the disputes of men." Having sung the service, he directly proceeded towards the council chamber, without devising any subterfuge, or any attempt to disguise the truth. To his dependents, who were desirous of withholding him, and who could not be persuaded but their cause was in danger, he said, "Know for certain, that I here visibly perceive those holy archbishops, Dunstan of Canterbury, and Oswald of York; who, defending me this day with their prayers, will darken the understandings of my gainsayers." Then giving his benediction to a monk, a man of little eloquence, but somewhat acquainted with the Norman language, on summing up his cause, he obtained, that he, who was before thought unworthy of the management of his own diocese, should be humbly entreated by the archbishop of York to condescend to visit those parts of his province, which he himself, through dread of enemies, or ignorance of the language, had refrained from approaching.

§ 304. But I will no longer torture the patience of my readers, who perhaps do not regard this matter with pleasure, as they are in expectation of the history of William's successors; though, if I am not too partial to myself, a variety of anecdote can be displeasing to no one, unless he be morose enough to rival the superciliousness of Cato. But whoever is so inclined will find such other matters in the fourth and fifth book; for here the third shall terminate.

PREFACE TO BOOK IV.

I AM aware, that many persons think it unwise in me, to have written the history of the kings of my own time, alleging that in a work of such a description, truth is often made shipwreck of, while falsehood meets with support; because to relate the crimes of contemporaries is attended with danger, their good actions with applause. Whence it arises, say they, that, as all things have now a natural tendency to evil rather than to good, the historian passes over any disgraceful transaction, however obvious, through timidity; and, for the sake of approbation, feigns the existence of good qualities when he cannot find them. There are others, who, judging of us by their own indolence, deem us unequal to so great a task, and brand our undertaking with malignant censure. Wherefore, impelled by the reasoning of the one, or the contempt of the other, I had long since voluntarily retired to leisure and to silence; but, after indulging in them for a time, the accustomed inclination for study again strongly beset me; as it was impossible for me to be unoccupied, and I knew not how to give myself up to those external avocations, which are beneath the notice of a literary character. To this must be added the incitements of my friends, to whose suggestions, though only implied, I ought to pay regard; and they indeed gently urged me, already sufficiently disposed, to prosecute my undertaking. Animated, therefore, by the advice of those whom I love most affectionately, I advance to give them a lasting pledge of friendship from the stores of my research. Grateful also to those who are in fear for me, least I should either excite hatred, or disguise the truth, I will, by the help of Christ, make such a return for their kindness, as neither to become odious, nor a falsifier. For I will describe, both what has been done well, or otherwise, in such wise, that, safely steering, as it were, between Scylla and Charybdis, my opinions shall not be concealed, though some matters may be omitted in my history. Moreover, to those who undervalue the labours of others, I make the same answer as St. Jerome formerly did to his critics; "Let them read if they like; if not, let them cast it aside;" because I do not obtrude my work on the fastidious, but I dedicate it to the studious, if any think it worthy of their notice; a matter which even these men will readily pronounce to be consonant to equity, unless they are of the number of those, of whom it is said, "Fools are easy to confute, but not so easy to restrain." I will relate, then, in this, the fourth book of my work, everything which may be said of William, the son of William the Great, in such manner, that neither shall the truth suffer, nor shall the dignity of the prince be obscured. Some matters also will be inserted in these pages, which in his time were calamitous in this country, or glorious elsewhere, as far as my knowledge extends: more especially, the pilgrimage of the Christians to Jerusalem, which it will be proper to annex in this place; because an expedition so famous in these times is well worth hearing, and will also be an incitement to valour. Not indeed that I have any confidence these transactions will be better treated by me than by others who have written on the subject; but that, what many write, many may read. Yet, lest so long a preface should disgust my reader, I will immediately enter on my work.

THE FOURTH BOOK OF WILLIAM OF MALMESBURY'S HISTORY OF THE KINGS OF ENGLAND.

BOOK IV.

Of King William Rufus, son of King William the First.

§ 305. WILLIAM then, the son of William, was born in Normandy many years before his father came to England, and being educated with extreme care by his parents, as he had naturally an ambitious mind he at length reached the summit of dignity. He would no doubt have been a prince incomparable in our time, had not his father's greatness eclipsed him; and had not the fates cut short his years too early for his maturer age to correct such errors as had been contracted by the licentiousness of power and the impetuosity of youth. When childhood was passed, he spent the period of youth in military occupations; in riding, throwing the dart, contending with his elders in obedience, with those of his own age in action; esteeming it injurious to his reputation, if he were not the foremost to take arms in military commotions; unless he were the first to challenge the adversary, or when challenged, to overcome him. To his father he was ever dutiful, always exerting himself in his sight in battle, ever at his side in peace. His hopes gradually expanding, he already aspired after the succession, especially on the abdication[1] of his elder brother, while the tender age of the younger gave him no uneasiness. Thus, adopted as his successor by his father during his last illness, he set out to take possession of the kingdom ere the king had breathed his last; where being gladly received by the people, and obtaining the keys of the treasury, he by these means subjected all England to his will. Archbishop Lanfranc, who had educated him and made him a knight,[2] favoured his pretensions; by whose authority and assistance he was crowned on the day of Saints Cosmas and Damian,[3] and passed the remainder of the winter quietly and with general favour.

[1] This act can scarcely be considered to have been voluntary on the part of Robert.

[2] At this period the custom of receiving knighthood from the hands of bishops or abbots yet obtained. There is a law of Henry I. prohibiting abbots from making knights.

[3] The feast of Saints Cosmas and Damian is the 27th of September. Florence of Worcester and other authorities state that William was crowned on Sunday, the 26th of September. According to the Saxon Chronicle it was "three days before Michaelmas day."

How King Rufus overcame his Opponents.

§ 306. At the expiration of this period, in the beginning of spring,[1] his first contention was with his uncle, Odo, bishop of Baieux. For when he, on his release from confinement, as I have related, had firmly established his nephew, Robert, in the duchy of Normandy, he came to England, and received from the king the earldom of Kent.[2] But when he saw everything in the kingdom managed, not at his own pleasure, as formerly, (for the administration of public affairs was now committed to William,[3] bishop of Durham,) moved with envy, he himself revolted from the king, and tainted many others by insinuating that the kingdom belonged to Robert, who was of gentler disposition, and whose youthful follies had been corrected by many adversities; that William, delicately brought up, and overbearing from that ferocity of mind which was manifest in his countenance, would dare everything, in defiance of right and equity; that it must soon come to pass, that they would lose the honours they had already obtained with so much difficulty; that nothing was gained by the father's death, if those whom he had cast into prison were to be killed by the son. To this effect he used, at first, secretly to whisper, together with Roger Montgomery, Geoffrey, bishop of Coutances,[4] with his nephew Robert earl of Northumberland and others; afterwards they were more open in their clamours, repeating and disseminating them by letters and by emissaries. Moreover, even William bishop of Durham, the confidential minister of the king, had joined in their treachery; which was a matter of great concern to William, it is said; because, together with the breach of friendship, he was disappointed of the resources of the distant provinces. Odo now carried off booty of every kind to Rochester, plundering the king's revenues in Kent, and especially the lands of the archbishop; breathing eternal hatred against him, because, he said, it was by his advice that his brother had cast him into chains. Nor was this assertion false; for when William the Elder formerly complained to Lanfranc, that he was deserted by his brother; "Seize, and cast him into chains," said he. "What!" replied the king, "he is a clergyman." Then the archbishop with playful archness, as Persius says,[5] "balancing the objection with nice antithesis," rejoined, "you will not seize the bishop of Baieux, but confine the earl of Kent." Bishop Geoffry with his nephew, depopulating Bath and Berkeley, and part of the county of Wilts, treasured up their spoils at Bristol. Roger Montgomery sending out his army with the Welsh from

---

[1] The conspiracy was formed in Lent; and as soon as Easter came, then went they forth. See the Sax. Chron. A.D. 1088.
[2] Odo was created earl of Kent, A.D. 1067.   [3] William de S. Carileph.
[4] Geoffrey de Montbray became bishop of Coutance in 1048. He was chief justiciary of England, and presided at the great trial in the county court held at Pinendene in Kent, between Lanfrank, archbishop of Canterbury, and Odo, bishop of Baieux. He died 4th of February, 1093. In Domesday Book he is described as "Constantiensis episcopus;" but in one place (fol. 165) he is called "Episcopus de Sancto Laudo" (St. Lo, a town in Lower Normandy), and, among the witnesses to a charter granted by the Conqueror to St. Augustine's monastery at Canterbury, is "Episcopus Galfrydus de Seynt Loth."   [5] Persius, Sat. i. 85.

Shrewsbury, plundered Worcestershire; and then attacked Worcester, when the king's soldiers who guarded it, though few in number, relying on the blessing of bishop Wulstan, to whom the custody of the castle was committed, dispersed this multitude; and after wounding and killing many, took some of them prisoners. Moreover, Roger Bigot at Norwich, and Hugo de Grentemesnil at Leicester, each with their party, were plundering in their respective neighbourhoods. In vain, however, did the whole power of revolt rage against a man, who was deficient neither in prudence nor in good fortune. For seeing almost all the Normans leagued in one furious conspiracy, he sent persuasive letters, summoning to him such brave and honest English as yet remained; and complaining to them on the subject of his wrongs, he bound them to his party, by promising them wholesome laws, a diminution of tribute, and free leave to hunt.[1] With equal cunning he circumvented Roger Montgomery, when riding with him, with dissembled perfidy; for taking him aside, he loaded him with odium, saying, that he would willingly retire from the government, if it seemed meet to him, and to the rest whom his father had left as his guardians; that he could not understand why they were so outrageous; if they wanted money, they might have what they pleased; if an increase of their estates, they might have that also; in short, they might have whatever they chose; only let them be careful that the judgment of his father was not called in question; for, if they thought it ought to be disregarded in the instance of himself, it might be a bad example for them; for the same person made him king who had made them earls. Influenced by these words and promises, the earl, who, next to Odô, had been the chief leader of the faction, was the first to desert. Proceeding, therefore, immediately against the rebels, he laid siege to the castles of his uncle at Tunbridge and at Pevensey, and seizing him in the latter, compelled him to swear, as he dictated, that he would depart from England and deliver up Rochester. To fulfil this promise he sent him forward with a party he could rely on, intending to follow at his leisure. At that time almost all the young nobility of England and Normandy were at Rochester: three sons of earl Roger, Eustace the younger of Boulogne, and many others not deserving notice. The royal party accompanying the bishop were few and unarmed,—for who could fear treachery where he was present? and going round the walls, they called to the townsmen to open the gates, for so the bishop in person and the absent king commanded. Observing from the wall, however, that the countenance of the bishop ill agreed with the language of the speakers, they suddenly sallied out, took horse in an instant, and carried away captive the bishop and the whole party. The report of this transaction quickly reached the king. Fierce from the injury, and smothering his indignation, he called together his English subjects, and ordered them to summon all their countrymen to the siege, unless any wished to be branded with the name of "Nithing,"[2]

[1] On their own lands, it should seem, from the statement of the Sax. Chron.

[2] Of this word Matt. Paris writes, "'Nithing,' which is the same as 'Nequam' in Latin;" and adds that the English consider nothing more contumelious or disgraceful than this vile word.

which implies " rascal." The English, who thought nothing more disgraceful than to be stigmatized by such an appellation, flocked in troops to the king, and rendered his army invincible. Nor could the townsmen longer delay submission, finding that a party, however noble or however numerous, could avail nothing against the king of England. Odo, now taken a second time, abjured England for ever: the bishop of Durham, of his own accord, retired beyond sea, the king allowing him to escape uninjured, out of regard to his former friendship: the rest were all admitted to fealty. During the interval of this siege, some of the king's fleet destroyed a party which the earl of Normandy had sent to assist the traitors, partly by slaughter and partly by shipwreck; the remainder, intent on escaping, endeavoured to make sail, but being soon after disappointed by its falling calm, they became matter for laughter to our people, but their own destruction; for, that they might not be taken alive, they leaped from their vessels into the sea.

§ 307. The next year, as the sense of injuries ever grows keener from reconsideration, the king began carefully to examine how he might revenge his griefs and repay his brother for this insult. In consequence, by his practices, bribing the garrison, he obtained possession of the castle of St. Valery,[1] the adjoining port, and the town which is called Albemarle. The earl had not the courage to resist, but by means of ambassadors acquainted his lord, the king of France, with the violence of his brother, and begged his assistance. He, inactive, and belching from his daily surfeit, came hiccupping, through repletion, to the war; but, as he was making great professions, the money of the king of England met him by the way, with which his resolution being borne down, he unbuckled his armour and went back to his gormandizing. In this manner Normandy, for a long time, groaned under intestine war, sometimes one party, sometimes the other, being victorious: the nobility, men of fickle temper and faithful to neither brother, exciting their mutual fury. A few, better advised, attentive to their own advantage, for they had possessions in both countries, were mediators of a peace; the basis of which was, that the king should get possession of Maine for the earl, and the earl should cede to the king those castles which he already held, and the monastery of Fescamp. The treaty was ratified and confirmed by the oath of the nobles on both sides.

§ 308. Not long after, the king went abroad to execute these conditions. Each leader made great efforts to invade Maine; but when they had completed their preparations, and were just ready to proceed, an obstacle arose, through the spirit of Henry, the youngest brother, loudly remonstrating against their covetousness, which had shared their paternal possessions between themselves, and blushed not at having left him almost destitute. In consequence, he took possession of Mount St. Michael, and harassed, with constant sallies, the besieging forces of his brothers. During this siege, a noble specimen of disposition was exhibited, both by the king and by the earl; of compassion in the one, and of magnanimity in the other. I shall subjoin these instances, for the information of my readers.

[1] See Sax. Chron. A D. 1090.

§ 309. The king, going out of his tent, and observing the enemy at a distance, proudly prancing, rushed unattended against a large party; spurred on by the impetuosity of his courage, and at the same time confident that none would dare resist him. Presently his horse, which he had that day purchased for fifteen marks of silver, being killed under him, he was thrown down, and for a long time dragged by his foot; the strength of his mail, however, prevented him from being hurt. The soldier who had unhorsed him was at this instant drawing his sword to strike him, when, terrified at the extremity of his danger, William cried out, " Hold, rascal, I am the king of England." The whole troop trembled at the well-known voice of the prostrate monarch; and immediately, respectfully raising him from the ground, brought him another horse. Leaping into the saddle without waiting for assistance, and darting a keen look on the by-standers : " Who unhorsed me ? " said he. While the rest were silent through fear, the bold perpetrator of the deed readily defended himself, saying, " 'Twas I, who took you, not for a king, but for a soldier." Soothed, and regaining the serenity of his countenance, the king exclaimed, " By the Face at Lucca,"[1] (for such was his usual oath,) " henceforth thou shalt be mine, and, placed on my roll, shalt receive the recompense of this gallant deed." Nobly done, magnanimous king! what encomium shall I pass on this speech? Equal to Alexander the Great in glory; who, through admiration of his courage, preserved unhurt a Persian soldier who had attempted to strike him from behind, but was frustrated in his design by the treachery of his sword.

§ 310. But now to relate the humanity of the earl. When the blockade had so far proceeded that the besieged were in want of water, Henry sent messengers to Robert, to expostulate with him on the thirst he endured, and to represent, that it was impious to deprive him of water, the common right of mankind : let him try his courage another way, if he chose, and not employ the violence of the elements, but the valour of a soldier. On which, wrought upon by the natural tenderness of his disposition, he ordered his party to be more remiss in their duty where they kept guard, that his thirsty brother might not be deprived of water : which circumstance, when related to the king, who was always inclined to warmth of temper, made him say to the earl, " You well know how to carry on war indeed, who allow your enemies plenty of water; and pray, how shall we subdue them, if we indulge them in food and drink ? " But he smiling, uttered this kind and truly laudable expression, " Oh shame! should I suffer my brother to die with thirst? and where shall we find another, if we lose him ? " On this the king, deriding the mild temper of the man, put an end to the war without

[1] These words have been frequently mistranslated into " By St. Luke's face !" whereas it means "By the Face at Lucca !" Lord Lyttleton says, "There is at Lucca in Tuscany an ancient figure of Christ, brought there miraculously, as they pretend. They call it 'Il santo volto di Lucca :' it is stamped on their coins with this legend, 'Sanctus vultus de Lucca.'" In an Italian book, called "Il Forestiere informato delle cose di Lucca," this legend is given in great detail. The author states that it was the work of Nicodemus, the author of the Gospel. See further on this subject, in the Rev. J. E. Tyler's interesting volume entitled, " Oaths, their Origin, Nature, and History;" London, 8vo. pp. 289—296.

accomplishing his design; and as the commotions of the Scots and Welsh required his presence, he retired with both his brothers to his kingdom.

§ 311. Leading immediately an expedition, first against the Welsh, and then against the Scots, he performed nothing worthy of his greatness; but lost many of his soldiers, and had his sumpter-horses intercepted. And not only at that time, but frequently in Wales, was fortune unfavourable to him; which may seem strange to any one, when the chance of war was generally on his side in other places. But it appears to me that the unevenness of the country, and the badness of the weather, as it assisted their rebellion, was also an impediment to his valour. But king Henry, who now reigns, a man of excellent talents, discovered a mode of counter-acting their designs; which was, by stationing in their country the Flemings, to be a barrier to them, and constantly keep them within bounds. At that time, by the industry of earl Robert, who had long since gained the good graces of the Scot, the basis of a peace was laid between Malcolm and William. But various grounds of difference still existing on both sides, and justice wavering through their mutual animosity, Malcolm came of his own accord to Glou-cester, earnestly soliciting peace, so that it were on equitable con-ditions: he obtained, however, nothing more than permission to return uninjured to his kingdom; for the king disdained to take a man by subtlety, whom he might have conquered by arms. But the next winter he was dispatched by the party of Robert earl of Northumberland, rather through stratagem than force. When his wife, Margaret, a woman distinguished for alms-giving and for chastity, heard of his death, disgusted with life, she earnestly en-treated of God to die. They were both remarkable for piety, but the queen more especially; for during her whole life, wherever she might be, she had twenty-four poor persons whom she supplied with meat and clothing. In Lent, waiting for the singing of the priests, she used to watch all night in the church, herself assisting at triple mattins—of the Trinity, of the Cross, of St. Mary; and afterwards repeating the Psalter; with tears bedewing her garments, and agitating her breast. Departing from the church, she used to feed the poor; first three, then nine, then twenty-four, at last three hundred: herself standing by with the king, and pouring water on their hands. Edgar his son, when expelled by his uncle, was restored by William; assuredly with a noble compassion, and be-coming so great a personage, who, forgetting the injuries of the father, replaced the son, when suppliant, on his throne.

§ 312. Greatness of soul was preeminent in the king, which in process of time he obscured by excessive severity; vices, indeed, in place of virtues, so insensibly crept into his bosom, that he could not distinguish them. The world doubted, for a long time, to which side he would incline; what tendency his disposition would take. At first, as long as archbishop Lanfranc survived, he abstained from every crime, so that it might be hoped he would be the very mirror of kings; after his death, for a time, he showed himself so variable, that the balance hung even betwixt vices and virtues: at last, however, in his latter years, the desire after good grew cold, and the crop of evil increased to ripeness: his liberality became prodigality; his magnanimity pride; his austerity cruelty. I may be allowed, with permission of the royal majesty, not to conceal the truth : for he feared God but little, man not at all. If any one shall say this is undiscerning, he will not be wrong : because wise men should observe this rule, " God ought to be feared at all times; but man, according to circumstances." He was, when abroad, and in public assemblies, of supercilious look, darting his threatening eye on the by-stander ; and with assumed severity and ferocious voice, assailing such as conversed with him. From apprehension of poverty, and of the treachery of others, as may be conjectured, he was too much given to lucre, and to cruelty. At home, and at table with his intimate companions, he gave loose to levity and to mirth. He was a most facetious railer at anything he had himself done amiss, in order that he might thus do away obloquy and make it matter of jest. But I shall dilate somewhat on that liberality, in which he deceived himself; and afterwards on his other propensities, that I may manifest what great vices sprang up in him under the semblance of virtues.

§ 313. For in fact, there are two kinds of givers : the one is denominated prodigal, the other liberal. The prodigal are such as lavish their money on those things, of which they will leave either a transient, or perhaps no memory at all in this world ; neither will they gain mercy by them from God: the liberal are those who redeem the captive from the plunderer, assist the poor, or discharge the debts of their friends. We must give, therefore, but with discrimination and moderation ; for many persons have exhausted their patrimony by giving inconsiderately. " For what can be more silly, than to take pains to be no longer able to do, that which you do with pleasure ?"[1] Some, therefore, when they have nothing to give, turn to rapine, and get more hatred from those from whom they take, than good-will from those to whom they give. We lament that thus it happened to this king; for, when in the very beginning of his reign, through fear of tumults, he had assembled soldiers, and denied them nothing, promising still greater remuneration hereafter, the consequence was, that as he had soon exhausted his father's treasures, and had then but moderate revenues, his substance failed, though the spirit of giving remained, which by habit had almost become nature. He was a man who knew not how to take off from the price of anything, or to judge of the value of goods; but the trader might sell him his commodity at whatever rate, or the soldier demand any pay, he pleased. He was anxious that the cost of his clothes should be extravagant, and angry if they were purchased at a low price. One morning, indeed, while putting on his new boots, he asked his chamberlain what they cost ; and when he replied, "Three shillings," indignantly and in a rage he cried out, " You son of a whore, how long has the king worn boots of so paltry a price ? go, and bring me a pair worth a mark of silver." He went, and bringing him a much cheaper pair, told him, falsely,

[1] Cicero de Officiis, ii. 15. Much of the argument is borrowed from the same source.

that they cost as much as he had ordered: "Ay," said the king, "these are suitable to royal majesty." Thus his chamberlain used to charge him what he pleased for his clothes; acquiring by this means many things for his own advantage.

§ 314. The fame of his generosity, therefore, pervaded all the West, and reached even to the East. Military men came to him out of every province on this side the mountains, whom he rewarded most profusely. In consequence, when he had no longer aught to bestow, poor and exhausted, he turned his thoughts to money-getting. The rapacity of his disposition was seconded by Ralph,[1] the inciter of his covetousness; a clergyman of the lowest origin, but raised to eminence by his wit and subtilty. If at any time a royal edict issued, that England should pay a certain tribute; it was doubled by this plunderer of the rich, this exterminator of the poor, this confiscator of other men's inheritance. He was an invincible pleader, as unrestrained in his words as in his actions: and equally furious against the meek as against the turbulent. Wherefore some people[2] used to laugh, and say, that he was the only man who knew how to employ his talents in this way, and cared for no one's hatred, so that he could please his master. At this person's suggestion, the sacred honours of the church, as the pastors died, were exposed to sale: for whenever the death of any bishop or abbot was announced, directly one of the king's clerks was despatched, who made an inventory of everything, and carried all future rents into the royal exchequer. In the meantime some person was sought out, fit to supply the place of the deceased; not from proof of morals, but of money; and at last, if I may so say, the empty honour was conferred, and even that purchased at a great price. These things appeared the more disgraceful, because in his father's time, after the decease of a bishop or abbot, all rents were reserved entire, to be given up to the succeeding pastor; and persons truly meritorious on account of their religion were elected. But in the lapse of a very few years, everything was changed. There was no man rich, except the money-changer; no clerk unless he was a lawyer; no priest unless (to use an expression hardly Latin) he was a farmer. Men of the meanest condition, or guilty of whatever crime, were listened to, if they could suggest anything likely to be advantageous to the king: the halter was loosened from the robber's neck, if he could promise any emolument to the sovereign. All military discipline being relaxed,[3] the courtiers preyed upon the property of the country people, and consumed their substance by taking the very meat from the mouths of these wretched creatures. Then was their flowing hair and extravagant dress, and then was invented the fashion of shoes with curved points:[4] then the model for young men was to rival women in

---

[1] Ralph Flambard, or Passeflabere. He was raised to the dignity of bishop of Durham, and was consecrated on the 5th June, 1099. See Anglia Sacra, i. 705.
[2] Some MSS. (A. and L.) read, "The king used to laugh."
[3] Compare Eadmer, Hist. Nov. p. 94.
[4] These shoes, which gave occasion for various ordinances for their regulation or abolition during several successive centuries, are said to have owed their invention to Fulco earl of Anjou, in order to hide his ill-formed feet,—Ordericus Vitalis,

delicacy of person, to mince their gait, to walk with loose gesture and half-naked. Enervated and effeminate, they unwillingly remained what nature had made them ; the assailers of others' chastity, prodigal of their own.[1] Troops of pathicks and droves of harlots followed the court, so that it was said, with justice, by a wise man, that England would be fortunate if Henry could reign ; led to such an opinion, because he abhorred obscenity from his youth.

§ 315. Here, were it necessary, I could add, that archbishop Anselm attempted to correct these abuses ; but failing of the co-operation of his suffragans, he voluntarily quitted the kingdom ; yielding to the depravity of the times. Anselm, than whom none ever was more tenacious of right ; none in the present time so thoroughly learned ; none so completely spiritual ; the father of his country, the mirror of the world : he, when just about to set sail, after waiting in port for a wind, was rifled, as though he had been a public robber ; all his bags and packages being brought out and ransacked. Of this man's injuries I could speak farther, had the sun witnessed anything more unjust than this single transaction, or were it not necessary to omit a relation, which has been anticipated by the eloquence of the very reverend Edmer.[2]

§ 316. Hence may be perceived how fierce a flame of evil burst forth from what the king conceived to be liberality. In repressing which, as he did not manifest so much diligence as negligence, he incurred a degree of infamy, not only great, but scarcely to be wiped out : I think undeservedly, however, because he never could have exposed himself to such disgrace, had he only recollected the dignity of his station. I pass over, therefore, these matters slightly, and hasten in my composition, because I blush to relate the crimes of so great a king; rather giving my attention to refute and extenuate them.

§ 317. The Jews in his reign gave proof of their insolence towards God : at one time, at Rouen, endeavouring to prevail on some converts, by means of presents, to return to Judaism ;[3] at p. 682; who also observes that the first improver, by adding the long curved termination, was a fellow (quidam nebulo) in the court of William Rufus, named Robert.

[1] Ordericus Vitalis censures the French, and particularly the Normans under Duke Robert, for nearly similar vices.

[2] Eadmer, besides making constant mention of Anselm in his Historia Novorum, wrote his Life, also, in a separate form, of which a translation will appear in the present series.

[3] The MSS. C. D. & E. followed by Saville, agree with the text ; but A. and L. here insert a story (borrowed from Eadmer, Hist. Novor. p. 47) to the following effect :—"A Jewish youth imagined that St. Stephen had appeared to him, and commanded him to be baptized : this he obeyed. His father immediately flew to the king, earnestly entreating an order for his son to be restored to the faith of his ancestors. The king not discovering any advantage as likely to accrue to himself, remained silent : on this the Jew offered him sixty marks, on condition that he would restore his son to Judaism. William then ordered the youth to be brought before him ; related his father's complaint, and commands him to renounce his baptism. The lad, astonished, replied, 'Your majesty is joking surely.' 'I joke with thee,' exclaimed the king, 'thou son of ordure ! begone, and obey my commands instantly, or by the face at Lucca, I will have thine eyes torn out.' The young man remaining inflexible, he drove him from his presence. The father was then ordered before the king, who desired him to pay down the money he had promised ; but, on the Jew's remonstrating that he had not reconverted his son, and the king's declaring that his labour was not to go unrewarded, it was agreed that he should receive half the sum."

another, at London, entering into controversy with our bishops : because the king (in jest, as I suppose) had said, that if they mastered the Christians in open argument, he would become one of their sect. The question therefore was agitated with much apprehension on the part of the bishops and clergy, fearful, through pious anxiety, for the Christian faith. From this contest, however, the Jews reaped nothing but confusion : though they used repeatedly to boast, that they were vanquished, not by argument, but by power.

§ 318. In later times, that is, about the ninth year of his reign, Robert earl of Normandy, at the admonition of pope Urban, as will be related hereafter, took the resolution of going to Jerusalem, and pawned Normandy to his brother, for the sum of ten thousand marks. In consequence, an edict for an intolerable tax was circulated throughout England. On this the bishops and abbots, in great numbers, went to court, to complain of the injury ; observing that they could not raise so great an impost, unless they drove away their wretched husbandmen altogether. To this the courtiers, with angry countenance, as usual, replied, " Have you not shrines adorned with gold and silver, full of dead men's bones ?" deigning the petitioners no other answer. In consequence, perceiving the drift of the reply, they took off the gold from the shrines of their saints ; robbed their crucifixes ; melted their chalices ; not for the service of the poor, but of the king's exchequer. For almost everything, which the holy parsimony of their ancestors had saved, was consumed by the rapacity of these freebooters.

§ 319. Just so, too, were their proceedings against their vassals; first taking their money, then their land : neither the poor man's poverty, nor the rich man's abundance, protecting him. He so restricted the right of hunting, which he had formerly allowed, that it became a capital offence to take a stag. This extreme severity, which was tempered by no affability, was the cause of many conspiracies, among the nobility, against his safety : one of whom, Robert de Molbrei, earl of Northumberland, in consequence of very high words between him and the king, retired to his province, with the intention of making powerful efforts against his lord ; but William pursuing him, he was taken, and doomed to perpetual captivity. Another, William de Ou, being accused of treachery towards the king, challenged his accuser to single combat ; but being unable to justify himself in the duel, he was deprived of his sight, and castrated. The same accusation involved many innocent and honourable men ; among whom was William de Alderea, a man of handsome person, who had stood godfather [1] with the king. Being sentenced to be hanged, he made his confession to Osmund bishop of Salisbury, and was scourged at every church of the town. Parting his garments to the poor, he went naked to the gallows, often making the blood gush from his delicate flesh by falling on his knees upon the stones. He satisfied the minds of the bishop, and of the people who followed him to the place of punishment, by exclaiming, " God help my soul, and deliver it from evil, as I am

[1] " Compater" sometimes means a friend or companion.

free from the charge of which I am accused : the sentence, indeed, passed upon me will not be revoked, but I wish all men to be certified of my innocence." The bishop then commending his soul to heaven, and sprinkling him with holy water, departed. At his execution, he manifested an admirable degree of courage ; neither uttering a groan before, nor even a sigh at the moment of his death.

§ 320. But still there are some proofs of noble magnanimity in the king, the knowledge of which I will not deny to posterity. As he was once engaged in hunting in a certain forest, a foreign messenger acquainted him that the city of Mans, which he had lately added to his dominions on the departure of his brother, was besieged. Unprepared as he was, he turned his horse instantly, and shaped his journey to the sea. When his nobles reminded him that it would be necessary to call out his troops and put them in array, "I shall see," said he, who will follow me: do you think I shall not have people enough? If I know the temper of the young men of my kingdom, they will even brave shripwreck to come to me." In this manner he arrived, almost unattended, at the sea coast. The sky at that time was overcast, the wind was contrary, and a tempest swept the surface of the deep. When he determined to embark directly, the mariners besought him to wait till the storm should subside and the wind be favourable. "Why," said William, "I have never heard of a king perishing by shipwreck : no, weigh anchor immediately, and you shall see the elements conspire to obey me." When the report of his having crossed the sea reached the besiegers, they hastily retreated. One Helias, the author of the commotion, was taken; to whom, when brought before him, the king said jocularly, "I have you, master." But he, whose haughty spirit, even in such threatening danger, knew not how to be prudent or to speak submissively, replied, "You have taken me by chance; if I could escape I know what I would do." At this William, almost beside himself with rage, and seizing Helias, exclaimed, "You scoundrel! and what would you do? Begone, depart, fly : I give you leave to do whatever you can; and by the Face at Lucca, if you should conquer me, I will ask no return for this favour." Nor did he falsify his word, but immediately suffered him to escape,[1] rather admiring than following the fugitive. Who could believe this of an unlettered man! And perhaps there may be some person who, from reading Lucan,[2] may falsely suppose that William borrowed these examples from Julius Cæsar; but he had neither inclination nor leisure to attend to learning; it was rather the innate warmth of his temper and his conscious valour, which prompted him to such expressions. And indeed, if our religion would allow it, as the soul of Euphorbus was formerly said to have passed into Pythagoras of Samos, so might it equally be asserted that the soul of Julius Cæsar had migrated into king William.

[1] Elias count of Maine, being taken by Robert de Bellesme in 1098, and delivered into the king's hands, purchased his liberty only by the surrender of the city of Mans, as testified by Ordericus Vitalis. [2] Pharsalia, lib. ii. 515; v. 580.

§ 321. He began and completed one very noble edifice, the palace in London;[1] sparing no expense to manifest the greatness of his liberality. His disposition therefore the reader will be able to discover from the circumstances we have enumerated. Should any one be desirous, however, to know the make of his person : he is to understand that he was well set ; his complexion florid, his hair yellow ; of open countenance ; different coloured eyes, varying with certain glittering specks ; of astonishing strength, though not very tall, and his belly rather projecting ; of no eloquence, but remarkable for an hesitation of speech, especially when angry. Many sudden and sorrowful accidents happened in his time, which I shall arrange singly, according to the years of his reign ; chiefly vouching for their truth on the credit of the Chronicles.

§ 322. In the second year of his reign, on the third of the ides of August [11th Aug. A.D. 1089], a great earthquake terrified all England with an horrid spectacle; for all the buildings were lifted up, and then again settled as before. A scarcity of every kind of produce followed ; the corn ripened so slowly, that the harvest was scarcely housed before the feast of St. Andrew [30th Nov.]

§ 323. In his fourth year [A.D. 1091], was a tempest of lightning, and a whirlwind : finally, on the ides of October [15th Oct.], at Winchelcumbe, a stroke of lightning beat against the side of the tower, with such force, that shattering the wall, where it joined to the roof, it opened a place wide enough to admit a man; entering there, it struck a very large beam, and scattered fragments of it over the whole church ; moreover it cast down the head of the crucifix, with the right leg, and the image of St. Mary. A stench so noisome followed, as to be insufferable to the human nostril. At length, the monks, with auspicious boldness, entering, defeated the contrivances of the devil, by the sprinkling of holy water.

§ 324. But what could this mean ? a matter before unknown in every age. A tempest of contending winds, from the south-east, on the sixteenth of the kalends of November [Oct. 17th], destroyed more than six hundred houses in London. Churches were heaped on houses, and walls on partitions. The tempest, proceeding yet farther, carried off altogether the roof of the church of St. Mary le Bow, and killed two men. Rafters and beams were whirled through the air, an object of surprise, to such as contemplated them from a distance ; of alarm, to those who stood nigh, lest they should be crushed by them. For, four rafters, six and twenty feet long, were driven with such violence into the ground, that scarcely four feet of them were visible. It was curious to see how they had perforated the solidity of the public street, maintaining there the same position which they had occupied in the roof from the hand of the workman, until, on account of their inconvenience to passengers, they

---

[1] It has been inferred from this passage that Malmesbury states the Tower of London was built by William Rufus. There appears, however, little doubt that the principal building, now called the White Tower, was commenced by the Conqueror, and finished by Rufus, under the superintendence of Gundulph bishop of Rochester.

were cut off level with the ground, as they could not be otherwise removed.

§ 325. In his fifth year [A.D. 1092], a similar thunder-storm at Salisbury entirely destroyed the roof of the church-tower, and much injured the wall, only five days after Osmund the bishop, of famed memory, had consecrated it.

§ 326. In his sixth year [A.D. 1093], there was such a deluge from rain, and such incessant showers, as none had ever remembered. Afterwards, on the approach of winter, the rivers were so frozen, that they bore horsemen and wagons; and soon after, when the frost broke, the bridges were destroyed by the drifting of the ice.

§ 327. In his seventh year [A.D. 1094], agriculture was neglected, on account of the heavy tribute, which the king had levied while in Normandy; of which the immediate consequence was a famine. This also gaining ground, a mortality ensued, so general, that the dying wanted attendance, and the dead, burial. At that time, too, the Welsh, fiercely raging against the Normans, and depopulating the county of Chester and part of Shropshire, obtained Anglesey by force of arms.

§ 328. In his tenth year [A.D. 1097], on the kalends of October [Oct. 1], a comet appeared for fifteen days, turning its larger train to the east, and the smaller to the south-east. Other stars also appeared, darting, as it were, at each other. This was the year in which Anselm, that light of England, voluntarily escaping from the darkness of error, went to Rome.

§ 329. In his eleventh year [A.D. 1098], Magnus king of Norway, with Harold, son of Harold formerly king of England, subdued the Orkney, Mevanian, and other circumjacent isles; and was now obstinately bent against England from Anglesey. But Hugh earl of Chester and Hugh earl of Shrewsbury opposed him; and ere he could gain the continent, forced him to retire. Here fell Hugh of Shrewsbury, being struck from a distance with a fatal arrow.

§ 330. In his twelfth year [A.D. 1099] an excessive tide flowed up the Thames, and overwhelmed many villages, with their inhabitants.

§ 331. In his thirteenth year [A.D. 1100], which was the last of his life, there were many adverse events; but the most dreadful circumstance was, that the devil visibly appeared to men, in woods and secret places, and spoke to them as they passed by. Moreover, in the county of Berks, at the village of Hamstead,[1] a fountain so plentifully flowed with blood for fifteen whole days, that it discoloured a neighbouring pool. The king heard of it, and laughed; neither did he care for his own dreams, nor for what others saw concerning him.

§ 332. They relate many visions and predictions of his death, three of which, sanctioned by the testimony of credible authors, I shall communicate to my readers. Edmer, the historian of our times, noted for his veracity, says that Anselm, the noble exile, with

---

[1] This is the reading of the MSS. A. C. D. E. L., but amongst his various readings Saville gives Finghamstede.

whom all religion was also banished, came to Marcigny, that he
might communicate his sufferings to Hugh, abbot of Clugny; where,
when the conversation turned upon king William, the abbot aforesaid observed, " Last night that king was brought before God ; and
by a deliberate judgment, incurred the sad sentence of damnation."
How he came to know this, he neither explained at the time, nor
did any of his hearers ask : nevertheless, out of respect to his piety,
not a doubt of the truth of his words remained on the minds of any
present.   Hugh led such a life and had such a character that all
regarded his discourse and venerated his advice, as though an oracle
from heaven had spoken.   And soon after, the king being slain as
we shall relate, there came a messenger to entreat the archbishop
to resume his see.

§ 333. The day before the king died he dreamed that he was let
blood by a surgeon, and that the stream, reaching to heaven,
clouded the light and intercepted the day. Calling on St. Mary for
protection, he suddenly awoke, commanded a light to be brought,
and forbade his attendants to leave him. They then watched with
him several hours until daylight. Shortly after, just as the day began to dawn, a certain foreign monk told Robert Fitz Hamo, one
of the principal nobility, that he had that night dreamed a strange
and fearful dream about the king : That he had come into a certain church, with menacing and insolent gesture, as was his custom,
looking contemptuously on the standers-by ; then violently seizing
the crucifix he gnawed the arms, and almost tore away the legs; that
the image endured this for a long time, but at length struck the
king with its foot in such a manner that he fell backwards ; from
his mouth, as he lay prostrate, issued so copious a flame that the
volumes of smoke touched the very stars. Robert, thinking that
this dream ought not to be neglected, as he was intimate with him,
immediately related it to the king. William, repeatedly laughing,
exclaimed, " He is a monk, and dreams for money, like a monk ;
give him an hundred shillings." Nevertheless, being greatly moved,
he hesitated a long while whether he should go out to hunt as he
had designed ; his friends persuading him not to suffer the truth of
the dreams to be tried at his personal risk. In consequence he
abstained from the chase before dinner, dispelling the uneasiness of
his unregulated mind by serious business. They relate, that, having
plentifully regaled that day, he soothed his cares with a more than
usual quantity of wine. After dinner he went into the forest,
attended by few persons ; of whom the most intimate with him was
Walter, surnamed Tirel,[1] who had been induced to come from
France by the liberality of the king. This man alone had remained
with him, while the others, employed in the chase, were dispersed

---

[1] The tradition of William having met his death by the hand of Sir Walter
Tirel, whilst hunting in the New Forest, is generally received; but Suger, a contemporary historian, and, as it seems, a friend of Tirel, in his life of Louis le Gros,
king of France, alluding to the death of Rufus, observes, "Some persons have
charged a certain noble named Walter Tyrell with having slain him with an
arrow; but I have often heard him swear when he had nothing either to fear or
hope from such an assertion, that on that particular day he neither was in the
part of the wood where the king was hunting, nor saw him at all in the wood." See
also Eadmer, Hist. Nov. p. 54, and Ord. Vit. Hist. Eccl. x. 783.

as chance directed.—The sun was now declining, when the king, drawing his bow and letting fly an arrow, slightly wounded a stag which passed before him; and, keenly gazing, followed it, still running, a long time with his eyes, holding up his hand to keep off the power of the sun's rays. At this instant Walter, conceiving a noble exploit,—which was, while the king's attention was otherwise occupied, to transfix another stag which by chance came near him, —unknowingly, and without power to prevent it, O gracious God! pierced his breast with a fatal arrow. On receiving the wound the king uttered not a word; but breaking off the shaft of the weapon where it projected from his body, and then falling upon the wound, he accelerated his death. Walter immediately ran up, but as he found him senseless and speechless he leaped swiftly upon his horse, and escaped by spurring him to his utmost speed. Indeed there was none to pursue him, some conniving at his flight, others pitying him, and all intent on other matters. Some began to fortify their dwellings, others to plunder, and the rest to look out for a new king. A few countrymen conveyed the body, placed on a cart, to the cathedral at Winchester, the blood dripping from it all the way. Here it was committed to the ground within the tower, attended by many of the nobility, though lamented by few. Next year the tower fell; though I forbear to mention the different opinions[1] on this subject, lest I should seem credulous of trifles : more especially as the building might have fallen through imperfect construction, even though he had never been buried there. He died in the year of our Lord's incarnation one thousand one hundred, of his reign the thirteenth, on the fourth of the nones of August [Aug. 2], aged above forty years; forming mighty plans, which he would have brought to effect, could he have spun out the thread of fate, or broken through and disengaged himself from the violence of fortune. Such was the energy of his mind, that he was bold enough to promise himself any kingdom whatever. Indeed, the day before his death, being asked where he would keep his Christmas, he answered, In Poictou; because the earl of Poictou, wishing anxiously to go to Jerusalem, was said to be about to pawn his territory to him. Thus, not content with his paternal possessions, and allured by expectation of greater glory, he grasped at honours not pertaining to him. He was a man much to be pitied by the clergy, for throwing away the soul they laboured to save; to be beloved by stipendiary soldiers for the multitude of his gifts; but not to be lamented by the people, because he suffered their substance to be plundered. I remember no council being held in his time wherein the health of the church was strengthened through the correction of abuses. He hesitated a long time ere he bestowed ecclesiastical honours, either for the sake of emolument or of weighing desert : so that, on the day he died, he held in his own hands three

---

[1] This is the reading of the MSS. C. D. E., followed by Saville; but A. and L. read as follows : "Nor did some hesitate to say that the fall of the tower, which happened some years after, was caused by the enormity of placing in a consecrated grave him who was grasping and dissolute all his life, and had died wanting the last offices of the Church." The Tower fell on the 7th of Oct. 1107. An. Winton, Ang. Sacr. i. 297.

bishoprics and twelve vacant abbeys. Besides, taking advantage of the schism between Urban in Rome and Guibert at Ravenna, he forbade the payment of the tribute[1] to the holy see; though he was more inclined to favour Guibert, because the ground and instigation of the discord between himself and Anselm was that this man, so dear to God, had pronounced Urban to be pope, the other an apostate.

§ 334. In his time began the Cistercian order, which is now both believed and asserted to be the surest road to heaven.[2] To speak of this order does not seem irrelevant to the work I have undertaken, since it redounds to the glory of England to have produced the distinguished man who was the author and promoter of that rule. To us he belonged, and in our schools passed the earlier part of his life. Wherefore, if we are not envious, we shall embrace his good qualities the more kindly, in proportion as we knew them more intimately : and, moreover, I am anxious to extol his praise, because it is a mark of an ingenuous mind to approve that virtue in others of which in yourself you regret the absence. He was named Harding, and born in England of no very illustrious parents. From his early years he was a monk at Shireburn; but when secular desires had captivated his youth, he grew disgusted with the monastic garb, and went first to Scotland and afterwards to France. Here, after some years exercise in the liberal arts, he became awakened to the love of God. For, when manlier years had put away childish things, he went to Rome with a clerk who partook of his studies; neither the length and difficulty of the journey, nor the scantiness of their means of subsistence by the way, preventing them, both as they went and returned, from singing, daily, the whole psalter. Indeed the mind of this celebrated man was already meditating the design which soon after, by the grace of God, he attempted to put in execution: for returning into Burgundy, he received the tonsure at Molesmes, a new and magnificent monastery, and readily admitted the first elements of the order, as he had formerly seen them; but when additional matters were proposed for his observance, such as he had neither read in the rule nor seen elsewhere, he began modestly, and as became a monk, to ask the reason of them, saying, " By reason the supreme Creator has made all things, by reason He governs all things, by reason the fabric of the world revolves, by reason even the planets move, by reason the elements are directed, and by reason, and by due regulation, our nature ought to conduct itself. But since, through sloth, she too often departs from reason, many laws were, long ago, enacted for her use; and latterly a divine rule has been promulgated by St. Benedict to bring back the deviations of nature to reason. In this, though some things are contained, the design of

---

[1] By this probably is to be understood the payment of Peter-pence. Anselm had offended the king, by acknowledging Urban without consulting him.

[2] —— In cœlum quos evehit optima summi
Nunc via processus.—Juv. Sat. i. 38.

A similar allusion to the Cistercian order being the surest road to heaven may be seen in the prologue to Richard of Devizes : "Quanto cella Cartusiœ celsior sit et cœlo vicinior claustro Wintoniœ."—Chron. Ric. Divis. cur. Stevenson.

which I cannot fathom, yet I deem it necessary to yield to authority. And though reason and the authority of the holy writers may seem at variance, yet still they are one and the same. For since God hath created and restored nothing without reason, how can I believe that the holy fathers, no doubt strict followers of God, could command anything but what was reasonable, as if we ought to give credit to their bare authority. See then that you bring reason, or at least authority, for what you devise; although no great credit should be given to what is merely supported by human reason, because it may be combated with arguments equally forcible. Therefore, from that rule, which, equally supported by reason and authority, appears as if dictated by the spirit of all just persons, produce precedents; which if you fail to do, in vain shall you profess his rule whose regulations you disdain to comply with."

§ 335. Sentiments of this kind, spreading as usual from one to another, justly moved the hearts of such as feared God, "lest haply they should or had run in vain." The subject then being canvassed in frequent chapters, ended by bringing over the abbot himself to the opinion that all superfluous matters should be passed by, and merely the essence of the rule be observed. Two of the fraternity, therefore, of equal faith and learning, were elected, who, by vicarious examination, were to discover the intention of the founder's rule; and when they had discovered it, to propound it to the rest. The abbot diligently endeavoured to induce the whole convent to give their concurrence, but as it is difficult to eradicate from men's minds what has early taken root, since they reluctantly relinquish the first notions they have imbibed, almost the whole of them refused to accept the new regulations, because they were attached to the old. Eighteen only, among whom was Harding, also called Stephen, persevering in their holy determination, together with their abbot, left the monastery, declaring that the purity of the institution could not be preserved in a place where riches and gluttony warred against even the heart that was well-inclined. They came, therefore, to Citeaux, a situation formerly covered with woods, but now so conspicuous from the abundant piety of its monks, that it is not undeservedly esteemed conscious of the Divinity himself. Here, by the countenance of the archbishop of Vienne, who is now pope,[1] they entered on a labour worthy to be remembered and venerated to the end of time.

§ 336. Certainly many of their regulations seem severe, and more particularly these: They wear nothing made with furs or linen, nor even that finely-spun woollen garment, which we call Staminium;[2] neither breeches, unless when sent on a journey, which at their return they wash and put away. They have two tunics with cowls, but no additional garment in winter; though, if they think fit, in summer they may lighten their garb. They sleep clad and girded, and never after Mattins return to their beds: but they so order the time of Mattins, that it shall be light ere the Lauds[3]

---

[1] Calixtus II. who occupied the papal chair from A.D. 1119 to 1124.
[2] A kind of woollen shirt.   [3] The concluding psalms of the Mattin service.

begin; so intent are they on their rule, that they think no jot or tittle of it should be disregarded. Directly after these hymns they sing the Prime: after which they go out to work for stated hours. They complete whatever labour or service they have to perform by day without any other light. No one is ever absent from the daily services, or from Complines, except the sick. The cellarer and hospitaller, after Complines, wait upon the guests, yet observing the strictest silence. The abbot allows himself no indulgence beyond the others: everywhere present, everywhere attending to his flock; except that he does not eat with the rest, because his table is with the strangers and the poor. Nevertheless, be he where he may, he is equally sparing of food and of speech: for never more than two dishes are served, either to him or to his company; lard and meat never but to the sick. From the ides of September till Easter, whatever festival may occur, they do not take more than one meal a day, except on Sunday. They never leave the cloister but for the purpose of labour; nor do they ever speak, either there or elsewhere, save only to the abbot or prior. They pay unwearied attention to the canonical[1] services, making no addition to them, except the Vigil for the defunct. They use in their divine service the Ambrosian chants[2] and hymns, as far as they were able to learn them from Milan. While they bestow care on the stranger and the sick, they inflict intolerable mortifications on their own bodies, for the health of their souls.

§ 337. The abbot, at first, both encountered these privations with much alacrity himself, and compelled the rest to do the same. In process of time, however, the man repented;[3] for he had been delicately brought up, and could not well bear such continued scantiness of diet. The monks, whom he had left at Molesmes, getting intimation as to his design either by messages or letters, for it is uncertain which, drew him back to the monastery, by his obedience to the pope, for such was their pretext: compelling him to a measure, to which he was already extremely well-disposed. For, as if wearied out by the pertinacity of their entreaties, he left the narrow confines of poverty, and resought his former magnificence. All followed him from Citeaux, who had gone thither with him, except eight. These, few in number, but great in virtue, appointed Alberic, one of their party, abbot, and Stephen, prior; the former not surviving more than eight years, was, by the will of Heaven, happily called away. Then, doubtless by God's appointment, Stephen, though absent, was elected abbot; the original contriver of the whole scheme; the especial and celebrated ornament of our times. Sixteen abbeys which he has already completed, and seven which he has begun, are sufficient testimonies of his

---

[1] The Horæ, or canonical services, were, Mattins, Primes, Tierce, Sexts, Nones, Vespers, and Complines.

[2] The Ambrosian Ritual prevailed pretty generally till the time of Charlemagne, who adopted the Gregorian. Durandus (V. 1.) has a curious account of an experiment, on the result of which was founded the general reception of the latter, and the confining the former chiefly to Milan, the church of St. Ambrose.

[3] The learned Mabillon appears much displeased with Malmesbury, for the motives here assigned for abbot Robert's quitting Citeaux. V. Ann. Benedictinorum.

abundant merit.   Thus, God speaking through him, as by a
trumpet, he directs the people around him, both by word and deed,
to heaven; acting fully up to his own precepts; affable in speech,
pleasant in look, and with a mind always rejoicing in the Lord.
Hence, openly, that noble joy of countenance; hence, secretly, that
compunction, coming from above; because despising this state of
a sojourner, he constantly desires to be in a place of rest.   For
these causes he is beloved by all; for God graciously imparts to the
minds of other men, a love for that man whom He loves.   Wherefore the inhabitant of that country esteems himself happy, if,
through his hands, he can transmit his wealth to God.   He receives
much, indeed; but expending little on his own wants, or those of
his flock, he immediately spends the rest on the poor, and in the
building of monasteries: for the purse of Stephen is the public
treasury of the indigent.   A proof of his abstinence is, that you
see nothing there, as in other monasteries, flaming with gold,
blazing with jewels or glittering with silver.   For as a Gentile says,
" Of what use is gold to a saint?"   We think it not enough in our
holy vases, unless the ponderous metal be eclipsed by precious
stones; by the flame of the topaz, the violet of the amethyst, and
the green shade of the emerald; unless the sacerdotal robes wanton
with gold; and unless the walls glisten with various coloured
paintings, and through the reflection of the sun's rays upon the
ceiling.   These men, however, placing those things which mortals
foolishly esteem the first, only in a secondary point of view, give all
their diligence to improve their morals, and love pure minds more
than glittering vestments; knowing that the best remuneration
for doing well, is to enjoy a clear conscience.   Moreover, if at any
time the laudable kindness of the abbot either desires, or feigns a
desire, to modify aught from the strict letter of the rule, they are
ready to oppose such indulgence; saying, that they have no long
time to live, nor shall they continue to exist so long as they have
already done; that they hope to remain steadfast in their purpose to the end, and to be an example to their successors, who
will transgress, if they should give way.   And indeed through
human weakness, the perpetual law of which is, that nothing
attained even by the greatest labour can long remain unchanged,
it will be so.   But to comprise, in one sentence, all things which
are, or can be said of them; the Cistercian monks, at the present
day, are a model for all monks, a mirror for the diligent, a spur to
the indolent.

*The Translation of the three Bishoprics of Wells, Chester, and
Thetford.*

§ 338.   At this time three sees in England were removed from
their ancient situations: Wells to Bath, by John: Chester to
Coventry, by Robert: Thetford to Norwich, by Herbert; all through
greater ambition than ought to have influenced men of such eminence.   Finally, to speak of the last first; Herbert, from his skill in

adulation, surnamed Losinga,[1] from being abbot of Ramsey, purchased the bishopric of Thetford, while his father, Robert, surnamed as himself, was intruded on the abbey of Winchester. This man, then, was the great source of simony in England; having craftily procured, by means of his wealth, both an abbey and a bishopric: for he hoodwinked the king's solicitude for the church by his money, and whispered great promises to secure the favour of the nobility: whence a poet of those times admirably observes,

A monster in the church from Losing rose,
Base Simon's sect, the canons to oppose.
Peter, thou'rt slow; see Simon soars on high;
If present, soon thou'd'st hurl him from the sky.[2]
Oh grief, the church is let to sordid hire,
The son a bishop, abbot is the sire.
All may be hoped from gold's prevailing sway,
Which governs all things; gives and takes away;
Makes bishops, abbots, basely in a day.

§ 339. Future repentance, however, atoned for the errors of his youth: he went to Rome, when he was of a more serious age, and there resigning the staff and ring which he had acquired by simony, had them restored through the indulgence of that most merciful see; for the Romans regard it both as more holy and more fitting, that the dues from each church should rather come into their own purse, than be subservient to the use of any king whatever. Herbert thus returning home, removed the episcopal see, which had formerly been at Helmam, and was then at Thetford, to a town celebrated for its trade and populousness, called Norwich. Here he settled a congregation of monks, famous for their numbers and their morals; purchasing everything for them out of his private fortune. For, having an eye to the probable complaints of his successors, he gave none of the episcopal lands to the monastery, lest they should deprive the servants of God of their subsistence, if they found anything given to them which pertained to their see. At Thetford, too, he settled Cluniac monks, because the members of that order, dispersed almost all over the world, are rich in worldly possessions, and of distinguished piety towards God. Thus by the great and extensive merit of his virtues, he shrouded the multitude of his former failings; and by his abundant eloquence and learning, as well as by his skill in secular affairs, he became a favourite also of the Roman pontiff. Herbert thus changed, became, (as Lucan observes of Curio,) "the changer and mover of all things;" and, as in the times of this king, he had been a pleader in behalf of simony, so was he, afterwards, its most strenuous opposer; nor did he suffer that to be done by others, which he lamented he had ever himself done through the presumption of juvenile ardour: ever having in his mouth, as they relate, the saying of St. Jerome, "We have erred when young; let us amend now we are old." Finally, who can sufficiently extol his conduct, who, though not a very rich bishop, yet built so noble a monastery; in which nothing remains

[1] From the French "losenge," adulation. A collection of his letters, edited by Robert Anstruther, was published at Brussels in 8vo. 1846.
[2] Alluding to the Legend of St. Peter and Simon Magus; who having undertaken, by means of enchantment, to fly, was, by the adjuration of St. Peter, dashed to the earth and killed. See Constit. Apostol. vi. 9, ap. Labb. Concil. i. 380.

to be desired, either in the beauty of the lofty edifice, the elegance of its ornaments, or in the piety and universal charity of its monks. These things soothed him with joyful hope while he lived, and when dead, if repentance be not in vain, conducted him to heaven.

§ 340. John was bishop of Wells ; a native of Touraine, and an approved physician, by practice, rather than education. On the death of the abbot of Bath, he easily obtained the abbey from the king, both because all things at court were exposed to sale, and his covetousness seemed palliated by some degree of reason, that so famed a city might be still more celebrated, by becoming the see of a bishop. He at first began to exercise his severity against the monks, because they were dull, and in his estimation barbarians ; taking away all the lands ministering to their subsistence, and furnishing them with but scanty provision by his lay dependents. In process of time, however, when new monks had been admitted, he conducted himself with more mildness; and gave a small portion of land to the prior, by which he might, in some measure, support himself and his inmates. And although he had begun austerely, yet many things were there by him both nobly entered on and completed, in decorations and in books; and more especially, in a selection of monks, equally notable for their learning and kind offices. But still he could not, even at his death, be softened far enough totally to exonerate the lands from bondage; leaving, in this respect, an example not to be followed by his successors.

§ 341. There was in the diocese of Chester a monastery, called Coventry,[1] which, as I have before related, the most noble earl Leofric, with his lady Godiva, had built; so splendid for its gold and silver, that the very walls of the church seemed too scanty to receive the treasures, to the great astonishment of the beholders. This, Robert, bishop of the diocese, eagerly seized on, in a manner by no means episcopal ; stealing from the very treasures of the church wherewith he might fill the hand of the donor, beguile the vigilance of the pope, and gratify the covetousness of the Romans. Continuing there many years, he gave no proof of worth whatever; for, so far from rescuing the tottering roofs from ruin, he wasted the sacred treasures, and became guilty of peculation ; and the bishop might have been convicted of illegal exactions, had an accuser been at hand. He fed the monks on miserable fare, made no attempts to excite in them a love for their profession, and suffered them to reach only a very common degree of learning: lest he should make them delicate by sumptuous living, or strictness of rule and depth of learning should inspire them to oppose him. Contented therefore with rustic fare, and humble literary attainments, they deemed it enough if they could only live in peace. Moreover, at his death, paying little attention to the dictates of the canons, by which it is enacted that bishops ought to be buried in their cathedrals, he commanded himself to be interred, not at Chester, but at Coventry; leaving to his successors by such a decision the task, not of claiming what was not due to them, but, as it were, of vindicating their proper right.

[1] See § 196.

§ 342. Here, while speaking of the times of William, I should be induced to relate the translation of the most excellent Augustine, the apostle of the English, and of his companions, had not the talents of the learned Goscelin [1] anticipated me; of Goscelin, who being a monk of St. Bertin, formerly came to England with Herman bishop of Salisbury, skilled equally in literature and music. For a considerable time visiting the cathedrals and abbeys, he left proofs of uncommon learning in many places. Second to none after Beda in the celebration of the English saints; next to Osberne too, he bore away the palm in music. Moreover he wrote innumerable lives of modern saints, and restored, in an elegant manner, such of those of the ancients as had been lost through the confusion of the times, or had been carelessly edited. He also so exquisitely wrought the process of this translation, that he may be said to have realized it to the present race, and given a view of it to posterity. Happy that tongue which ministered to so many saints! happy that voice which poured forth such melody! more especially as in his life his probity equalled his learning. But, as I have hitherto recorded disgraceful transactions of certain bishops, I will introduce other contemporaneous bishops of different lives and dispositions, that our times may not be said to have grown so dark as not to produce one single saint. Such as are desirous may find this promise completed in a subsequent book, after the narrative of king Henry's transactions.

§ 343. I shall now describe the expedition to Jerusalem, relating in my own words what was seen and endured by others. Besides, too, as opportunity offers, I shall select from ancient writers accounts of the situation and riches of Constantinople, Antioch, and Jerusalem, in order that he who is unacquainted with these matters, and meets with this work, may have something at hand to communicate to others. But for such a relation needs a more fervent spirit, in order to complete effectually what I begin with such pleasure. Invoking, therefore, the Divinity, as is usual, I begin as follows.

§ 344. In the year of the Incarnation 1095, pope Urban the second, who then filled the papal throne, passing the Alps, came into France. The ostensible cause of his journey was, that, being driven from Rome by the violence of Guibert, he might prevail on the churches on this side the mountains to acknowledge him. His more secret intention was not so well known; this was, by Boamund's advice, to excite almost the whole of Europe to undertake an expedition into Asia, that in such a general commotion of all countries, auxiliaries might easily be engaged, by whose means both Urban might obtain Rome, and Boamund, Illyria and Macedonia. For Guiscard, his father, had conquered those countries from Alexis, and also all the territory extending from Durazzo to Thessalonica; wherefore Boamund claimed them as his due since he obtained not the inheritance of Apulia, which his father had given to his younger son, Roger. Still, nevertheless, whatever might

[1] Goscelin's "Life and Translation of St. Augustine" is printed in the "Acta Sanctorum" of the Bollandists, 26 Maii.

be the cause of Urban's journey, it turned out of great and singular advantage to the Christian world. A council, therefore, was assembled at Clermont, which is the most noted city of Auvergne. The number of bishops and abbots was three hundred and ten. Here at first, during several days, a long discussion was carried on concerning the Catholic faith, and the establishment of peace among contending parties. For, in addition to those crimes in which every one indulged, all on this side of the Alps had arrived at such a calamitous state as to take each other captive on little or no pretence; nor were they suffered to go free, unless ransomed at an enormous price. Again, too, the snake of simony had so reared her slippery crest, and cherished, with poisonous warmth, her deadly eggs, that the whole world became infected with her mortal hissing, and tainted the honours of the church. At that time, I will not say bishops to their sees merely, but none aspired even to any ecclesiastical degree, except by the influence of money. Then, too, many persons putting away their lawful wives, procured divorces, and invaded the marriage-couch of others. Wherefore, as in both these cases, there was a mixed multitude of offenders, the names of some powerful persons were singled out for punishment. Not to be tedious, I will subjoin the result of the whole council, abbreviating some parts, in my own language.

§ 345. In a council at Clermont,[1] in the presence of pope Urban, these articles were enacted: "That the Catholic church shall be pure in faith, free from all servitude; that bishops, or abbots, or clergy of any rank, shall receive no ecclesiastical dignity from the hand of princes, or of any of the laity; that clergymen shall not hold prebends in two churches or cities; that no one shall be bishop and abbot at the same time; that ecclesiastical dignities shall be bought or sold by no one; that no person in holy orders shall be guilty of carnal intercourse; that such as not knowing the canonical prohibition had purchased canonries should be pardoned, but that they should be taken from such as were known to possess them by their own purchase, or that of their relations; that no layman from Ash Wednesday, no clergyman from Quadragesima to Easter shall eat flesh; that, at all times, the first fast of the Ember weeks should be in the first week of Lent; that orders should be conferred at all times on the evening of Saturday, or on a Sunday, continuing fasting;[2] that on Easter-eve, service should not be celebrated till after the ninth hour; that the second fast should be observed in the week of Pentecost; that from our Lord's Advent to the octave of the Epiphany, from Septuagesima to the octaves of Easter, from the first day of the Rogations to the octaves of Pentecost, and from the fourth day of the week at sunset, at all

---

[1] The council of Clermont, in Auvergne, continued from 18th to 28th of Nov. A. D. 1095; wherein the decrees of the councils held by pope Urban at Amalfi, Benevento, Troie, and Plaisance, were confirmed, and many new canons made. Malmesbury's is perhaps the best account now known of that celebrated council. See the acts of the council of Clermont. See Labb. Concil. x. 506.

[2] If orders could not be completely conferred on Saturday, the ceremony might be performed on Sunday, and the parties continuing to fast, the two days were considered as one only.—Durand.

times, to the second day in the following week at sunrise, the truce of God [1] be observed; that whoever laid violent hands on a bishop should be excommunicated; that whoever laid violent hands on clergymen or their servants should be accursed; that whoever seized the goods of bishops or clergymen at their deaths, should be accursed; that whoever married a relation, even in the seventh degree of consanguinity, should be accursed; that none should be chosen bishop except a priest, deacon, or subdeacon, who was of noble descent, unless under pressing necessity and licence from the pope; that the sons of priests and concubines should not be advanced to the priesthood, unless they first made their vow; that whosoever fled to the church or the cross should, being insured from loss of limb, be delivered up to justice, or if innocent, be released; that every church should enjoy its own tithes, nor convey them away to another; that laymen should neither buy nor sell tithes; that no fee should be demanded for the burial of the dead." In this council the pope excommunicated Philip, king of France, and all who called him king or lord, and obeyed him or spoke to him, unless for the purpose of correcting him; in like manner too his accursed consort and all who called her queen or lady, till they so far reformed as to separate from each other; [2] and also Guibert of Ravenna, who called himself pope; and Henry, emperor of Germany, who supported him.

§ 346. Afterwards a clear and forcible discourse, such as should come from a priest, was addressed to the people, on the subject of an expedition of the Christians against the Turks. This I have thought fit to transmit to posterity, as I have learned it from those who were present, preserving its sense unimpaired. For who can preserve the force of that eloquence? We shall be fortunate if, treading an adjacent path, we come to its meaning even by a circuitous route.

§ 347. " You recollect," [3] said he, " my dearest brethren, many things which have been decreed for you at this time; how some matters have in our council been commanded, others inhibited. A rude and confused chaos of crimes required the deliberation of many days; an inveterate malady demanded a sharp remedy; for while we give unbounded scope to our clemency, our papal office finds numberless matters to proscribe, none to spare. But it has

[1] The truce of God was first invented in Aquitain in 1032. It was so called from the eagerness with which its first proposal was received by the suffering people of every degree: during the time it endured; no one dared to infringe it by attacking his fellows. It was blamed by some bishops as an occasion of perjury, and rejected by the Normans as contrary to their privileges. Ducange, Gloss. vi. 682—685.

[2] "It is beyond doubt that king Philip and his concubine Bertrade were anathematized by Urban in the council of Clermont; but we are not acquainted with any writer prior to Alberic, monk of Trefontaines, and a writer of the 13th century, who asserts that it was forbidden to any one to obey him or call him lord or king; and history refutes the assertion, for we do not read that any of the French, who considered Philip as lawfully divorced from his consort, withdrew their allegiance from him on that account."—Note in Bouquet, xiii. 6.

[3] There are other orations, said to have been delivered by Urban in this council, remaining; and Labb. (Concil. x. 511, 514) has printed two from a Vatican MS.: but they are both very inferior to the narrative of Malmesbury.

hitherto arisen from human frailty that you have erred, and that,
deceived by the speciousness of vice, you have exasperated the long-
suffering of God by too lightly regarding his forbearance. It has
arisen too from human wantonness, that disregarding lawful wedlock, you have not duly considered the heinousness of adultery.
From too great covetousness, also, it has arisen that, as opportunity
offered, making captive your brethren, bought by the same great
price, you have outrageously extorted from them their wealth. To
you, however, now suffering this perilous shipwreck of sin, a secure
haven of rest is offered, unless you neglect it. A station of perpetual safety will be awarded you, for the exertion of a trifling
labour against the Turks. Compare now the labours which you
underwent in the practice of wickedness, and those which you will
encounter in the undertaking I advise. The intention of committing adultery or murder begets many fears (for, as Solomon says,
' There is nothing more timid than guilt ') and many labours ; for
what is more toilsome than wickedness ? But, ' He who walks
uprightly walks securely.' Of these labours, of these fears, the
end was sin ; the wages of sin is death ; the death of sinners is
most dreadful. Now the same labours and apprehensions are required from you for a better consideration. The cause of these
labours will be charity ; if thus warned by the command of God,
you lay down your lives for the brethren ; the wages of charity will
be the grace of God ; the grace of God is followed by eternal life.
Go then prosperously ; go then with confidence to attack the
enemies of God ; for they long since (O sad reproach to Christians !) have seized on Syria, Armenia, and lastly all Asia Minor,
the provinces of which are Bithynia, Phrygia, Galatia, Lydia, Caria,
Pamphylia, Isauria, Licia, Cilicia, and now they insolently domi-
neer over Illyricum, and all the hither countries, even to the sea,
which is called the straits of St. George. Nay, they usurp even
the sepulchre of our Lord, that singular assurance of faith, and sell
to our pilgrims admissions to that city which ought, had they a
trace of their ancient courage left, to be open to Christians only.
This alone might be enough to cloud our brows ; but now, who
except the most abandoned or the most envious of Christian reputation can endure that we do not divide the world equally with
them ? They inhabit Asia, the third portion of the world, as their
native soil, which was not improperly esteemed by our ancestors
equal, by the extent of its tracts and greatness of its provinces, to
the two remaining parts. There formerly sprung up the branches
of our religion ; there all the apostles, except two, consecrated their
deaths ; there, at the present day, the Christians, if any survive,
sustaining life by a wretched kind of agriculture, pay these miscreants tribute, and even with stifled sighs long for the participation of your liberty since they have lost their own. They hold
Africa also, another quarter of the world, already possessed by their
arms for more than two hundred years ; which, on this account,
I pronounce derogatory to Christian honour, because that country
was anciently the nurse of celebrated geniuses, who, by their divine
writings, will mock the rust of antiquity as long as there shall be a

person who can relish Roman literature;[1] the learned know the truth of what I say. Europe, the third portion of the world, remains; of which how small a part do we Christians inhabit, for who can call all those barbarians who dwell in remote islands of the Frozen Ocean, Christians, since they live after a savage manner? Even this small portion of the world, belonging to us, the Turks and Saracens oppress. Thus for three hundred years Spain and the Balearic isles being subjugated to them, the possession of the remainder is eagerly anticipated by feeble men, who, not having courage to engage in close encounter, love a flying mode of warfare; for the Turk never ventures upon close fight, but when driven from his station, bends his bow at a distance, and trusts the winds with his meditated wound; and as he uses poisoned arrows, venom, and not valour, inflicts death on the man he strikes. Whatever he effects, then, I attribute to fortune, not to courage, because he wars by flight and by poison. It is apparent, too, that every race born in that region, being scorched with the intense heat of the sun, abounds more in reflection than in blood; and, therefore, they avoid coming to close quarters, because they are aware how little blood they possess. Whereas the people who are born amid the polar frosts and distant from the sun's heat are less cautious indeed; but, elate from their copious and luxuriant flow of blood, they fight with the greatest alacrity. You are a nation born in the more temperate regions of the world, who may be both prodigal of blood in defiance of death and wounds, and are not deficient in prudence. For you are equally obedient in camp, and prudent in battle. Thus endued with skill and with valour, you undertake a memorable expedition. You will be extolled throughout all ages if you rescue your brethren from danger. To those present, in God's name, I command this; to the absent I enjoin it. Let such as are going to fight for Christianity put the form of the cross upon their garments, that they may outwardly demonstrate their devotion to their inward faith; enjoying by the gift of God and the privilege of St. Peter, absolution from all their crimes; and, in the mean time, let this joyful consideration soothe the labour of their journey, that they shall obtain after death the advantages of a blessed martyrdom. Putting an end to your crimes then, that Christians may at least live peaceably in these countries, go, and employ in a more righteous war that valour and that sagacity which you used to waste in civil broils: go, soldiers everywhere renowned in fame, go, and subdue these dastardly nations. Let the noted valour of the French advance, which, accompanied by its adjoining nations, shall affright the whole world by the single terror of its name. But why do I delay you longer by detracting from the courage of the Gentiles? Rather bring to your recollection the saying of God, 'Narrow is the way which leadeth to life.' Be it then that the track to be followed is narrow, replete with death, and terrible with dangers; still this path will lead to your lost country; for 'by much tribulation you must enter into the kingdom of God.' Expect, then,

---

[1] He alludes to St. Cyprian, St. Augustine, and the other fathers of the African church.

if you shall be made captive, torments and chains; nay, every possible suffering that can be inflicted: undergo, for the firmness of your faith, even horrible punishments; that so, if it be necessary, you may redeem your souls at the expense of your bodies. Do you fear death, you men of exemplary courage and intrepidity? Surely human wickedness can devise nothing against you worthy to be put in competition with heavenly glory; 'for the sufferings of the present time are not worthy to be compared to the glory which shall be revealed to us hereafter.' Know you not, ' that for men to live is wretchedness, but to die is gain?' This doctrine, if you remember, you imbibed with your mother's milk, through the preaching of the clergy: and this doctrine your ancestors, the martyrs, held out by their example. Death sets free from its filthy prison the human soul, which then takes flight for the mansions fitted to its virtues. Death accelerates their country to the good; death cuts short the wickedness of the ungodly. By means of death, then, the soul made free is either soothed with joyful hope, or is punished without farther apprehension of worse. So long as it is fettered to the body, it derives from it earthly contagion; and to speak more truly, is dead. For, earthly with heavenly, and divine with mortal, ill agree. The soul, indeed, even now in its state of union with the body, is capable of great efforts; it gives life to its instrument, secretly moving and animating it to exertions almost beyond mortal nature: but when freed from the clog which drags it to the earth, it regains its proper station, it partakes of a blessed and perfect energy, communicating in some measure with the invisibility of the divine nature. Discharging a double office, therefore, it ministers life to the body when it is present, and the cause of its change when it departs. You must observe how pleasantly the soul wakes in the sleeping body, and, apart from the senses, sees many future events by reason of its relationship to the Deity. Why then do ye fear death who love the repose of sleep, which resembles death? Surely it must be madness, through lust of a transitory life, to deny yourselves that which is eternal. Rather, my dearest brethren, should it so happen, lay down your lives for the brotherhood: rid God's sanctuary of the wicked: expel the robbers: bring in the pious. Let no love of relations detain you, for man's chiefest love ought to be towards God. Let no attachment to your native soil be an impediment, because in different points of view all the world is exile to the Christian, and all the world his country: thus exile is his country, and his country exile. Let none be restrained from going by the largeness of his patrimony, for a still larger is promised him, not of such things as soothe the miserable with vain expectation, or flatter the indolent disposition with the mean advantages of wealth, but of such as are shown by perpetual example and approved by daily experience. Yet these, too, are pleasant but vain, and which to such as despise them produce reward an hundred-fold. These things I publish, these I command; and for their execution I fix the end of the ensuing spring. God will be gracious to those who undertake this expedition, that they may have a favourable year, both in abundance of produce and in serenity of season. Those who may die will enter the mansions of heaven, while the living shall behold the sepulchre of the Lord. And what can be greater happiness than for a man, in his life-time, to see those places which the Lord of heaven visited in his human nature? Blessed are they, who, called to these occupations, shall inherit such a recompense ; fortunate are those who are led to such a conflict, that they may partake of such rewards."

§ 348. I have adhered to the tenour of this address, retaining some few things unaltered, on account of the truth of the remarks, but omitting many. The bulk of the auditors, being extremely excited, attested their sentiments by a shout ; pleased with the speech, and inclined to the pilgrimage: and immediately, in presence of the council, some of the nobility, falling down at the knees of the pope, consecrated themselves and their property to the service of God. Among these was Aimar, the very powerful bishop of Puy, who afterwards ruled the army by his prudence, and augmented it through his eloquence. In the month of November, then, in which this council was held, each departed to his home. The good news soon becoming generally reported, refreshed as with a gentle breeze the minds of the Christians: and being universally diffused, there was no nation so remote or secluded, as not to contribute its portion : for this ardent devotion not only inspired the continental provinces, but even all who had heard the name of Christ, whether in the most distant islands, or savage countries. The Welshman left his hunting ; the Scot his fellowship with vermin ; the Dane his drinking party ; the Norwegian his raw fish. Lands were deserted of their husbandmen ; houses of their inhabitants ; even whole cities migrated. There was no regard to relationship ; affection to their country was held in little esteem ; God alone was placed before their eyes. Whatever was stored in granaries, or hoarded in chambers, to answer the hopes of the avaricious husbandman, or the covetousness of the miser, all was deserted ; they hungered and thirsted after Jerusalem alone. Joy attended such as went; while grief oppressed those who remained. But why do I say remained? You might see the husband departing with his wife, indeed, with all his family; you would smile to see the whole household laden on a carriage, about to proceed on their journey.[1] The road was too narrow for the passengers, the path too confined for the travellers; so thickly were they thronged with endless multitudes. The number surpassed all human imagination, though the itinerants were estimated at six millions.[2] Doubtless, never did so many nations unite in one opinion ; never did so immense a population subject their

[1] The rustic, observes Guibert, shod his oxen like horses, and placed his whole family on a cart ; where it was amusing to hear the children, on the approach to any large town or castle, inquiring, if that were Jerusalem. Guib. Novigent. Opera, p. 482.

[2] Fulcher of Chartres estimates the number at six hundred thousand pilgrims able to bear arms, besides priests, monks, women, and children. He says that those who assumed the cross amounted to six millions ; but that multitudes returned home ere they passed the sea. Gesta Dei per Francos, pp. 387—389, Guibert (556) censures the credulity of Fulcher upon this point. By Urban II. the number is only rated at three hundred thousand pilgrims. Epist. xvi. ; Concil. x. 438.

unruly passions to one, and almost to no, direction. For the strangest wonder to behold was, that such a countless multitude marched gradually through various Christian countries without plundering, though there was none to restrain them. Mutual regard blazed forth in all; so that, if any one found in his possession what he knew did not belong to him, he exposed it everywhere for several days, to be owned; and the desire of the finder was suspended, till perchance the wants of the loser might be repaired.[1]

§ 349. The long looked-for month of March was now at hand, when, the hoary garb of winter being laid aside, the world, clad in vernal bloom, invited the pilgrims to the confines of the East; nor, such was the ardour of their minds, did they seek delay. Godfrey duke of Lorrain proceeded by way of Hungary: second to none in military virtue, and, descended from the ancient lineage of Charles the Great, he inherited much of Charles, both in blood and in mind: he was followed by the Frisians, Lorrainers, Saxons, and all the people who dwell between the Rhine and the Garonne.[2] Raimund[3] earl of St. Giles, and Aimar bishop of Puy, nobly matched in valour, and alike noted for valour and piety, took the route of Dalmatia: under their standard marched the Goths and Gascons, and all the people scattered throughout the Pyrenees and the Alps. Before them, by a shorter route, went Boamund, an Apulian by residence, but a Norman by descent: for embarking at Brindisi, and landing at Durazzo, he marched to Constantinople by roads with which he was well acquainted: under his command Italy, and the whole adjacent province, from the Tuscan sea to the Adriatic, joined in the war. All these assembling, at the same time, at Constantinople, partook somewhat of mutual joy. Here, too, they found Hugh the Great, brother of Philip king of France: for having inconsiderately, and with a few soldiers, entered the territories of the emperor, he was taken by his troops, and detained in free custody. But Alexis, emperor of Constantinople, alarmed at the arrival of these chiefs, willingly, but, as it were, induced by their entreaties, released him. Alexis was a man famed for his duplicity, and never attempted anything of importance unless by stratagem. He had taken off Guiscard, as I before related,[4] by poison, and had corrupted his wife by gold; falsely promising by his emissaries to marry her. Again, too, he allowed William earl of Poictou to be led into an ambush of the Turks, and, after losing sixty thousand[5] soldiers, to escape almost unattended; being incensed at his reply, when he refused homage to the Greek. In after time, he laid repeated snares for Boamund, who was marching against him to avenge the injuries of the crusaders; and when these failed he bereaved him of his brother Guido, and of almost all his army; making use of his usual arts, either in poisoning the rivers or

---

[1] However repugnant this representation may be to the generally received opinion, it is that of an eye-witness, when describing the army assembled at Constantinople. Fulch. Carnot. p. 389.

[2] It should probably be the Elbe, as he appears to describe the people of northern Germany.　　　[3] See § 388.

[4] See § 262; and Bouquet, xiii. 7, note ᶜ.

[5] See also § 383. Orderic. Vitalis writes "three hundred thousand soldiers followed the earl of Poictou."

their garments : but of this hereafter. Now, however, removing the army from the city, and mildly addressing the chiefs, his Grecian eloquence proved so powerful, that he obtained from them all, homage, and an oath that they would form no plot against him ; and that, if they could subdue the cities pertaining to his empire, they would restore them to him : thus purchasing another's advantage at the expense of their own blood. The credit of maintaining his liberty, appeared more estimable to Raimund alone : so that he neither did homage to him, nor took the oath. Collecting, then, all their forces, they made an attack on Nicea, a city of Bithinia : for they chose to assault this first, both as it was an obstacle to the crusaders, and as they were eager to revenge the death of those pilgrims who had recently been slain there. For, one Walter, a distinguished soldier, but precipitate, (for you will scarcely see prudence and valour united in the same person, as one retards what the other advances,) incautiously roaming around the walls, had perished with a numerous party, which Peter the Hermit had allured from their country by his preaching.

§ 350. Now, too, in the month of September, Robert earl of Normandy, brother of king William whose name is prefixed to this book, earnestly desiring to enter on the expedition, was accompanied by Robert of Flanders, and Stephen of Blois, who had married his sister. They were three earls all of noble lineage, and corresponding valour. Under their command were the English and Normans, the Western Franks, and people of Flanders, and all the tribes lying between the British Ocean and the Alps. Proceeding on their journey, at Lucca they found pope Urban, who, being enraged at Guibert, as I have said, was, by the assistance of Matilda, carrying war into Italy, and around the city of Rome. He had now so far succeeded, that the Roman people, inclining to his party, were harassing that of Guibert, both by words and blows ; nor did the one faction spare the other, either in the churches or in the streets, until Guibert, being the weaker, left the see vacant for Urban, and fled to Germany

§ 351. Of Rome, formerly the mistress of the globe, but which now, in comparison with its ancient state, appears a small town ; and of the Romans, once "sovereigns over all, and the toga-clad nation,"[1] but now the most slothful of men, bartering justice for gold, and dispensing with the canons for money ; of this city and its inhabitants, I say, whatever I might attempt to write has been anticipated by the verses of Hildebert, first, bishop of Mans, and afterwards archbishop of Tours :[2] which verses I insert, not to assume the honour acquired by another man's labour, but rather as a proof of a liberal mind, inasmuch as, not envying his fame, I give testimony to his graceful eloquence :—

> Rome, thy grand ruins, still beyond compare,
> Thy former greatness mournfully declare,

---

[1] Virg. Æneid. i 281.

[2] Hildebert was translated to Tours A. D. 1125, upon the death of Gislebert, who died at Rome about the middle of Dec. 1124, in the same week with Pope Calixtus. Orderic. Vital. p. 882. This poem is printed in his works, col. 1334.

Though time thy stately palaces around
Hath strew'd, and cast thy temples to the ground.
Fall'n is the pow'r, the pow'r Araxes dire
Regrets now gone, and dreaded when entire;
Which arms and laws, and e'en the gods on high
Bade o'er the world assume the mastery;
Which guilty Cæsar rather had enjoy'd
Alone, than e'er a fostering hand employ'd.
Which gave to foes, to vice, to friends its care,
Subdued, restrain'd, or bade its kindness share.
This growing pow'r, the holy fathers rear'd,
Where near the stream the fav'ring spot appear'd.
From either pole, materials, artists meet,
And rising walls their proper station greet;
Kings gave their treasures, fav'ring too was fate,
And arts and riches on the structure wait.
Fall'n is that city, whose proud fame to reach,
I merely say, "Rome was," there fails my speech.
Still neither time's decay, nor sword, nor fire,
Shall cause its beauty wholly to expire.
Human exertions raised that splendid Rome,
Which gods in vain shall strive to overcome.
Bid wealth, bid marble, and bid fate attend,
And watchful artists o'er the labour bend,
Still shall the matchless ruin art defy
The old to rival, or its loss supply.
Here gods themselves their sculptured forms admire,
And only to reflect those forms aspire;
Nature unable such like gods to form,
Left them to man's creative genius warm;
Life breathes within them, and the suppliant falls,
Not to the god, but statues in the walls.
City thrice bless'd! were tyrants but away,
Or shame compell'd them justice to obey.

§ 352. Are not these sufficient to point out in such a city, both the dignity of its former advantages and the majesty of its present ruin? But that nothing may be wanting to its honour, I will add the number of its gates and the multitude of its sacred relics; and, that no person may complain of his being deprived of any knowledge by the obscurity of the narrative, the description shall run in an easy and familiar style.[1]

The first is the Cornelian gate, which is now called the gate of St. Peter and the Cornelian way. Near it is situated the church of St. Peter, in which his body lies, decked with gold and precious stones; and no one knows the number of the holy martyrs who rest in that church. On the same way is another church, in which lie the holy virgins Rufina and Secunda. In a third church are Marius and Martha, and Audifax and Abacuc, their sons.

The second is the Flaminian gate, which is now called the gate of St. Valentine[2] and the Flaminian way, and when it arrives at the Milvian bridge it takes the name of the Ravennanian way, because it leads to Ravenna; and there, at the first stone without the gate, St. Valentine rests in his church.

The third is called the Porcinian[3] gate, and the way, the same; but where it joins to the Salarian it loses its name, and there, nearly in the spot which is called Cucumeris, lie the martyrs,

---

[1] For a very interesting account of the walls and gates of Rome, see Lumisden's "Remarks on the Antiquities of Rome."
[2] Now Porta del Popolo.   [3] Porta Pinciana.

Festus, Johannes, Liberalis, Diogenes, Blastus, Lucina, and, in one sepulchre, the two hundred and sixty,[1] in another the thirty. The fourth is the Salarian[2] gate and way, now called St. Silvester's. Here, near the road, lie St. Hermes and St. Vasella, and Protus and Jacinctus, Maxilian, Herculanu, Crispus; and in another place, hard by, rest the holy martyrs Pamphilus and Quirinus, seventy steps beneath the surface. Next is the church of St. Felicitas, where she rests, and Silanus her son; and not far distant, Boniface the martyr. In another church there are Crisantus, and Daria, and Saturninus, and Maurus, and Jason, and their mother Hilaria, and others innumerable. And in another church are St. Alexander, Vitalis, Martialis, sons of St. Felicitas, and seven holy virgins, Saturnina, Hilarina, Duranda, Rogantina, Serotina, Paulina, and Donata. Next comes the church of St. Silvester, where he lies under a marble tomb; and the martyrs, Celestinus, Philippus, and Fœlix; and there too, the three hundred and sixty-five martyrs rest in one sepulchre; and near them lie Paulus and Crescentianus, Prisca, and Semetrius, Praxedis, Potentiana.

The fifth is called the Numentan[3] gate. There lies St. Nicomede, priest and martyr; the way too is called by the same name. Near the road are the church and body of St. Agnes; in another church, St. Emerentiana and the martyrs Alexander, Felix, and Papias; at the seventh mile-stone, on this road, rests the holy pope Alexander, with Eventius and Theodolus.

The sixth is the Tiburtine[4] gate and way, which is now called St. Lawrence's; near this way lies St. Lawrence in his church, and Abundius the martyr; and near this, in another church, rest these martyrs, Ciriaca, Romanus, Justinus, and Crescentianus; and not far from hence is the church of St. Hippolitus, where he himself rests, and his family, eighteen in number; there too repose St. Trifena, the wife of Decius, and his daughter Cirilla, and her nurse Concordia. And in another part of this way, is the church of Agapitus the martyr.

The seventh is called, at present, the Greater gate,[5] formerly the Siracusan, and the way the Lavicanian, which leads to St. Helena. Near this are buried Peter, Marcellinus, Tyburtius, Geminus, Gorgonius, and the forty soldiers,[6] and others without number, and a little farther the Four Coronati.[7]

The eighth is the gate of St. John,[8] which by the ancients was called Assenarica. The ninth gate is called Metrosa;[9] and in front of both these runs the Latin way. The tenth is called the Latin gate,[10] and way. Near this, in one church, lie the martyrs, Gor-

---

[1] The two hundred and sixty are said to have been shot with arrows in the amphitheatre, by order of Claudius. The thirty suffered under Dioclesian.
[2] Porta Salaria.   [3] Porta Pia.
[4] Porta di San Lorenzo.   [5] Porta Maggiore.
[6] The forty soldiers suffered martyrdom under Licinius at Sebaste in Armenia.
[7] So called, because for a long time after they had suffered martyrdom, (martyrio coronati) their names were unknown; and though afterwards their real names were revealed to a certain priest, yet they still continued to retain their former designation.   [8] Porta di San Giovanni.
[9] There is no notice of this in Lumisden; it is probably now destroyed.
[10] Porta Latina.

dianus and Epimachus, Sulpicius, Valerianus, Quintus, Quartus, Sophia and Triphenus. Near this, too, in another spot, Tertullinus; and not far distant, the church of St. Eugenia, in which she lies, and her mother Claudia, and pope Stephen, with nineteen of his clergy, and Nemesius the deacon.

The eleventh is called the Appian gate[1] and way. There lie St. Sebastian, and Quirinus, and formerly the bodies of the apostles rested there. A little nearer Rome, are the martyrs Januarius, Urbanus, Xenon, Quintinus, Agapitus, and Felicissimus; and in another church, Tyburtius, Valerianus, and Maximus. Not far distant is the church of the martyr Cecilia; and there are buried Stephanus, Sixtus, Zepherinus, Eusebius, Melchiades, Marcellus, Eutichianus, Dionysius, Anteros, Pontianus, pope Lucius, Optacius, Julianus, Colocerus, Parthenius, Tarsicius, and Policamus, martyrs; there too are the church and body of St. Cornelius; and in another church St. Sotheris; and not far off rest the martyrs, Hyppolitus, Adrian, Eusebius, Maria, Martha, Paulina, Valeria, and Marcellus, and, near, pope Marcus in his church. Between the Appian and Ostiensian way is the Ardeano way, where are Marcus and Marcellianus. And there lies pope Damasus in his church; and near him St. Petronilla, and Nereus, and Anchilleus, and many more.

The twelfth gate and way was called the Ostian, but, at present, St. Paul's,[2] because he lies near it in his church. There too is the martyr Timotheus; and near, in the church of St. Tecla, are the martyrs Felix, Audactus, and Nemesius. At the Three Fountains[3] is the head of the martyr St. Anastasius.

The thirteenth is called the Portuan[4] gate and way, near which in a church are the martyrs, Felix, Alexander, Abdon, and Sennes, Symeon, Anastasius, Polion, Vincentius, Milex, Candida, and Innocentia.

The fourteenth is the Aurelian[5] gate and way, which now is called the gate of St. Pancras, because he lies near it in his church, and the other martyrs, Paulinus, Arthemius, and St. Sapientia, with her three daughters, Faith, Hope, and Charity. In another church are Processus and Martinianus; and, in a third, two Felixes; in a fourth St. Calixtus and Calepodius; in a fifth St. Basilides. At the twelfth mile-stone within the city, on Mount Celius, are the martyrs Johannes and Paulus, in their house, which was made a church after their martyrdom; and Crispin and Crispinianus, and St. Benedicta. On the same mount is the church of St. Stephen, the first martyr; and there are buried the martyrs Primus and Felicianus; on Mount Aventine St. Boniface, and on Mount Nola St. Tatiana rests.

§ 353. Such are the Roman sanctuaries, such the sacred pledges upon earth; and yet in the midst of this heavenly treasure, as it were, a people drunk with senseless fury, at the very time the cru-

---

[1] Porta di San Sebastiano.   [2] Porta di San Paolo.
[3] Aquas Saluias, now Trefontane. The tradition is, that St. Paul was beheaded on this spot: that his head, on touching the ground, rebounded twice, and that a fountain immediately burst forth from each place where it fell. See Lumisden.
[4] Porta Portese.   [5] Porta di San Pancrazio.

saders arrived, were disturbing everything with wild ambition, and
when unable to satisfy their lust of money, pouring out the blood
of their fellow-citizens over the bodies of the very saints. The earls,
confiding them in Urban's benediction, having passed through Tuscany and Campania, came by Apulia to Calabria, and would have
embarked immediately had not the seamen, on being consulted,
forbade them, on account of the violence of the south winds. In
consequence, the earls of Normandy and Blois passed the winter
there, sojourning each among their friends as convenient. The
earl of Flanders, alone, ventured to sea, experiencing a prosperous
issue to a rash attempt; wherefore part of this assembled multitude
returned home through want, and part of them died from the
unwholesomeness of the climate. The earls who remained however, when at the beginning of the spring they saw the sea sufficiently calm for the expedition, set sail, and, by Christ's assistance,
landed safely at two ports. Thence, through Thessaly, the metro-
polis of which is Thessalonica and Thracia, they came to Constantinople. Many of the lower order perished on the march through
disease and want; many lost their lives at the Devil's-ford, as it is
called from its rapidity; and more indeed would have perished had
not the advanced cavalry been stationed in the river to break the
violence of the current, by which means the lives of some were
saved, and the rest passed over on horseback. The whole multitude then, to solace themselves for their past labours, indulged in
rest for fifteen days, pitching their camp in the suburbs of the city;
of which, as the opportunity has presented itself, I shall briefly
speak.

§ 354. Constantinople was first called Bizantium; which name
is still preserved by the imperial money called Bezants. St. Aldhelm, in his book on Virginity,[1] relates that it changed its appellation by divine suggestion; his words are as follow. As Constantine
was sleeping in this city, he imagined that there stood before him
an old woman, whose forehead was furrowed with age; but that
presently, clad in an imperial robe, she became transformed into a
beautiful girl, and so fascinated his eyes, by the elegance of her
youthful charms, that he could not refrain from kissing her; that
Helena, his mother, being present, then said, "She shall be yours
for ever; nor shall she die till the end of time." When he awoke,
the emperor obtained from heaven, by fasting and almsgiving, an
explanation of the dream. For behold, within eight days, being
cast again into a deep sleep, he thought he saw pope Silvester, who
died some little time before, regarding his convert[2] with complacency, and saying, "You have acted with your customary prudence,
in waiting for a solution from God of that enigma which was
beyond the comprehension of man. The old woman you saw is
this city, worn down by age, whose time-struck walls, menacing

---

[1] Cap. 25, edit. Hen. Wharton, with some slight variations. See note [1], p. 26,
ante.

[2] The legend of Constantine's baptism at Rome thirteen years before his death
was invented in the eighth century. He seems to have been baptized and received
the imposition of hands for the first time during his last illness. Euseb. in Vit.
Constant. lib. iv. c. 61.

approaching ruin, require a restorer.   But you, renewing its walls and its affluence, shall signalize it also with your name, and here shall the imperial progeny reign for ever.   You shall not, however, lay the foundations at your own pleasure ; but mounting the horse on which, when in the noviciate of your faith, you rode round the churches of the apostles at Rome, you shall give him the rein, and liberty to go whither he please ; you shall have, too, in your hand, your royal spear, whose point shall describe the circuit of the wall on the ground.   You will regard, therefore, the track of the spear as the direction in which you are to lay the foundations of the wall."

§ 355. The emperor eagerly obeyed the vision, and built a city equal to Rome ; alleging that the emperor ought not to reign in Rome, where the martyred apostles, from the time of Christ, held dominion.   He built in it two churches, one of which was dedicated to Peace, the other to the Apostles ; bringing thither many bodies of saints, who might conciliate the assistance of God against the incursions of its enemies.   He placed in the circus, for the admiration and ornament of the city, the statues of triumphal heroes, brought from Rome, and the images of heathen deities to excite the contempt of the beholders, and the tripods from Delphi. They relate that it was highly gratifying to the emperor to receive a mandate from heaven,[1] to found a city in that place, where the fruitfulness of the soil, and the temperature of the atmosphere, conduced to the health of its inhabitants ; for as he was born in Britain,[2] he could not endure the burning heat of the sun.   Thracia is a province of Europe, as the poets observe, extremely cool, " From Hebrus' ice and the Bistonian North," and near to fruitful Mœsia, where, as Virgil remarks,[3] " With wonder Gargara the harvests sees."   But Constantinople, washed by the sea, obtains the mingled temperature both of Europe and of Asia, because the Asiatic east wind coming only from a short distance, tempers the severity of the northern blast.   The city is surrounded by a vast extent of walls, yet the influx of strangers is so great, as to make it crowded.   In consequence, they form a mole in the sea, by throwing in masses of rock and loads of sand ; and the space obtained by this new device, straightens the ancient waters.   The sea looks wonderingly at fields unknown before, amid its glassy waves, and surrounds and supplies its city with all the conveniences of the earth.   The town is encompassed on every side, except the north,

---

[1] In one of his laws, Constantine has been careful to instruct posterity that, in obedience to the command of God, he laid the everlasting foundations of Constantinople : the words are, " pro commoditate urbis quam æterno nomine, jubente Deo, donavimus."   (Cod. Theod. lib. xiii. tit. v. leg. 7.)

[2] The place of Constantine's birth, as well as the condition of his mother Helena, have been the subject not only of literary but of national disputes.   There are three opinions with regard to his birth.   The English antiquaries claim the honour for Britain on the words of his panegyrist, ' Britannias, illic oriendo, nobiles fecisti ;' but these words may with as much propriety refer to the accession as to the nativity of Constantine.   Modern Greek writers ascribe the honour of his birth to Depranum, a town on the Gulf of Nicomedia, where his mother's father kept an inn ; but Nassius in Dacia is the place where he was most probably born. Its claim is supported by contemporary authority.   [3] Geor. i. 103.

by the ocean, and is full of angles in the circuit of its walls, where it corresponds with the windings of the sea, which walls contain a space of twenty miles in circumference. The Danube, which is likewise called the Ister, flows in hidden channels underground into the city; and on certain days being let out by the removal of a plug, it carries off the filth of the streets into the sea.[1]   All vied with the emperor in noble zeal to give splendour to this city, each thinking he was bound to advance the work in hand, one contributing holy relics, another money; Constantine all things.

§ 356. After Constantine the Great, the following emperors reigned here. Constantine his son; Julian the apostate; Jovinian, Valens, Theodosius the elder; Archadius, Theodosius the younger; Marcianus, Leo the First; Leo the Younger; Zeno, Anastasius, Justin the Elder; Justinian (who, famed for his learning and his wars, built a church in Constantinople to the Divine Wisdom, that is, to the Lord Jesus Christ, and called it Hagia Sophia, a structure, as they report, surpassing every other edifice in the world, and where ocular inspection proves it superior to its most pompous descriptions;) Justin the Younger; Tiberius, Mauricius, the first Greek; Focas, Heraclius, Constantine, the son of Heraclius; Heracleonas, and Constans (this last coming to Rome and purloining all the remains of ancient decoration, stripped the churches even of their brazen tiles, anxiously wishing to gain renown at Constantinople, even from such spoils as these; his covetousness, however, turned out unfortunately for himself, for being shortly after killed at Syracuse, he left all these honourable spoils to be conveyed to Alexandria by the Saracens;) Constantine, Justinian, Leontius, Tiberius, another Justinian, Philippicus, Anastasius, Theodosius, Leo the Third; all these[2] reigned both at Constantinople and at Rome; the following in Constantinople only: Constantine, Leo, Constantine, Nicephorus, Stauratius, Michael, Leo, Michael, Theophilus, Michael, Basilius, Leo, Alexander, Constantine, two of the name of Romanus, Nicephorus, Focas, John, Basil, and Constantine, Romanus, Michael, Michael, Constantine, Theodora the empress, Michael, Sachius,[3] Constantine, Romanus Diogenes, Nicephorus Butanius, and Michael,[4] who, driven from the empire by Alexis, secretly fled to Guiscard in Apulia, and surrendering to him his power, imagined he had done something prejudicial to Alexis; hence Guiscard's ambition conceived greater designs; falsely persuading himself that he might acquire by industry what the other had lost by inactivity; how far he succeeded the preceding book hath explained. In the same city is the cross of our Saviour, brought by Helena from Jerusalem. There, too, rest the apostles, Andrew, James the brother of our Lord; Matthias; the

[1] The Danube empties itself through six mouths into the Euxine. The river Lycus, formed by the conflux of two little streams, pours into the harbour of Constantinople a perpetual supply of fresh water, which serves to cleanse the bottom, and to invite the periodical shoals of fish to seek their retreat in that capacious port.

[2] The definitive separation of the empires of the east and west took place much earlier, under the sons of Theodosius the Great, A.D. 395.

[3] Isaac Comnenus.

[4] Michael VII. preceded Nicephorus Botaniates, who was expelled by Alexis.

prophets Elizeus, Daniel, Samuel, and many others; Luke the evangelist; martyrs innumerable; the confessors Johannes Chrysostom, Basil, Gregorius Nazianzen, and Spiridion; the virgins Agatha and Lucia, and lastly all the saints whose bodies the emperors were able to transport thither out of every country.

§ 357. The earls, then, of Normandy and Blois did homage to the Greek; for the earl of Flanders had already passed on, disdaining to perform this ceremony from the recollection that he was freely born and educated. The others giving and receiving promises of fidelity, proceeded in the first week of June to Nicea, which the rest had already besieged from the middle of May. Uniting, therefore, their forces, much carnage ensued on either side, since every kind of weapon could easily be hurled by the townsmen on those who were beneath them, and the arm even of the weakest had effect on persons crowded together. Moreover the Turks dragged up with iron hooks numberless dead bodies of our people, to mangle them in mockery, or to strip them of their raiment. The Franks were grieved at this; nor did they cease venting their rage by slaughter till the Turks, wearied by extremity of suffering, on the day of the summer solstice surrendered themselves to the emperor by means of secret messengers. He, accustomed to consult only his own advantage, gave orders to the Franks to depart; choosing rather that the city should be reserved for the undisguised disloyalty of the Turks than the distrusted power of the Franks. He ordered, however, silver and gold to be distributed to the chiefs, and copper coin to those of inferior rank, lest they should complain of being unrewarded. Thus the Turks, who passing the Euphrates had now for the space of fifty years been possessed of Bithynia, which is that part of Asia Minor which is called Romania, betook themselves to flight to the eastward. Nevertheless, when the siege was ended, they attempted, at the instigation of Soliman,[1] who had been sovereign of all Romania, to harass the army on its advance. This man collecting, as is computed, three hundred and sixty thousand archers, attacked our people, expecting anything rather than hostility, with such violence, that, overwhelmed and terrified by the iron shower of arrows, they immediately fled. At that time, by chance, duke Godfrey and Hugh the Great, and Raimund had taken another route, that they might plunder the enemies' country to a wider extent, and obtain forage with more facility. But the Norman, sensible of his extreme danger, by means of expeditious messengers on a safe track, acquainted Godfrey and the rest of the approach of the Turks. They, without a moment's delay, turned against the enemy, and delivered their associates from danger: for these were now indiscriminately slaughtered in their tents, unprepared for resistance, and filling the air with prayers and lamentations. Nor did the enemy take any particular aim, but trusting his arrows to the wind, he never, from the thickness of the ranks, drew his bow vain. What alone

---

[1] His Turkish name was Kilidge-Arslan: his kingdom of Roum extended from the Hellespont to the confines of Syria, and barred the pilgrimage of Jerusalem. (See De Guignes, iii. ; ii. 10—30.)

retarded destruction was, that the attack took place near a thicket
of canes, which prevented the Turkish cavalry from acting freely. At
length, however, perceiving the advanced guard of the approaching
chiefs, the Christians left the thicket, and shouting the military
watch-word, " It is the will of God,"[1] they attack the scattered
ranks of the enemy, making a signal to their companions at the same
time to assail them in the rear. Thus the Turks, pressed on either
side, forthwith fled, shrieking with a dreadful cry, and raising a yell
which reached the clouds: nor had they recourse to their customary
practice of a flying battle, but throwing down their bows they
manifested, by a flight of three successive days, something greater
than mere human apprehension. But there was no one capable of
following them, for our horses, scarce able to support life on the
barren turf, were unequal to a vigorous pursuit ; showing immediately their want of strength by their panting sides. Asia was
formerly, it is true, a land most fruitful in corn ; but, both in ancient
and in recent times it had been so plundered by the savage Turks,
that it could scarcely suffice for the maintenance of a small army,
much less of a multitude so vast as to threaten the devouring of
whole harvests and drinking of rivers dry. For when they departed
from Nicea they were still estimated at seven hundred thousand ;
of the remainder, part had been wasted by the sword, part by sickness, and still more had deserted to their homes.

§ 358. Thence, then, they arrived at Heraclea by the route of
Antioch and Iconium, cities of Pisidia. Here they beheld in the
sky a portent fashioned like a flaming sword, the point of which extended towards the East. All the period from the kalends of July
[July 1], when they left Nicea, till the nones of October [Oct. 7,] had
elapsed when they arrived at Antioch in Syria. The situation of
this city I should describe, had not my wish in this respect been anticipated by the eloquence of Ambrosius in Hegesippus ;[2] and were I
not also fearful that I might be blamed for the perpetual digressions
of my narrative. Still, however, I will relate so much as the labour
I have undertaken seems to require.

§ 359. The city of Antioch, which was named after his father,
Antiochus, by Seleucus king of Asia, is surrounded with a vast
wall, which even contains a mountain within it. Next to Rome,
and Constantinople, and Alexandria, it obtains precedence over the
cities of the world. It is secure by its walls, difficult of access
from its hilly situation ; and if ever taken, it must be more by
stratagem than force. The nearest river to it, which I learn is now
called Fernus though originally Orontes, falls into the sea twelve
miles from the city; its tide, impetuous and growing colder from
its rapidity, ministering to the health of the inhabitants by its effect

---

[1] When Urban II. addressed the multitude from a lofty scaffold in the market-
place of Clermont, inciting the people to undertake the Crusade, he was frequently
interrupted by the shout of thousands in their rustic idiom exclaiming "Deus lo
volt !"   "It is indeed the will of God !" replied the pope; "and let those words,
the inspiration surely of the Holy Spirit, be for ever adopted as your war-cry."

[2] Hegesippus wrote an ecclesiastical history, an account of the Jewish War, and
of the destruction of Jerusalem ; said to have been translated into Latin by St.
Ambrose. See Cave, Hist. Liter. i. 255.

on the atmosphere. Capable, too, of receiving supplies by shipping for the service of its citizens, it can at all times mock the efforts of its besiegers. Here the venerable title of Christian was first conceived;[1] hence, first St. Paul, the spring and spur of this religion, went forth to preach; here the first bishopric was filled by St. Peter, in honour to whom the church there founded remained uninjured through the whole domination of the Turks: and another dedicated to St. Mary equally struck the spectators with its beauty, exciting wonder that they should reverence the church of Him whose faith they persecuted.

§ 360. This city, then, the Franks invested from October till June,[2] pitching their tents around the walls after they had passed the river. Foreseeing, however, the difficulty of taking it, and judging it expedient to provide against the cowardice of certain of their party, the chiefs, in common, took an oath that they would not desist from the siege till the city should be taken by force, or by stratagem. And, that they might more easily complete their design, they built many fortresses on this side the river, in which soldiers were placed to keep guard. Aoxianus, too, the governor of the city, observing that the Franks acted neither jestingly nor coldly, but set heartily to besiege it, sent his son Sansadol to the sultan,[3] the emperor, to make known the boldness of the Franks and to implore assistance. The Persian sultan, a title equivalent to Augustus among the Romans, is commander of all the Saracens, and of the whole East. I imagine this empire has continued so long, and still increases, because the people, as I have related, are unwarlike, and being deficient in active blood, know not how to cast off slavery when once admitted; not being aware, as Lucan says,[4] that

"Arms were bestow'd that men should not be slaves."

But the Western nations, bold and fierce, disdain long-continued subjugation to any people whatever, often delivering themselves from servitude, and imposing it on others. Moreover the Roman empire first declined to the Franks, and after to the Germans; the Eastern continues ever with the Persians.

§ 361. Sansadol, therefore, being despatched to the chief of this empire, hastened his course with youthful ardour; and his father in the meantime was by no means wanting to the duties of a commander in the protection of the city. The valour of the besieged was not content merely to defend their own party, but voluntarily harassed ours, frequently and suddenly attacking them when foraging, or marketing; for, making a bridge of the vessels which they found there, they had established a mart beyond the river. Through Christ's assistance, therefore, becoming resolute, they seized their arms, and boldly repelled their enemies, so that they never suffered them to reap the honour of the day. To revenge this disgrace, the Turks wreaked their indignation on the Syrian and Armenian inhabitants

[1] Acts xi. 26.
[2] The siege of Antioch commenced 21st Oct. 1097, and ended 3d of June, 1098.
[3] Here A. and L., supported by Saville, add, "of Persia."
[4] Pharsalia, iv. 579.

of the city, throwing, by means of their balistæ[1] and petraries, the heads of those whom they had slain, into the camp of the Franks, that by such means they might wound their feelings.

§ 362. And now, everything which could be procured for food being destroyed around the city, a sudden famine, which usually makes even fortresses give way, began to oppress the army; so much so, that the harvest not having yet attained to maturity, some persons seized the pods of beans before they were ripe, as the greatest delicacy; others fed on horse-flesh, or hides soaked in water; others passed parboiled thistles through their bleeding jaws into their stomachs. Others sold mice, or such like dainties, to those who required them; content to suffer hunger themselves so that they could procure money. Some, too, there were who even stuffed carcase into carcase, feeding on human flesh; but at a distance and on the mountains, lest others should be offended at the smell of their cookery. Many wandered through unknown paths, in expectation of meeting with sustenance, and were killed by robbers acquainted with the passes. But not long after, the city was surrendered.

§ 363. For Boamund, a man of superior talents, had, by dint of very great promises made by his emissaries, induced a Turkish chief who had the custody of the principal tower, on the side where his station lay, to deliver it up to him.[2] And he, too, to palliate the infamy of his treachery by a competent excuse, gave his son as an hostage to Boamund; professing that he did so by the express command of Christ, which had been communicated to him in a dream. Boamund, therefore, advanced his troops to the tower, having first craftily obtained from the chiefs the perpetual government of the city, in case he could carry it. Thus the Franks, on a stormy night, scaled the walls by rope ladders, and displaying on the top of the tower the crimson standard of Boamund, repeated with joyful accents the Christian watch-word, " It is the will of God! It is the will of God!" The Turks awaking, and weary from want of rest, took to flight through narrow passages; and our party, following with drawn swords, made dreadful slaughter of the enemy. In this flight fell Aoxianus, governor of the city, being beheaded by a Syrian peasant: his head, when brought to the Franks, excited both their laughter and their joy.

§ 364. Not long rejoicing in this complete victory, they had, the next day, to lament being themselves besieged by the Turks from without. For the forces which had been solicited by Sansadol, were now arrived under the command of Corbaguath, an Eastern nobleman, who had obtained from the emperor of Persia three hundred thousand men,[3] under twenty-seven commanders.

---

[1] The balista was a warlike engine for casting either darts or stones: the petrary for throwing large stones only.

[2] Phirouz, a Syrian renegade, has the infamy of this foul treason.

[3] In describing the host of Kerboga, most of the Latin historians, the author of the Gesta (p. 17), Robertus Monachus (p. 56), Baldric (p. 111), Fulcherius Carnotensis (p. 392), Guibert (p. 512), William of Tyre (VI. iii. 714), Bernardus Thesaurarius (xxxix. 695), are content with the vague expressions of "infinita multitudo," "immensum agmen," "innumeræ copiæ," "innumeræ gentes." The numbers of

Sixty thousand of these ascended over the rocks to the citadel, by desire of the Turks, who still remained in possession of it.   These woefully harassed the Christians by frequent sallies : nor was there any hope left, but from the assistance of God, since want was now added to the miseries of war ; want, always the earliest attendant on great calamities.   Wherefore, after a fast of three days, and earnest supplications, Peter the Hermit was sent ambassador to the Turks, who spake, with his usual eloquence,[1] to the following effect : That the Turks should now voluntarily evacuate the Christian territory, which they had formerly unjustly invaded ; that it was but right, as the Christians did not attack Persia, that the Turks should not molest Asia ; that they should therefore, either voluntarily return home, or expect an attack on the following morning ; and suggested that each side should try its fortune, by two, or four, or eight champions, and not jeopardise the whole army.

§ 365.   Corbaguath condescended not to honour the messenger even with a reply; but, playing at chess and gnashing his teeth, dismissed him as he came, merely observing, that the pride of the Franks was at an end.   Hastily returning, Peter apprised the army of the insolence of the Turk.   Each then animating the other, it was publicly ordered that every person should, that night, feed his horse as plentifully as possible, lest he should falter in the various evolutions of the following day.   And now had the morning dawned, when, drawn up in bodies, they proceeded with hostile standard against the enemy.   The first band was led by the two Roberts, earls of Normandy and Flanders, and Hugh the Great ; the second by Godfrey; the third by the bishop of Puy; Boamund brought up the rear, as a support to the rest.   Raimund continued in the city, to cover the retreat of our party, in case it should be necessary. The Turks, from a distance observing their movements, were at first dubious what they could mean.   Afterwards, recognising the standard of the bishop, (for they were extremely afraid of him, as they said he was the pope of the Christians and the fomenter of the war,) and seeing our people advancing so courageously and quickly, they fled ere they were attacked.   Our party, too, exhilarated with unexpected joy, slew the fugitives, as far as the strength of the infantry or exertion of the cavalry would permit.   They imagined, moreover, that they saw the ancient martyrs, George and Demetrius, who had formerly been soldiers, and who had gained eternal life in reward for their death, come down from the mountains with upraised banners, hurling darts against the enemy, but assisting the Franks. Nor is it to be denied, that the martyrs did assist the Christians, as the angels formerly did the Maccabees,[2] fighting for the self-same cause.   When the Franks returned for the purpose of plunder, they found in the Turkish camp sufficient to satisfy, or even totally to glut, the covetousness of the greediest army.   This battle took place

the Turks are fixed by Albertus Aquensis at two hundred thousand (IV. x. 242), and by Radulphus Cadomensis (lxxii. 309) at four hundred thousand horse.   Gibb. Decl. Rom. Emp. vii. 364-5.

[1] William of Tyre (I. ii. 637-8) thus describes the hermit : " He was weak and of mean appearance, but of a lively disposition ; he had a clear and pleasing eye, and was gifted with a naturally flowing eloquence."   [2] 2 Maccab. viii. 20.

An. Dom. 1098, on the fourth of the kalends of July [June 28]; for the city had been taken the day before the nones of July [July 6]. Soon after, on the kalends of the ensuing August [Aug. 1], the bishop of Puy, the leader of the Christians, and chief author of this laudable enterprise, died peacefully; and Hugh the Great, by permission of the chiefs, as it is said, returned to France, alleging as a reason a perpetual bowel complaint.

§ 366. But when, by a long repose of seven months at Antioch, they had obliterated the memory of their past labours, they began to think of proceeding on their route. And first of all Raimund, never idle, and whose pride it was ever to be first in the field; and next to him the two Roberts, and Godfrey, proceeded upon the march. Boamund alone for a time deferred his advance, lured by the prospect of a magnificent city, and the love of wealth. A plausible reason, however, lay concealed beneath his covetousness, when he alleged that Antioch ought not to be exposed to the Turks without a chief, as they would directly attack it. He therefore took up his residence in the city; and this harsh governor drove Raimund's followers, who occupied one of the streets, without the walls. The others, however, passing through Tripoli,[1] and Berytus, and Tyre, and Sidon, and Accaron, and Caiphas, and Cæsarea in Palestine, where they left the coast to the right hand, came to Ramula; being kindly received by some of the cities, and signalizing their valour by the subjugation of others. For their design was to delay no longer, as it was now the month of April, and the produce of the earth had become fully ripe. Ramula is a very small city, without walls: and, if we credit report, the place of the martyrdom of St. George; whose church, originally founded there, the Turks had somewhat defaced: but at that time, through fear of the Franks, they had carried off their property and retreated to the mountains. The next morning at early dawn, Tancred the nephew of Boamund, a man of undaunted courage, and some others, taking arms, proceeded to Bethlehem, desirous of exploring the neighbourhood. The Syrians of the place, who came out to meet them, manifested their joy with weeping earnestness, through apprehension for their safety, on account of the smallness of their numbers; for few more than an hundred soldiers were of the party. But our people having devoutly prayed in the sacred edifice,[2] immediately stretch anxiously forward towards Jerusalem. The Turks, confident in their force, fiercely sallied out, and for some time skirmished with our troops, for the whole army had now come up; but they were soon repulsed by the exertions of the Franks, and sought security within their walls.

§ 367. The numbers who have already written on the subject, admonish me to say nothing of the situation and disposition of Jerusalem, nor is it necessary for my narrative to expatiate on such a field. Almost every person is acquainted with what Josephus,

---

[1] The greatest part of their march is most accurately traced in Maundrell's journey from Aleppo to Jerusalem (pp. 11—67).
[2] The church of St. Mary at Bethlehem contained within its walls a sort of grotto, in which it was pretended Christ was born. See Beda, E. H. § 405

Eucherius, and Beda have said: for who is not aware that it was called Salem, from Melchisedek; Jebus, from the Jebusites; Jerusalem, from Solomon? Who has not heard how often, falling from adverse war, it buried its inhabitants in its ruins, through the different attacks of Nabugodonosor, of Titus, or of Adrian? It was this last who rebuilt Jerusalem, called Helia after his surname, enclosing it with a circular wall of greater compass, that it might embrace the site of the sepulchre of our Lord, which originally stood without: Mount Sion, too, added to the city, stands eminent as a citadel. It possesses no springs;[1] but water collected in cisterns prepared for that purpose supplies the wants of the inhabitants; for the site of the city, beginning from the northern summit of Mount Sion, has so gentle a declivity, that the rain which falls there does not form any mire, but running like rivulets, is received into tanks, or flowing through the streets, augments the brook Kedron. Here is the church of our Lord, and the temple which they call Solomon's; by whom built is unknown, but religiously reverenced by the Turks; more especially the church of our Lord, where they daily worshipped, and prohibited the Christians from entering, having placed therein a statue of Mahomet. Here also is a church of elegant workmanship, containing the holy sepulchre, built by Constantine the Great, and which has never suffered any injury from the enemies of our faith, through fear, as I suppose, of being struck by that celestial fire which brightly shines in lamps, every year, on the vigil of Easter.[2] When this miracle had a beginning, or whether it existed before the times of the Saracens, history has left no trace. I have read in the writings of Bernard[3] the monk, that about two hundred and fifty years ago, that is in the year of our Lord 870, he went to Jerusalem, and saw that fire, and was entertained in the hospital which the most glorious Charles the Great had there ordered to be built, and where he had collected a library at great expense. He relates that, both in Egypt and in that place, the Christians under the dominion of the Turks enjoyed such security, that if any traveller lost a beast of burden by accident, in the midst of the high road, he might leave his baggage, and proceed to the nearest city for assistance, and would most certainly find everything untouched at his return. Still, from the suspicion that they might be spies, no foreign Christian could live there securely, unless protected by the signet of the emperor of

[1] Jerusalem was possessed only of the torrent of Kedron, dry in summer, and of the little brook or spring of Siloe. (Reland, i. 294, 300.) Tacitus mentions a perennial fountain, an aqueduct, and cisterns of rain-water. The aqueduct was conveyed from the rivulet Tekoe, or Etham, which is likewise mentioned by Bohadin (in Vit. Saladin, p. 238).

[2] It was pretended that the lamps in the church of the Holy Sepulchre were miraculously ignited on Easter-eve. Mosheim, in his Dissertations on Ecclesiastical History (ii. 214—306), has separately discussed this pretended miracle. He ascribes the invention of the pious fraud to the Franks, soon after the decease of Charlemagne.

[3] Bernard with two companions sailed from Italy to Alexandria, and travelled thence by land to Jerusalem in the year 870. Their travels are printed in Mabillon's Acta Benedictinorum, iv. 523—526, ed. Paris. The account is short, but has several interesting particulars. There is also a good MS. in the British Museum, Bib. Cott. Faust. B. 1, where, by a mistake of the scribe, it is dated A.D. 970, but this is clearly wrong, for Bernard mentions Lewis king of Italy as then living, and he died A.D. 875. See Hist. Lit. de la France, v. 375.

Babylon. The natives purchased peace from the Turks at the expense of three talents, or bezants, annually. But as Bernard mentions the name of Theodosius the then patriarch, this gives me an occasion of enumerating the whole of the patriarchs.

§ 368. James, the brother of our Lord, and son of Alpheus; Simon, son of Cleophas, the cousin of Christ, (for Cleophas was the brother of Joseph;) Justus, Zaccheus, Tobias, Benjamin, John, Machabæus, Philip, Seneca, Justus, Levi, Effrem, Justus, Judas; (these fifteen were circumcised;) Mark, Cassian, Publius, Maximus, Julian, Gaius; (the latter first celebrated Easter and Lent after the Roman manner:) Symacus, Gaius, Julian, Capito, Maximus, Antonius, Valens, Docilianus, Narcissus, Dius, Germanio, Gordius, Alexander, Mazabanus, Irmeneus, Zabdas, Ermon, Macharius (in whose time the holy cross was found by St. Helenä:) Ciriacus, Maximus, Cirillus, who built the church of the Holy Sepulchre, and of Mount Calvary, and of Bethlehem, and of the valley of Josaphat. All these were called bishops. After them came the patriarchs: Cirillus the first patriarch; Johannes,[1] Prailius, Juvenalis, Zacharias (in whose time Chosdroe[2] king of Persia came to Jerusalem, and destroyed the churches of Judea and Jerusalem, and slew with his army six and thirty thousand of the Christians:) Modestus (who was appointed patriarch by the emperor Heraclius, when he returned victorious from Persia:) Sophronius, (in whose time the Saracens came, and thrust out all the Christians from Jerusalem, except the patriarch, whom they suffered to remain, out of reverence to his sanctity: this was the period when the Saracens overran the whole of Egypt, and Africa, and Judea, and even Spain, and the Balearic Isles. Part of Spain was wrested from them by Charles the Great, but the remainder, together with the countries I have enumerated, they have possessed for nearly five hundred years, down to the present day:) Theodorus, Ilia, Georgius, Thomas, Basilidis, Sergius, Salomontos, Theodosius; whom Bernard relates to have been an abbot, and that he was torn from his monastery, which was fifteen miles distant from Jerusalem, and made patriarch of that city: then, he says, Michael was patriarch of Babylon, over Egypt; the patriarchate of Alexandria being removed to Babylon: Ilia, Sergius, Leonthos, Athanasius, Christodolus, Thomas, Joseph, Orestes, (in whose time came Sultan Achim, the nephew of the patriarch Orestes, from Babylon, who sent his army to Jerusalem, destroyed all the churches, that is to say, four thousand, and caused his uncle, the patriarch, to be conveyed to Babylon, and there slain;) Theophilus, Nicephorus, (who built the present church of the Holy Sepulchre, by the favour of Sultan Achim;) Sophronius, (in his time the Turks coming to Jerusalem, fought with the Saracens, killed them all and took possession of the city; but the Christians continued there under the dominion of the Turks;) Euthimius and Simeon; in

[1] No patriarch of this name is known at this period. Anastasius succeeded Juvenal A.D. 458. The names of the eleven successive patriarchs prior to Zacharias (A.D. 458—609) are omitted by Malmesbury.

[2] Cosroes, or Chosroes, the Second, king of Persia.

[3] The church of Jerusalem was vacant after the death of Sopronius (A.D. 644) until the year 705, when John V. succeeded, whom Theodorus followed, A.D. 754.

whose time came the Franks, and laid siege to Jerusalem, and rescued it from the hands of the Turks and of the king of Babylon. § 369. [A.D. 1099.] In the fourth year, then, of the expedition to Jerusalem, the third after the capture of Nicea, and the second after that of Antioch, the Franks laid siege to Jerusalem; a city well able to repay the toils of war, to soothe its labours, and to requite the fondest expectation. It was now the seventh day of June; nor were the besiegers apprehensive of wanting food or drink for themselves, as the harvest was on the ground, and the grapes were ripe upon the vines; the care alone of their cattle distressed them, which, from the nature of the place, and of the season, had no running stream to support them: for the heat of the sun had dried up the secret springs of the brook Siloe, whose refreshing stream only runs at uncertain periods. This brook, when at any time swollen with rain, increases that of Kedron; and then passes on, with impetuous current, into the valley of Josaphat: but this is extremely rare; for there is no certain period for its augmentation or decrease. In consequence, the enemy, suddenly darting from their caverns, frequently killed our people, when straggling abroad for the purpose of watering their cattle. In the meantime the chiefs were each observant at their respective posts; and Raimund actively besieged the tower of David.[1] This fortress, defending the city on the west, and strengthened, nearly half-way up, by courses of squared stone soldered with lead, was a source of confidence against the invaders, although the garrison was small. As they saw, therefore, that the city was difficult to carry on account of the steep precipices, the strength of the walls and the fierceness of the enemy, they ordered engines to be constructed. But before this, indeed, on the seventh day of the siege, they had tried their fortune with scaling-ladders, and shooting arrows against their opponents: but, as the ladders were few, and perilous to those who mounted them, since they were exposed on all sides and nowhere protected from wounds, they changed their design. There was one engine which we call the Sow, the ancients, Vineæ; because the machine, which is constructed of slight timbers, the roof covered with boards and wicker-work, and the sides defended with undressed hides, protects those who are within it, who, after the manner of a sow, undermine the foundations of the walls. There was another, which for want of timber was but a moderate sized tower, constructed after the manner of houses:[2] they call it Berefreid: this was to equal the summit of the walls in height. The making of this machine delayed the siege, on account of the unskilfulness of the workmen, and the scarcity of wood. And now the fourteenth day of July arrived, when some bringing up the Vineæ began to undermine the wall; others to move forward the tower. To do this more conveniently, they took it towards the works in separate pieces; and putting it together again at such a distance as to be out of bow-

---

[1] The Tower of David was the old tower Psephina, or Neblosa; it was likewise called Castellum Pisanum, from the patriarch Daimbert. D'Anville, pp. 19—23.

[2] That is to say with several floors, or apartments, one above the other; each of which contained soldiers.

shot, it was advanced on wheels, nearly close to the wall.   In the
meantime, the slingers with stones, the archers with arrows, and
the cross-bow-men with bolts, each intent on their department,
began to press forward and dislodge their opponents from the
ramparts; soldiers too, unmatched in courage, ascend the tower,
waging nearly equal war against the enemy with spears and with
stones.   Nor, indeed, were our foes at all amiss; but trusting their
whole security to their valour, they poured down grease and burning
oil upon the tower, and slung stones on the soldiers; rejoicing in
the completion of their desires, by the destruction of multitudes.
During the whole of that day, the battle was such, that neither
party seemed to think it had been worsted; on the following, which
was the fifteenth of July, the business was decided.   For the Franks
becoming more experienced from the event of the attack of the
preceding day, threw fagots, flaming with oil, on a tower adjoining
the wall, and on the party who defended it; the flames blazing by
the action of the wind, first seized the timber and then the stones,
and drove off the garrison.   Moreover, the beams which the Turks
had left hanging down from the walls in order that, being forcibly
drawn back, they might, by their recoil, batter the tower in pieces,
in case it should advance too near, were by the Franks dragged to
them, after cutting away the ropes: and being projected from the
engine to the wall, and covered with hurdles, they formed a bridge
of communication between the ramparts to the tower.   Thus, what
the infidels had contrived for their defence, became the means
of their destruction.   Then the enemy, dismayed by the smoky
masses of flame and by the courage of our soldiers, began to give
way.   These advancing on the wall, and thence into the city,
manifested the excess of their joy by the strenuousness of their
exertions.   This success took place on the side of Godfrey and of
the two Roberts; Raimund knew nothing of the circumstance, till
the cry of the fugitives, and the alarm of the people, throwing
themselves from the walls, (who thus met death while flying from
it,) acquainted him that the city was taken.   On seeing this, he
rushed with drawn sword on the runaways, and hastened to avenge
the injuries of God, until he had satiated his own animosity.   Moreover, having regard to the advantages of immediate repose, he sent
unhurt to Ascalon five hundred Ethiopians, who, retreating to the
citadel of David, had given up the keys of the gates under promise
of personal safety.   There was no place of refuge for the Turks, so
indiscriminately did the insatiable rage of the victors sweep away
both the suppliant and the resisting.   Ten thousand were slain in
the temple of Solomon; more were thrown from the tops of the
churches, and of the citadel.   After this, the dead bodies were
heaped up, and evaporated by means of fire; lest, putrifying in the
open air, they should pour contagion on the flagging atmosphere.
The city being thus expiated by the slaughter of the infidels, they
proceeded with hearts contrite, and bodies prostrate, to the Sepulchre
of the Lord, which they had long so earnestly sought after, and for
which they had undergone so many labours.   By what ample
incense of prayer they propitiated heaven, or by what repentant

tears they once again brought back the favour of God, none; I am confident, can describe: no; not if the splendid eloquence of the ancients could revive, or Orpheus himself return; who, as it is said, bent even the listening rocks to his harmonious strain. Be it imagined, then, rather than expressed.

§ 370. So remarkable was the example of forbearance exhibited by the chiefs, that, neither on that, nor on the following day, did any of them, through lust of spoil, withdraw his mind from following up the victory. Tancred alone, beset with ill-timed covetousness, carried off some very precious effects from the temple of Solomon; but, afterwards, reproved by his own conscience, and the address of some other persons, he restored, if not the same things, yet such as were of equal value.[1] At that time, if any man, however poor, seized an house, or riches of any kind, he did not afterwards encounter the brawlings of the powerful, but held what he had once possessed, as his hereditary right. Without delay, then, Godfrey, that brilliant mirror of Christian nobility, in which, as in a splendid ceiling, the lustre of every virtue was reflected, was chosen king;[2] all, in lively hope, agreeing, that they could in no wise better consult the advantage of the church; deferring, in the meantime, the erection of a patriarch, who was to be appointed by the determination of the Roman Pontiff.[3]

§ 371. But the emperor of Babylon—not the city built by Nembroth, and said to have been enlarged by Semiramis, but that which Cambyses, son of Cyrus, built in Egypt, on the spot where Thaphnis formerly stood—the emperor of Babylon, I say, venting his long-conceived indignation against the Franks, sent the commander of his forces, to drive them, as he said, out of his kingdom. Hastening to fulfil the command, when he heard that Jerusalem was taken, he redoubled his diligence, though he had by no means been indolent before. The design of the barbarian was to besiege the Christians in Jerusalem, and after the victory, which he falsely presaging, already obtained in imagination, to destroy utterly the Sepulchre of our Lord. The Christians, who desired nothing less than again to endure the miseries of a siege, taking courage through God's assistance, marched out of the city towards Ascalon, to oppose the enemy; and carried with them part of the cross of Christ, which a certain Syrian, an inhabitant of Jerusalem, had produced, as it had been preserved in his house, in succession from father to son. This truly was a fortunate and a loyal device, that the secret should be all along kept from the Turks. Obtaining moreover a great booty of sheep and cattle, near Ascalon, they issued a general order, to leave the whole of it in the open plain, lest it should be an impediment when engaging the next morning, as they would have

---

[1] Interested motives and conduct, it is to be observed, are several times imputed to the adventurers from Sicily and Calabria.

[2] This devout pilgrim rejected the name and ensigns of royalty in a city where his Saviour had been crowned with thorns: he contented himself with the modest title of "Defender and Baron of the Holy Sepulchre."

[3] Pope Urban did not live to hear of the memorable event; he died 29th of July 1099, fourteen days after the conquest of Jerusalem. Daimbert, archbishop of Pisa, was installed without a competitor, patriarch of Jerusalem. (See William of Tyre, IX. xv—xviii., and x. iv. vii. ix.; Jaffé, p. 477.)

spoil more than enough if they conquered, so that, free from incumbrance, they might avenge the injuries of heaven. In the morning, therefore, as the army was on its march, you might see, I believe by divine instinct, the cattle with their heads erect, proceeding by the side of the soldiers, and not to be driven away by any force. The enemy perceiving this at a distance, and their sight being dazzled by the rays of the sun, lost their confidence ere the battle could commence, as they thought the multitude of their opponents was countless : yet were they, themselves, by no means deficient in numbers, and by long exercise trained to battle. They endeavoured therefore to hem in the Franks, who were proceeding at a slow rate, by dividing their force into two bodies, and by curving their wings. But the leaders, and more especially Robert the Norman, who was in the advanced guard, eluding stratagem by stratagem, or rather cunning by valour, leading on their archers and infantry, broke through the centre of the heathen. Moreover the Lorrain cavalry, which was stationed with its commander in the rear, advancing by the flanks, prevented their flight, and occupied the whole plain. Thus the Turks, penetrated in the front, and hemmed in on every side, were slain at the pleasure of the victors; the remainder escaping through favour of approaching night. Many golden utensils were found in their camp; many jewels, which, though from their scarcity unknown in our country, there shine in native splendour : nor was there ever a more joyful victory for the Christians, because they obtained the most precious spoil without loss.

§ 372. Returning therefore to Jerusalem, when, by a rest of many days, they had recruited their strength, some of them, sighing for their native country, prepared to return by sea. Godfrey and Tancred only remained; princes, truly noble, and to whose glory, posterity, if it judge rightly, never can set limits ; men, who, from the intense cold of Europe, plunged into the insupportable heat of the east; prodigal of their own lives, so that they could succour suffering Christianity : who, besides the fears of barbarous incursions, in constant apprehension from the unwholesomeness of an unknown climate, despised the security of rest and of health in their own country; and although very few in number, kept in subjection so many hostile cities by their reputation and prowess. They were memorable patterns, too, of trust in God ; not hesitating to remain in that climate, where they might either suffer from pestilential air, or be slain by the rage of the Saracens. Let the panegyrics of the poets then give way ; nor let ancient fiction extol her earliest heroes. No age hath produced aught comparable to the fame of these men. For, if the ancients had any merit, it vanished after death with the smoke of their funeral pile, because it had been spent, rather on the vapour of earthly reputation, than in the acquisition of substantial good. But the utility of these men's valour will be felt, and its dignity acknowledged, as long as the world shall revolve, or pure Christianity shall flourish. What shall I say of the good order and forbearance of the whole army? There was no gluttony, no lewdness, which was not directly corrected by the authority of the commanders, or the preaching of the bishops

There was no wish to plunder as they passed through the territories of the Christians; no controversy among themselves which was not easily settled by the examination of mediators. Wherefore, since the commendation of an army so well ordered, redounds to the glory of its conductors, I will signalize in my narrative the exploits and the adventures of each chief; nor will I subtract anything from the truth, as I received it on the faith of my relators. But let no one who has had a fuller knowledge of these events accuse me of want of diligence, since we, who are secluded on this side the British ocean, hear but the faint echo of Asiatic transactions.

§ 373. King Godfrey takes the lead in my commendation; he was the son of Eustace earl of Boulogne, of whom I have [1] spoken in the time of king Edward, but more ennobled maternally, as by that line he was descended from Charles the Great. For his mother, named Ida, daughter of the ancient Godfrey duke of Lorrain, had a brother called Godfrey, after his father, surnamed Bocard. This was at the time when Robert Friso, (of whom I have spoken [2] above,) on the death of Florence, duke of Friesland, married his widow Gertrude; advancing Theodoric, his son-in-law, to the succession of the duchy. Bocard could not endure this; but expelling Friso, subjected the country to his own will. Friso, unable to revenge himself by war, did it by stratagem, killing Bocard through the agency of his Flemings, who drove a weapon into his posteriors as he was sitting for a natural occasion. In this manner the son-in-law succeeded to the duchy, by the means of the victory of his father-in-law. The wife of this Godfrey was the marchioness Matilda, mentioned in the former book,[3] who on her husband's death spiritedly retained the duchy in opposition to the emperor; more especially in Italy, for of Lorrain and the hither-countries he got possession. Ida then, as I began to relate, animated her son Godfrey with great expectations of getting the earldom of Lorrain; for the paternal inheritance had devolved on Eustace her eldest son; the youngest, Baldwin, was yet a boy. Godfrey arriving at a sufficient age to bear arms, dedicated his services to the emperor Henry, who is mentioned [4] in the preceding book. Acquiring his friendship, therefore, by unremitting exertions, he received from the emperor's great liberality the whole of Lorrain as a recompense. Hence it arose that when the quarrel broke out between the pope and Henry, he went with the latter to the siege of Rome; was the first to break through that part of the wall which was assigned for his attack, and made a great breach for the entrance of the besiegers. Being in extreme perspiration and panting with heat, he entered a subterraneous vault which he found in his way, and by quenching his violent thirst by an excessive draught of wine, brought on a quartan fever. Others say that he fell a victim to poisoned wine, as the Romans and men of that country are used to poison whole casks. Others report that a portion of the walls fell to his lot, where the Tiber flowing, exhales destructive vapours in the morning; that by this fatal pest, all his soldiers, with the exception of ten, lost their lives; and that himself, losing his nails

[1] See § 199.   [2] See §§ 256, 257.   [3] See § 289.   [4] See § 262.

and his hair, never entirely recovered. But be it which it might of these, it appears that he was never free from a slow fever, until hearing the report of the expedition to Jerusalem, he made a vow to go thither, if God would kindly restore his health : the moment this vow was made the strength of the duke revived ; so that recovering the use of his limbs and rising with expanded breast, and casting off, as it were, his years of decrepitude, he shone with renovated youth.   In consequence, grateful for the mercies of God showered down upon him, he went to Jerusalem the very first, or among the first, leading a numerous army to the war : and though he commanded an hardy and experienced band, yet none was esteemed readier to attack, or more efficient in the combat than himself.   Indeed it is known, that, at the siege of Antioch, with a sword of Lorrain, he cut asunder a Turk, who had demanded single combat, and that one-half of the man lay panting on the ground, while the horse at full speed, carried away the other ; so firmly the miscreant sate.   Another also who attacked him he clave asunder from the neck to the groin, by taking aim at his head with a two-handed sword ; nor did the dreadful stroke stop here, but cut entirely through the saddle and the back-bone of the horse.   I have heard a man of veracity relate that he had seen what I here subjoin.   During the siege one of the duke's soldiers had gone out to forage ; and being attacked by a lion, avoided destruction for some time by the interposition of his shield : Godfrey, grieved at this sight, transfixed the ferocious animal with an hunting-spear. Wounded, and becoming fiercer from the pain, it turned against the prince with such violence as to hurt his leg with the iron which projected from the wound ; and had he not hastened with his sword to rip it up, this pattern of valour must have perished by the tusk of a wild beast.   Renowned from these exploits, he was exalted to be king of Jerusalem, more especially because he was conspicuous in rank and courage without being arrogant.   His dominion was small and confined, containing, besides the few surrounding towns, scarcely any cities : for the king's bad state of health, which attacked him immediately after the Babylonish war, caused a cessation of warlike enterprise ; so that he made no acquisitions ; yet, by able management, he so well restrained the avidity of the barbarians for the whole of that year, that nothing was lost.   They report that the king, from being unused to a state of indolence, fell again into his original fever ; but I conjecture that God; in his own good time, chose early to translate to a better kingdom, a soul, rendered acceptable to Himself and tried by so many labours, lest wickedness should change his heart or deceit beguile his understanding.   Revolving time thus completing a reign of one year, he died placidly, and was buried on Mount Golgotha.[1]   A king, whose spirit was as unconquerable in death as in battle, often kindly repressing the tears of the by-standers ; and when asked who was to succeed him, he mentioned no person by name, but said merely, " whoever was worthy."   He never would wear the ensign of

---

[1] The church of Golgotha contains within it the rock on which the cross was fixed for the crucifixion. Beda, E. H. § 405.

royalty, saying that it would be the height of arrogance for him to be crowned for glory, in that city, in which God had been crowned in mockery. He died [1] on the fifteenth of the kalends of August.

§ 374. On Godfrey's decease, Tancred and the other chiefs declared that Baldwin, his brother, who was at that time settled in Mesopotamia, should be king; for Eustace, the elder brother, who came to Jerusalem with Godfrey, had long since returned to his native land. The acts of Baldwin shall be related briefly, but with perfect truth; supported in their credibility by the narrative of Fulcher [2] of Chartres, who was his chaplain, and wrote somewhat of him, in a style not altogether unpolished, but, as we say, without elegance or correctness, and which may serve to admonish others to write more carefully. Baldwin undertaking the holy pilgrimage with the rest, had for companions many knights of disposition similar to his own; confiding in these associates, he began to levy fresh troops for his purpose; to watch for brilliant opportunities wherein to manifest his prowess; at last, not content with that commendation which was common to all, leaving the rest and departing three days' journey from Antioch, he got possession, by the consent of its in- habitants, of Tarsus, a noble city of Cilicia : Tarsus, formerly the nursing-mother of the apostle Paul, in honour of whom the cathe- dral there is dedicated. The Tarsians voluntarily submitted to his protection, as they were Christians, and hoped by his aid to be defended from the Turks. The Cilicians, therefore, eagerly yielded to his power, more especially after the surrender of Turbexel, a town fortified by nature, and one whose example sways the inferior towns. This being yielded, as I have said, the others followed its decision. And not only Cilicia, but Armenia and Mesopotamia, eagerly sought alliance with this chief; for these provinces were almost free from the domination of the Turks, though infested by their incursions. Wherefore the prince of the city of Edessa, who was alike pressed by the hatred of the citizens and the sword of the enemy, sent letters to Baldwin, descriptive of his difficulties, de- siring him to come with all speed, and receive a compensation for the labour of his journey, by his adoption, as he had no issue of either sex. This is a city of Mesopotamia in Syria, very noted for the fruit- fulness of its soil and for the resort of merchants, twenty miles dis- tant from the Euphrates, and an hundred from Antioch. The Greeks call it Edessa, the Syrians Rothasia. Baldwin, therefore, exacting an oath of fidelity from the ambassadors, passed the Euphrates with only eighty horsemen; a thing much to be wondered at, whether we call it courage or rashness, that he did not hesitate to proceed among the surrounding nations of barbarians, whom any other person, with so small a force, would have distrusted either for their race or their unbelief. By the Armenians and Syrians, indeed, coming out to meet him on the road with crosses and torches, he

---

[1] He died 18 July, 1100.

[2] Fulcher wrote an account of the transactions in Syria, where he was present, from A.D. 1095 to A.D. 1124. Malmesbury condenses much of his narrative with his usual ability. It is printed in the Gesta Dei per Francos, and, ap. Duchesne, Hist. Franc. Scriptor. tom. iii.

was received with grateful joy and kindly entertained. But the Turks, endeavouring to attack his rear, were frustrated in all their attempts by the skill of Baldwin; the Samosatians setting the first example of flight. Samosata is a city beyond the Euphrates, from which arose Paul of Samosata,[1] the confutation of whose heresy, whoever is desirous may read in the history of Eusebius.[2] And, if I well remember, Josephus says that Antony was laying siege to this city when Herod came to him. The Turks, inhabiting that city, then, who were the first instigators of outrage against the Franks, were the first to give way. Thus, Baldwin, coming safely to Edessa, found nothing to disappoint his expectations; for being received with surpassing favour by the prince, and soon after, on the latter being killed by his faithless citizens, obtaining the lawful sovereignty of the city, he was engaged in hostilities for the whole time during which the Franks were labouring at Antioch and at Jerusalem; worsting his opponents in repeated attacks. But in the month of November being reminded by Boamund, prince of Antioch, that they ought now to set out for Jerusalem, he prepared for marching, and by the single display of the white standard, which was his ensign in battle, overthrowing the Turks who had broken the peace on his expected departure, he left Antioch to the right, and came to Laodicea. Here, by the liberality of earl Raimund, who presided over the city, getting, at a cheap rate, a sufficiency of supplies for his people, he passed Gibellum, and followed the recent track of Boamund, who had encamped and awaited him. Daibert, archbishop of Pisa, joined them for the march; he had landed his confederate party at Laodicea, as did also two other bishops. These forces when united were estimated at five-and-twenty thousand; many of whom, when they entered the territories of the Saracens, were, through the scarcity of commodities, overtaken by famine, and many were dismounted from their horses being starved. Their distress was increased by an abundance of rain; for in that country it pours down like a torrent in the winter months only. In consequence, these poor wretches, having no change of garments, died from the severity of the cold, never getting under cover during several successive days. For this calamity, indeed, there was no remedy, as there was a deficiency both of tents and of wood; but they in some measure appeased their hunger by constantly chewing the sweet reeds which they call Cannamel;[3] so denominated from Cane and Honey. Thus, twice only, obtaining necessaries at an exorbitant price from the inhabitants of Tripoli and Cæsarea, they came to Jerusalem on the day of the winter

---

[1] Paul of Samosata, bishop of Antioch, A.D. 260. He was better pleased with the title of Ducenarius than with that of Bishop. His heresy, like those of Noetus and Sabellius in the same century, tended to confound the mysterious distinction of the divine Persons. He was degraded from his see in 270 by the sentence of eighty bishops, and altogether deprived of his office in 274 by Aurelian.

[2] Euseb. Hist. Ecclesiast. vii. 30.

[3] The sugar cane. "This kind of herb is annually cultivated with great labour. When ripe they pound it in a mortar, strain off the juice, and put it in vessels until it coagulates, and hardens in appearance like snow or white salt. This they use scraped and mixed with bread, or dissolved in water. The canes they call Zucra."—Albertus Aquensis, ap. Gesta Dei, p. 270.

solstice. They were met at the gates by king Godfrey with his brother Eustace, whom he had detained till this time, who showed them every degree of respect and generosity. Having performed in Bethlehem all the accustomed solemnities of our Lord's nativity, they appointed Daibert patriarch; to which transaction I doubt not that the consent of pope Urban was obtained; for he was reverend from age, eloquent, and rich. After the circumcision of our Lord, therefore, assuming palms[1] in Jericho, which antiquity has made the ensign of pilgrims, each one hastily endeavoured to reach his home. The cause of their speed was the stench of the unburied dead bodies, the fumes of which exhaled in such a manner as to infect the sky itself. In consequence, a contagious pestilence spreading in the atmosphere, swept off many of the new comers. The rest quickened their march, by the cities on the coast, that is to say, Tiberias and Cæsarea Philippi; for they were urged by scantiness of provision and the fear of the enemy. Their want, as I have said, was remedied by the celerity of their march; and to the fury of three hundred soldiers who harassed them from the town of Baldac, they opposed a military stratagem : for feigning flight for a short time, that by leaving the narrow passes themselves they might induce the Turks to enter them, they retreated purposely, and then returning, routed the straggling enemy at their pleasure. They had supposed our people unprepared for fight, as their shields and bows were injured by the excessive rains; not being aware, that among men, victory is not obtained by reliance on arms, or armour, but by the predominance of mental energy and bare physical exertion.

§ 375. At that time, indeed, Baldwin returned safely to Edessa, and Boamund to Antioch. But in the beginning of the month of July, a vague report reached the ears of Baldwin, that the pearl of our princes was shorn of its splendour; Boamund being taken, and cast into chains by one Danisman, an heathen, and a potentate of that country. In consequence, collecting a body of the people of Edessa and Antioch, he was in hopes of revenging this singular disgrace of the Christians. Moreover the Turk (who had taken this chieftain more by stratagem and chance than by courage or military force, as he had come with a small party to get possession of the city of Mellentinia) aware that the Franks would use their utmost efforts against him for the disgrace of the thing, betook himself to his own territories : marshalling his troops, not as though he intended to retreat, but rather to exhibit a triumph. Baldwin then proceeding two days' march beyond Mellentinia, and seeing the enemy decline the hazard of a battle, thought fit to return; but, first, with the permission of Gabriel the governor, brought over the city to his own disposal.

§ 376. In the mean time, intelligence reaching him of his brother's death, and of the general consent of the inhabitants and chiefs to his election, he entrusted Edessa to Baldwin, his nearest relation by blood, and moreover a prudent and active man, and prepared for receiving the crown of Jerusalem. Wherefore col-

---

[1] In token of victory, or the completion of their purpose, by having visited the Holy Sepulchre. V. Albertus Aquensis, ubi sup. p. 290.

lecting two hundred horse and seven hundred foot, he proceeded on a march pregnant with death and danger; whence many, whom he falsely supposed faithful, as soon as they saw what a hazardous attempt it was, clandestinely deserted. He, with the remainder, marched forward to Antioch, where, from the resources of his sagacious mind, he became the cause of great future advantage to this distressed people, by advising them to choose Tancred as their chief. Thence he came to Tripoli, by the route of Gibel and Laodicea. The governor of this city, a Turk by nation, but naturally of a kind disposition, afforded him the necessary provisions without the walls; at the same time kindly intimating that he should act cautiously, as Ducah, king of Damascus, had occupied a narrow pass through which he had heard he was to march. Ashamed of being moved by the threats of the Saracen, he resolutely proceeded on his destination: but when he came to the place, he found that the governor's information was correct; for about five miles on this side the city of Berytus there is a very narrow passage near the sea, so confined by steep precipices and narrow defiles, that were an hundred men to get possession of the entrance, they might prevent any number, however great, from passing. Such as travel from Tripoli to Jerusalem have no possible means of avoiding it. Baldwin, therefore, arriving on the spot, sent out scouts to examine the situation of the place and the strength of the enemy. The party returning, and hardly intelligible through fear, breathlessly related the difficulty of the pass, and the confidence of the enemy who had occupied it. But Baldwin, who fell little short of the best soldier that ever existed, feeling no alarm, boldly drew up his army and led it against them. Ducah then despatched some to make an onset, and lure the party unguardedly forward, retaining his main body in a more advantageous position. For this purpose at first they rushed on with great impetuosity, and then made a feint to retreat, to entice our people into the defile. This stratagem could not deceive Baldwin, who, skilled by long-continued warfare, made a signal to his men to make show of flight; and to induce a supposition that they were alarmed, he commanded the baggage which they had cast down to be again taken up, and the cattle to be goaded forward, as well as the ranks to be opened, that the enemy might attack them. The Turks at this began to exult, and, raging so horribly that you might suppose the furies yelling, pursued our party. Some getting into vessels took possession of the shore, others riding forward began to kill such pilgrims, as were incautiously loitering near the sea. The Franks continued their pretended flight till they reached a plain which they had before observed. No confusion deprived these men of their judgment; even the very emergency by which they had been overtaken nurtured and increased their daring; and though a small body, they withstood innumerable multitudes both by sea and land. For, the moment it appeared they had sufficiently feigned alarm, they closed their ranks, turned their standards, and hemmed in the now-charging enemy on all sides: thus the face of affairs was changed, the victors were vanquished, and the vanquished became victors.

The Turks were hewn down with dreadful carnage; the remainder anxiously fled to their vessels, and when they had gotten more than a bow-shot out to sea, they still urged them forward as fiercely with their oars, as though they supposed they could be drawn back to land by their adversaries' hands. And, that you may not doubt that this was a real and not a fancied miracle, this victory was obtained by the loss of only four Christian soldiers. Wherefore, I assert, that the Christians would never be conquered by the pagans, were they to implore the Divine assistance on their courage ere they entered the conflict; and, when in battle, conciliate the friendly powers of heaven to their arms. But since in peace they glut themselves in every kind of vice, and in battle rely only upon their courage, therefore, it justly happens that their valour is often unsuccessful. The earl then, rejoicing in his splendid victory, on returning to spoil the slain, found several Turks alive, whom he dismissed without personal injury, but despoiled them of their wealth. To avoid any hidden stratagem, he, that night, retreated with his party, and rested under the shelter of some olive-trees. Next day, at dawn, he approached the defile with the light troops, to survey the locality; and finding everything safe, and making a signal by smoke, as had been agreed upon, he intimated to his associates the departure of the enemy; for the Turks, who the day before were wantonly galloping around the hill, perceiving the carnage of their companions, had all fled in the dead of the night. Laying aside every delay, they instantly followed their commander. The governor of Berytus sent them food on their march, astonished at the valour of so small a force. The Tyrians, and Sidonians, and Acharonites, who were also called Ptholoamites, acted in the same manner; venerating, with silent apprehension, the bravery of the Franks. Nor were Tancred's party, in Caiphas, less generous, although he was absent. The ancient name of this town I am unable to discover, because all the inland cities, which we read of in Josephus as formerly existing, are either not in being, or else, changed into inconsiderable villages, have lost their names; whereas those on the coast remain entire. In this manner, by Cæsarea of Palestine, and Azotus, they came to Joppa. Here he was first congratulated on his kingdom, the citizens with great joy opening the gates to him.

§ 377. Being afterwards accompanied by the inhabitants of Joppa to Jerusalem, where he was favourably received, he indulged in a repose of seven days. Then, that the Turks might be convinced that the spirit of his reign would tend to their signal disadvantage, he led his troops towards Ascalon. When at a short distance from that city, he proudly displayed his forces, and with very little exertion compelled the attacking Ascalonites to retreat; waiting a favourable opportunity for accomplishing his designs. Finally, conceiving his glory satisfied for that time by their repulse, he drew off to the mountains to pursue the enemy, and also, at their expense, to procure necessaries for his troops, who were famished with hunger from the barrenness of the land; for a scanty harvest had that year denied sustenance, deceiving the expectations of the province by a meagre produce.   He ascended, therefore, the mountainous districts, whither the Turkish inhabitants of the country had retreated on leaving their towns, concealing the Syrians with them in sequestered caverns.   The Franks, however, discovered ˙a mode of counteracting the device of the fugitives, by filling the caverns with smoke; by which the miscreants were dislodged, and came out one by one.   The Turks were killed to a man ; the Syrians were spared. The army turning aside thence, and marching towards Arabia, passed by the sepulchres of the patriarchs Abraham, Isaac, and Jacob; and of their three wives, Sarah, Rebecca, Leah.   The place is in Hebron, thirteen miles distant from Jerusalem ; for the body of Joseph lies at Neapolis, formerly called Sichem, covered with white marble, and conspicuous to every traveller ; there, too, are seen the tombs of his brothers, but of inferior workmanship.   The army then came into the valley where God formerly overthrew Sodom and Gomorrah, darting fire from heaven on the wicked.   The lake there extends for eighteen miles, incapable of supporting any living creature, and so horrible to the taste as to distort the mouths of such as drink it, and distend their jaws with its bitter taste.   A hill overhangs the valley, emitting, in various places, a salt scum, and all over transparent, as it were with congealed glass : here is gathered what some call nitre, some crystal salt.   Passing the lake, they came to a very opulent town, abundant in those luscious fruits which they call dates ; in devouring which they were hardly able to satisfy their hunger or restrain the greediness of their palates, they were so extremely sweet.   Everything else had been taken away, through the alarm of the inhabitants, except a few Ethiopians, the dark wool of whose hair resembled smut; whom our people, (thinking it beneath their valour to kill persons of this description,) treated, not with indignation, but with contempt.   Beneath this town is a valley, where, to this day, is seen the rock which Moses struck, to give water to the murmuring tribes.   The stream yet runs so plentifully, and with such a current, as to turn the machinery of mills.   On the declivity of the hill stands a church, built in honour of the lawgiver Aaron : where, through the mediation and assistance of his brother, he used to hold converse with God.   Here learning from guides conversant in the roads, who from Saracens had been converted to Christianity, that from hence to Babylon was all barren country, and destitute of every accommodation, they returned to Jerusalem, to consecrate to God the first-fruits of a kingdom acquired by the subjugation of so many hostile countries.

§ 378.   The royal insignia being prepared, Baldwin was crowned with great ceremony, in Bethlehem, on Christmas-day,[1] by Daibert the patriarch ; all wishing him prosperity.   For both at that time and afterwards, he deserved, by his own exertions, and obtained, through the favour of others, every degree of royal respect, though sovereign of a very small, and I had almost said, a despicable kingdom.   Wherefore the Christians ought to regard the mercy of our Lord Christ, and to walk in the contemplation of his power, through whose assistance they were objects of apprehension, though unable

[1] Dec. 25, A.D. 1100.

to do harm ; for there were scarcely in the whole service four hundred horsemen and as many foot, to garrison Jerusalem, Ramula, Caiphas, and Joppa. For those who came thither by sea, with minds ill at ease amid so many hostile ports, after having adored the saints, determined to return home, as there was no possibility of proceeding by land. Moreover, an additional difficulty was, that in the month of March, Tancred had departed to assume the government of Antioch, nor could he or the king aid each other, by reason of the length of the journey; indeed, should necessity require it, neither of them could, without fear of irreparable loss, march his troops from one town to another. I pronounce it therefore to be a manifest miracle, that, safe alone through God's protection, he was an object of dread to such a multitude of barbarians.

§ 379. In this year, (which was A.D. 1101,) the sacred fire which used to signalize the vigil of Easter, delayed its appearance longer than usual. For on the Saturday, the lessons being read, alternately in Greek and Latin, the "Kyrie eleeson" repeated thrice ; and the fine Syrian music resounding, still when no fire appeared, and the sun was setting, the night closing in, then all departed sorrowful to their homes. It had been determined after mature deliberation, that on that night no person should remain in the church of the holy sepulchre, lest any impure person should irritate God still more, through his irreverent intrusion. But at day-break, a procession of the Latins was ordered to the Temple of Solomon, that by prayer they might invoke the mercy of God : the same was performed around the sepulchre of our Lord, by the Syrians, plucking their beards, and hair, through violence of grief. The mercy of God could endure no longer, light being instantly sent into one lamp of the sepulchre. When a Syrian perceived it glittering through a window, he expressed his joy by the clapping of his hands, and accelerated the advance of the patriarch. He, opening the recess of the sepulchral chamber by the keys which he carried, and lighting a taper, brought forth the celestial gift,[1] imparting it to all who crowded round him for that purpose ; afterwards the whole of the lamps, throughout the church, were divinely lighted up, the one which was next to be illumined evidencing its approaching ignition, by emitting smoke in a miraculous manner. Thus, doubtless, the constant manner of Christ has been to chasten those whom He loveth, that He may again kindly soothe them, and that the dread of his power may redound to his praise. For since even the common gifts of God are lightly esteemed by men, merely from their constant recurrence, He often enhances the grant of his indulgences by withholding them, in order that what is most ardently desired may be more gratefully regarded.

§ 380. At that time a fleet of Genoese and Pisans had touched at Laodicea, and thence made a prosperous voyage to Joppa ; and the crews, drawing their vessels on shore, spent Easter with the

[1] Bernard the monk notices the custom of imparting the holy light, in order that the bishops and people might illuminate their several residences from it. Fulcher describes this event at great length, and observes that each person had a wax taper in his hand, for the purpose of receiving the holy fire. Gesta Dei p. 407.

king at Jerusalém. He, bargaining for their services, engaged to give them the third of the spoil of each city they could take, and any particular street they might choose. Thus he impelled them, inconsiderate and blinded, more through lust of gold than love of God, to barter their blood, and lay siege immediately to Azotus, which they constrained to surrender after three days. Nor did the townspeople yield very reluctantly, as they feared the anger of the king, should they be taken by storm ; for, the preceding year, assisted by the machination of fortune, they had vigorously repulsed Godfrey when making a similar attempt ; for when, by means of scaling-ladders, he had advanced his forces on the walls, and they, now nearly victorious, had gotten possession of the parapet, the sudden fall of a wooden tower, which stood close to the outside of the wall, deprived them of the victory and killed many, while still more were taken and butchered by the cruelty of the Saracens. Leaving Azotus, Baldwin laid siege to Cæsarea of Palestine, with his whole force and with determined courage ; but perceiving the resolution of its citizens, and the difficulty of the enterprise, he ordered engines to be constructed. Petraries were therefore made, and a great tower built, twenty cubits higher than the wall. Our people, however, impatient of delay and of such lingering expectation, erecting their ladders, and attempting to overtop the wall, arrived at the summit by the energy of their efforts ; indignant, with conscious valour, that they had now been occupied in conflict with the Saracens during fifteen days, and had lost the whole of that time ; and although the Cæsareans resisted with extreme courage, and rolled down large stones on them as they ascended, yet despising all danger, they broke through the close ranks of their opponents, using their strength of arm and their drawn swords. The Turks, unable longer to sustain the attack, and taking to flight, either cast themselves down headlong, or fell by the hand of their enemies. Many were reserved for slavery ; a few for ransom : among the latter was the governor of the city, and a bishop named Archadius. It was a laughable spectacle for a by-stander, to see a Turk disgorging bezants,[1] when struck on the neck by the fist of a Christian ; for the wretched males, through fear of extreme indigence, had hid money in their mouths ; the females, in parts not to be particularized : you perceive that my narrative blushes to speak plainly, but the reader understands what I wish, or rather what I wish not, to express.

§ 381. Still, however, the emperor of Babylon could not be at rest, but would frequently send commanders and armies to attack the Franks. Arriving at Ascalon on ship-board, they scoured about Ramula, taking advantage of the king's occupation, who was then

---

[1] Fulcher relates, with great coolness, that he saw the bodies of the Turks, who were slain at Cæsarea, piled up and burnt, in order to obtain the bezants which they had swallowed. Hist. Hierosol. ap. Du Chesne, iv. 845. This practice of swallowing money is referred to by pope Urban, and, by his account, the merely burning dead bodies to obtain the hoard was a very humble imitation of the Saracen custom, with respect to those who visited Jerusalem before the Crusades : which was to put scammony in their drink to make them vomit, and if this did not produce the desired effect, they proceeded to immediate incision ! Guibert Abbas. Opera, p. 379.

busied in the contest with Cæsarea. They frequently, therefore, by depopulating the country, irritated him to engage. But he, with equal subtlety, that their mad impetuosity might subside, suffered them, when eagerly advancing, to grow languid by declining battle: by this procrastination he caused many, weary of delay, to withdraw; he then attacked the remainder, consisting of eleven thousand horse and twenty-one thousand infantry, with his own two hundred and fifty cavalry and less than seven hundred foot. Addressing a few words to his soldiers, to whom he pledged victory if they persevered, and fame if they fell; and calling to their recollection, that if they fled France was a great way off, he dashed first against the enemy; and, the contest continuing for some time, when he saw his ranks giving way, he remedied circumstances which seemed almost bordering on desperation. Thus, dismaying the Turks by his well-known appearance, he laid their leader prostrate with his lance; on whose death the whole army fled. Our soldiers, who in the onset were so hemmed in as to be unable to see each other, then exercised their valour in such wise, under the ensign of the Holy Cross which preceded them, that they killed five thousand. Eighty of the cavalry, and rather more of the infantry, were slain on the side of the Franks. However, subsequent successes consoled them, as they dispatched five hundred Arabian horse. These had been traversing before Joppa for two days; but effecting little, they were returning to Ascalon, and seeing our troops at a distance, and hoping they were their own, were approaching to congratulate them on their victory: but at length perceiving by the weapons hurled against them that they were Franks, they turned pale; and to use the words of the poet,[1] became like him, who,

"with unshod foot had trod upon a snake."

In consequence, unnerved with astonishment, they fled before their destroyers. Thus, the king coming to Joppa, corrected, by a true account, the falsity of the letter which had been sent to Tancred by the people of that city, erroneously declaring that the king had perished with his army. And, indeed, already had Tancred prepared for his march to Jerusalem; when a messenger arriving, and showing the royal signet, dispelled his sorrow, and restored his satisfaction.

§ 382. It would be tedious were I to relate all his contests; to tell how he subdued Tiberias, Sidon, Accaron, that is Ptolemais, and, ultimately, all the cities on the coast; or, how he distinguished almost each day by the slaughter of the Turks, either through secret attack or open warfare. The relation of his exploits requires the exclusive labours of a man of lofty eloquence, and undisturbed leisure: I have neither; and, what chiefly acts as an obstacle, want clear information on the subject. For it is by no means the part of an historian of veracity to give entire credit to flattering reports, or to deceive the credulity of his readers. Consequently, I shall only subjoin what I have found recorded, whereby this man's exalted devotion may be clearly proved, and his good report live for ever.

[1] Juvenal, Sat. i. 43.

This I may be bold to assert, that he often, with an inconsiderable
force, engaged in mighty conflicts, and that he never fled from the
field, except at Ramula and at Accaron. And indeed signal victories
ensued to each of these flights, because they proceeded more from
rash valour than from fear ; as the reader will discover from the
insertion of a few facts.

§ 383. In the month of September, on the seventh of the ides of
which [Sep. 7th], the battle aforesaid took place, William, earl of
Poictou, proceeded towards Jerusalem, leading with him a large army
estimated at sixty thousand [1] horse and a still larger number of foot.
There accompanied him, Stephen, earl of Burgundy, and Hugh de
Lusignan, brother of earl Raimund, Hugh the Great, and Stephen
of Blois, anxious to atone for the disgrace of their former desertion,
by renovated and determined valour.   Proceeding, therefore, by
Constantinople, after he had by an insolent answer, as I [2] before
related, offended Alexis, he fell into the snares of Solyman ; the
emperor rather procuring than preventing his disaster.   For Solyman, aware that the army was suffering from hunger and thirst, as
they had been wandering about the marshes and desolate places for
several days, encountered them with three hundred thousand
archers.   Never was there conflict more disastrous to the Franks ;
as it was impossible for flight to save the coward, or courage to
rescue the bold from danger: for the battle was fought in a confined
situation, and nothing could prevent the effect of clouds of arrows
on men who were crowded together.   More than an hundred thousand were slain ; and all the booty carried off.   Thus Solyman,
obtaining splendid offerings to the manes of his countrymen from
the spoils of the Franks, revenged the loss of Nicea.   But, as they
had proceeded by many roads, all were not slain ; nor was everything plundered.   For, except the Poictevin, who was nearly stript
to the skin, the other earls had boldly defended their baggage. All,
therefore, except Hugh the Great, who died, and was entombed in
the city of Tarsus, collecting again their soldiers after the flight,
hastened to Antioch. Tancred, a knight of distinguished piety, gave
them ample proof of his generosity; assisting them all, as far as he
was able, with money: more especially William, whom the inconstancy of fortune had now as deeply depressed as she had formerly
highly exalted, who, in addition to the loss of treasure, by which he
was not so much affected, as it was transitory and capable of
reparation, was left almost the sole survivor of so many valorous
soldiers.   Proceeding on their march with renovated courage, they
sought every opportunity of giving battle. The city of Tortosa was
the first to feel their rage ; by attacking and plundering which, they
in a great degree compensated their former losses.   Thence they
came to the defile, which I have mentioned above, where the king
had long waited them, in order to give assistance in case the Turks
should oppose their passage. Defended by his valour, and meeting
with kind entertainment at Joppa, they proceeded the following
Easter to Jerusalem, where they joyfully beheld, and reverently
adored, the sacred fire. Returning afterwards to Joppa, they took

---

[1] See note [2], p. 298.   [2] See § 349.

ship, each designing to revisit his native land. The Poictevin, the wind being favourable all the way, reached home; the rest were violently driven back.

§ 384. But now, in the beginning of May, the Turks and Arabs laid siege to Ramula; recruiting the losses of their army in the former year, by making up its original numbers. The bishop of the city, prudently watching an opportunity, retired from the place and went secretly to Joppa. Baldwin had already gone out, relying on a false assertion that the enemy did not exceed five hundred: in consequence of which, he neither put his forces in order, nor called out his infantry, the trumpeters merely sounding for the cavalry to follow the king; though his friends earnestly advised him to be on his guard against the subtlety of the Turks. The two Stephens, him of Blois, and the other of Burgundy, followed the king on horseback, that, instead of being branded as indolent and cowardly, they might return to their respective homes partakers of the credit of the triumph; far different, however, from their expectations, were the glory and the victory which the fates were preparing for them. For Baldwin, perceiving the multitude of the enemy and finding himself deceived in his opinion, filled with rage, and fierce in conscious valour, hesitated what was to be done. If he gave way, he saw that his former renown would be tarnished; if he fought, he foresaw the destruction of his followers. Nevertheless, his innate courage prevailed, and fear had already yielded, when, swayed by the advice of his comrades, he acquiesced in a plan of retiring, through the midst of the enemy, into a castle. The rest, following with loud clamour, broke through the thickest ranks, consecrating their souls to God, and selling their lives dearly; the earls, too, so wearied with striking that their hands grew stiff upon their swords, were slain. The king escaping to the fortress, had some few companions remaining out of the two hundred he had led forth: who entreating that he would deign to protract his life by flight, and observing that their danger was of little consequence to the world, while his life was of advantage to many, inasmuch as he would be an example of valour to every age, by his singular constancy in adversity, he consented to save himself. Wherefore, accompanied by five knights, he eluded his assailants by stealing away to the mountains. One of them was an Englishman named Robert, as I said before; the remoteness of time and place has left us in ignorance of the names of the others: he, with three more, was taken; the fifth escaped with the king. The Turks vented the whole of their fury on those who had retired to the castle, among whom was Hugh de Lusignan and Geoffrey de Vincennes: only three survivors told their mournful tale to the people of Jerusalem. The king, concealing himself during the day, urged his jaded courser and arrived at Azotus, by the singular and miraculous protection of God; as the Turks had but just departed, after having been plundering around the city for the space of two days. Coming thence by sea to Joppa, he despatched a letter to the people of Jerusalem, assuring them of his safety. The bearer of the epistle was a low Syrian fellow, who, even had he been discovered, would have deceived the enemy, from the meanness of his garb, and his using the common language of the country. Escaping the hands of the infidels by lone paths with which he was acquainted, he arrived the third day at Jerusalem. Upon this the cavalry who garrisoned the city, taking with them the bands of auxiliary infantry, and purposing to proceed to Joppa, took a route close to the sea ; avoiding the inland districts : the rear, however, of the party, were cut off by the Turks pressing on them, as they were left unprotected either by horse or foot. Thus collecting ninety horse from Jerusalem, and eighty from Tiberias, which Hugh, that most intrepid commander, had brought to their assistance, the attendants also, through necessity, were advanced to the rank of knights. The battle was delayed only till the next day, the Turks being now so ferocious as to prepare their engines, and to meditate an attack on the walls of Joppa. This was prevented by the activity of Baldwin, and by the Cross of Christ preceding them, which had been wanting in the former battle. They then, with all the forces, rushed eagerly on the enemy, and the contest was fierce ; but they, after their usual custom, surrounding our troops, thought they had completely overcome the Christians, and shouted with cheerful cry : but the Lord Jesus was present, who at length looked down from heaven, and inspiriting the Franks, put the enemy, driven from the field, to flight. It had happened in the preceding action, that, though frequently driven from their tents, they afterwards conquered through their numbers ; but now, as the infantry wounded them from a distance with their arrows, and the cavalry close at hand with their lances, they relied only on their speed, and continued their flight.

§ 385. He fought another battle in later years, in which our soldiers, pressed by the numbers of the Turks and compelled to fly, lost even their protecting standard : but after they had fled some distance, they rallied ; shame animating the timid to repel such ignominy. Then indeed the contest was strenuous ; fighting foot to foot, and breast to breast. Our party recovered the Cross ; routing the enemy, and regaining the field. Many fell here with whom I had been acquainted ; among these was Godfrey, Baldwin's bastard grand-nephew, who from a boy manifested valour in his countenance, and truth in his soul. In the beginning, indeed, both retreats were, it may be said, the source of ignominy ; but in the end, true food for glory : the one more celebrated ; the other more advantageous. Finally, to repair his losses and also to be united with him in marriage, the countess of Sicily came shortly after to Jerusalem, pouring such treasures into the royal palace, that it was matter of surprise whence a woman could accumulate such endless heaps of precious utensils :[1] and at this time, indeed, he married her, but shortly after he put her away. It is said that she was afflicted with a cancerous complaint, which preyed upon her womb.[2]

---

[1] Among a variety of instances adduced of her wealth, it is stated that the mast of the vessel which conveyed her to Palestine, was covered with pure gold. Albertus Aquensis, ap. Gesta Dei, p. 373.

[2] Some authors assign a different reason for the divorce. His second wife (daughter of Taphnuz, prince of Armenia), whom he had repudiated about the

This, however, is well known, that the king had no issue; nor is it wonderful, that a man to whom leisure was burthensome should be averse to the embraces of a wife, as he passed all his time in war. By these exertions his admirable, and almost godlike valour, operated as an incitement to the present race, and was a marvel to posterity. He died, during an expedition into Arabia, in the month of April, and was publicly buried at Jerusalem, near his brother, in the fourth month of the eighteenth year of his reign [A. D. 1118.] He was a man who gained his reputation by repeated labours, and on whose fame envy hath cast no shade, except it be, that he was too sparing of his money; though there is a ready and well-founded excuse for such a fault, if it be considered, that the necessary largesses to such as remained with him prevented him from purchasing the favour of those who departed.

§ 386. He was succeeded by his kinsman, Baldwin, prince of Edessa, already celebrated for his former campaigns, whom he had, when dying, named as king. Spiritedly defending the kingdom for many years, he augmented it with the sovereignty of Antioch, which he obtained when Roger, the son of Richard, was killed.[1] He governed both countries with laudable conduct; with less presumptuous haughtiness, perhaps, but with great and consummate prudence; though there are some who wound his fair fame, accusing him of excessive parsimony. Wherefore, last year, when the Turks had taken him while riding a short distance from Jerusalem, his people grieved but little for him, and for nearly a year it remained unknown both to subjects and even to tale-bearers, whither he was taken, or whether or not he was still alive. However, the people of Jerusalem, nothing discouraged on account of his absence, refused either to elect a king, or to change the order or command of the army, till the certainty of the matter could be known. At last, the place where he lay captive being discovered, some knights of surpassing boldness, assuming the guise of merchants, and hiding weapons beneath their garments, entered the town, and rescued the king from jeopardy; protesting that they did not act thus through respect for his niggardliness, but out of gratitude to Gozelin of Turbexel,[2] who never hesitated to bestow all he possibly could upon the military. He has now lived long, a provident man, and subject to no other imputation.[3] The princi-

---

[1] year 1105, and confined in the convent of St. Anne of Jerusalem, was then living. The marriage with the countess of Sicily, his third wife, was therefore set aside by the pope; after which she returned, in 1117, to Sicily, and died there, shortly after Baldwin. (Albertus Aquen. XII. xxiv.; Will. Tyr. II. i. and xv.) His first wife who accompanied him on the Crusade, but died before her arrival at Antioch, was the daughter of Raoul II. lord of Toëni, and had been separated from her former husband, Robert comte de Meulent.

[1] Roger, prince regent of Antioch, son of Richard seneschal of Apulia, married Hodierna, sister of Baldwin II. He was slain in 1119.

[2] This account appears in some measure incorrect. Gozelin and the king were both confined in the same castle. On its being seized, Gozelin escaped, and collected troops to liberate his friends, who were now themselves besieged. But ere his arrival, the Turks had made themselves masters of the fortress, and carried off the king, who did not recover his liberty for some time, and then only by paying a considerable ransom. Fulch. Carnot. and Will. Tyr. ap. Gesta Dei.

[3] Baldwin died A. D. 1135.

pality of Antioch pertains to the son of Boamund,[1] of whom I proceed to speak.

§ 387. Boamund[2] was the son of Robert Guiscard by a Norman woman ; he had another son named Roger,[3] born of an Apulian, who was, by his father, surnamed " Purse," because his paternal and attentive observation had discovered that, from a mere child, he had pleasure in counting money. As to Boamund, who was somewhat older, he never could retain anything, but even gave away his childish presents. Roger, therefore, received Apulia, which seemed to belong to him in right of his mother ; Boamund went with his father to the Durazzian war. And when the townspeople, through confidence of their walls, boasted that the city was called Durachium,[4] because it could endure all sieges undismayed ; and, " I," said Guiscard, " am called Durandus ; and I will remain besieging it, until I take away the name from the city ; so that henceforth it shall no longer be called Durachium, but Mollicium." The firmness of this answer so terrified them that they immediately opened their gates. Thus, secure in his rear, he subdued, with the less difficulty, the other cities as far as Thessalonica. He had now arrived there, and had already, both by himself and by his son, taught Alexis that he might be overcome ; when, beguiled by the treachery of his wife, he failed, by death, of a noble enterprise. Boamund, then, returning to Apulia, possessed some castles through his brother's indulgence, and acquired many others by his own courage and prudence. Indeed the dukedom had fallen to his brother only in appearance ; all the most warlike spirits following him. Nor was this of light importance ; for, observant of his father's purpose, he was averse to Guibert and strongly espoused the cause of Urban, urging him when hesitating, to proceed into France to the council of Clermont, whither the letters of Raimund earl of Provence and of the bishop of Chorges invited him. The council being ended, he readily embraced the opportunity, and transported his forces into Greece ; and thence moving forward his army, he quietly awaited Raimund and Godfrey. Joining them on their arrival, he inspired the rest with great confidence by reason of his military skill and courage, which was never surpassed. But, as what he performed in company with others only entitles him to a share in the general praise, and my former narrative has[5] related how he had been taken prisoner, it may be proper to mention in what manner he rescued himself from captivity. When Danisman perceived that no advantage resulted to him from detaining so great

---

[1] Bohemond II. son of Bohemond I. and Constance, daughter of Philippe I. of France.

[2] Bohemond, the son of Guiscard by his first wife Alberade, was baptized Mark; but his father, hearing a tale related of a giant Buamund, gave him that appellation. Ord. Vital. p. 817.

[3] Roger, afterwards king of Sicily, was the son of Guiscard by his second wife Sikelgaite, daughter of Gaimar IV. prince of Salerno.

[4] The Romans had changed the inauspicious name of Epi-damnus to Dyrrachium (Plin. iii. 26), and the vulgar corruption of Durachium bore some affinity to "duritia," implying "hardness." One of Robert's names was Durand, a durando. (Alberic. Monach. in Chron. apud Muratori, Annali d'Italia, ix. 137.) There is a play upon the words, "non Durachium sed Mollicium," intended to contrast the soft and hard,—the "mollis" and "durus."   [5] See § 375.

a man in confinement, changing his intentions, he began sedulously to treat of terms of peace; for he was neither inclined to put him to death, lest he should concentrate the fierce hatred of the Christians on himself; nor would he set him at liberty[1] without the hope of a lasting peace. Boamund, therefore, promising the infidel perpetual amity, returned to Antioch, bringing with him the silver fetters with which he had been confined; and being favourably received by his people, he took possession of Laodicea, and the other cities which Tancred, lest he should have been thought slumbering in indolence while his uncle was sighing in prison, had acquired during his captivity. Not long after he came into France, offering up, in honour of St. Leonard,[2] the chains with which he had been burdened; for this saint is said to be so especially powerful in loosing fetters that the captive may freely carry away his chains, even in the sight of his enemies, who dare not mutter a syllable. Then, marrying one of the daughters of the king of France and sending another to Tancred, he sought Apulia, followed by the French nobility, who deserted their country in hope of greater advantages, as well as that they might be eye-witnesses of what could be effected by that energetic valour which was so universally extolled by fame. Wherefore arranging his affairs in Apulia, he again attacked Alexis, alleging as a cause his cruelty to the crusaders, for which he was very noted: but being deceived by the subtlety of the emperor, who, as I have already mentioned, alienated his commanders from him by bribery, or took them off by poison, he had little or no success. Dejected at this, he returned to Apulia, where, in a few days, while purposing to proceed to Antioch, he died, not an old man, yet equal to any in prudence, leaving a son of tender age. He was a man firm in adversity and circumspect in prosperity; for he had even provided himself with a preservative from poison of which he was apprehensive. It was a knife, which, placed before him when eating, strange to tell, indicated, by the moistness of its handle, whenever poison was brought into the apartment. After him Tancred succeeded to the principality of Antioch, a nephew worthy of such uncle; he treading the common path of mortals by an early death, Roger the son of Richard succeeded. Though rivalling the fame of his predecessors in battle, yet he incurred the disgrace of being avaricious: in consequence of this, when the soldiery avoided him, he engaged the Turks with a trifling stipendiary, and a small native force, and fell selling his life dearly; for being taken by them, stripped of his armour, and commanded to yield up his sword, he refused to deliver it to any but the commander, as he considered all present unworthy to receive the surrender of one of his dignity. The unhappy chief gave credit

---

[1] Orderic. Vital. p. 797, gives a different account of his deliverance, and which has quite a romantic air.

[2] Leonard was godson to Clovis king of France, and obtained, through the favour of that monarch, that, whenever he should see any one who was in chains, he should be immediately set at liberty. At length it pleased God to honour him to that degree, that, if any person in confinement invoked his name, their chains immediately fell off, and they might depart; their keepers themselves having no power to prevent them. Vide Surius Vitæ Sanct. Nov. 6.

to his specious words, and having taken off his helmet, stretched out his hand to receive Roger's sword; when, indignant, and mustering all his remaining powers for the effort, he cut off the Turk's head, and being immediately stabbed, escaped the disgrace of slavery by the act his courage had suggested. Baldwin the Second, king of Jerusalem, revenging his death in a signal manner, faithfully reserved the dominion of the city, and his own daughter,[1] for Boamund the son of Boamund.

§ 388. Raimund was the son of the most noble William,[2] count of Tholouse, who being a man of enterprise and ability, rendered his country, which had been obscured through the indolence of his predecessors, illustrious by his own good qualities. His wife, Almodis,[3] was repeatedly married to different persons, and had a numerous issue by them all; a woman of such sad, unbridled lewdness, that, when one husband became disgusting to her from long intercourse, she would depart and take up her abode with another; to sum up all, she had been first united to the count of Arles;[4] presently, becoming weary of him, she connected herself with this William; and then, after bearing him two sons, she lured the earl of Barcelona[5] to marry her. Moreover, William, when at the point of death, gave to his son of his own name, but not of his own disposition, the county of Tholouse, because, though he was of slender talents, the people of Tholouse would attempt no innovation against him, as they were accustomed to the government of his family. But Raimund, who was of brighter abilities, received Querci, and increased it not a little by the addition of Arles, Narbonne, Provence, and Limoges. Again, he purchased Tholouse of his brother, who went to Jerusalem many years previous to the grand crusade; but these things were achieved by a considerable lapse of time, and a life expended on the labour. Thus, ever engaged in war, he had no desire for a legitimate wife, enjoying himself in unrestrained concubinage. Finally, he condescended to honour with his adoption and inheritance, Bertrand, his son by one of his mistresses; as he, in some respects, resembled his father. To this son he married the niece[6] of Matilda the Marchioness, a native of Lombardy, that by such affinity he might secure his possessions on that side. In the latter part of his life, too, he himself espoused the daughter of the king of Tarragona, covenanting for a noble dowry, namely, the perpetual peace of the

---

[1] The accession of Bohemond II. and his marriage with Alix, daughter of Baldwin II. king of Jerusalem, were subsequent to the year 1126. L'Art de Vérifier les Dates, i. 442.

[2] More correctly "Pontii." Raymond was the brother of William, and son of Pontius count of Thoulouse. To Pontius therefore should be referred all that Malmesbury here relates of William. Raymond count of St. Giles and Thoulouse, took his name of St. Giles from the place of his birth, or first appanage. It is situated in the Lower Languedoc, between Nismes and the Rhone. He was also duke of Narbonne and marquis of Provence.

[3] She was the daughter of Bernard count of La Marche en Limosin. Her first husband was Hugh V. sire de Luzignan, from whom she was divorced, and afterwards married Pontius count of Thoulouse.

[4] More correctly Hugh de Luzignan.

[5] Raymond Berenger I. comte de Barcelone.

[6] Eluta or Helena, daughter of Otho I. duke of Burgundy.

adjacent provinces. Soon after this, on contemplating his grey hairs, he made a vow to go to Jerusalem, in order that his bodily powers, though decayed and feeble, might still, though late, enter into the service of God. The chief promoter of this was the bishop of Chorges, by whose especial exertions he had always been thwarted; he had also lost an eye in a duel, which deformity, so far from concealing, he was ever anxious to show, boasting of it, as a proof of his valour. But now, leagued in mutual friendship, that they might employ their old age in religious services, they stimulated Urban, already inclined to preach the crusade, to pass the Alps and summon a council at Clermont, more especially as it was a city adjacent to their territories, and convenient for persons coming from every part of France. The bishop, however, died on his way to the council. To his influence succeeded the bishop of Puy, of whom we have before spoken : animated by whose advice, and protected by whose assistance, Raimund was the first layman who assumed the cross, making this addition to his vow, that he would never return to his country; but endeavour to lessen the weight of his past offences by perpetual exertion against the Turks. He had already given many proofs of his prowess on the way, being the first to labour and the last to rest; many also of forbearance, as he readily relinquished those places he had first occupied at Antioch to Boamund, and the Tower of David to Godfrey. But at length, his patience being worn out by the unreasonable demands of certain persons, he departed from his usual practice on the subject of the surrender of Ascalon. For, on the first arrival of the Franks, the townspeople, examining the disposition of our several commanders made choice of him for their patron ; because many men, who had come thither before, by sea, from Montpellier, to trade, had extolled his sincerity and courage to the skies. In consequence, delivering him their keys, they compelled him to make oath that he would never give up the command of the city to any other of the Christians, should he himself be either unwilling or unable to retain it. A murmuring then arose among the chiefs, who required the surrender of the city to the king, saying that his kingdom would be of little value unless he had possession of Ascalon, which would be a receptacle for the enemy and an obstacle to our party. The king indeed set forth the matter mildly, as he did everything else, with a placid countenance, consistent with his manners; the others rather more violently. However, he paid little attention to their words, obviating their allegations by very substantial reasons, saying that all his associates had secured a place of retreat, part of them had returned home, part were occupying the provinces they had acquired ; that he alone, having abjured his native country, could neither return thither, nor did he possess a place of refuge here ; that he had yielded in other points, but they must allow him to retain Ascalon, under fealty to the Holy Sepulchre, as he had taken an oath not to give it up. On hearing this, all began to clamour and to call him interested and faithless ; indeed, they could scarcely abstain from laying hands on him. The earl, indignant at this reproach, failed in the duty of a just and

upright man, delivering the keys to the enemies of God, and compensating the fear of perjury by the blood of many a man in after
time; for, to this day, that city has never been taken, either by
force or by stratagem.   Moreover, many of his people, delighted
with the unbounded affluence of the place, by denying their faith
obtained the friendship of its citizens.   Thus leaving Jerusalem, he
came to Laodicea, and having subdued it, continued there some
little time.   Afterwards, when he had gone to Constantinople,
Tancred obtained Laodicea, though it is dubious whether by force
or favour.   In the meantime, remaining at Byzantium, he contrived
by his consummate prudence to insinuate himself into the favour
of Alexis : whence it happened, that, through the kindness of the
emperor, getting a safe passage, he escaped sharing those calamities
which, as we have before related, befel William of Poictou and the
others, with whom he took the city of Tortosa, and, when the rest
proceeded onwards, retained possession of it.   To extend his power,
he fortified a town over against Tripoli, called Pilgrim's Castle,
where he appointed abbot Herbert, bishop : and that the shattered
strength of his followers might recruit by repose, he made a seven
years' league with the Tripolitans.   Nevertheless, ere the time
appointed, the peace was broken, on account of a certain townsman
being found within the castle, with a poisoned dagger concealed
beneath his garments.   And now truly would he have put the
finishing hand to the conquest of Tripoli, had he not died just as
he was on the point of accomplishing his great designs.   On learning his decease, William of Montpellier, and the other chiefs of the
province, provided that William the pilgrim, scarcely four years of
age, whom he had begotten on a Spanish woman during the siege,
should be conveyed home, to be educated for the succession, in
accordance with the universal desire.   Nor did Bertrand hear of
this transaction with displeasure, although he had never been consulted, as it enabled him to renew his father's fame.   Wherefore,
heading a vast army, and chiefly supported by the Genoese and
Pisans, who were allied to his wife, he attacked Tripoli by sea and
land, and, when exhausted by a protracted siege, reduced it to his
dominion.   To him succeeded Pontius, his son by a Lombard woman,
a youth who rivalled the glory of his ancestors, and who obtained
in marriage the relict of Tancred, formerly prince of Antioch.
This, when dying, he had commanded, affirming that the youth
would grow up a support to the Christians and an utter destruction
to the Turks.   Pontius therefore reigns at Tripoli, professing himself the servant of the Holy Sepulchre; in this respect following
the example of his grandfather and father.

§ 389. Robert, son of William the First, king of England, was
born in Normandy, and already considered as a youth of excellent
courage when his father came to England ; of tried prowess, though
of small stature and projecting belly.   He passed his early years
amid the warlike troops of his father, obedient to him in every
respect : but in the vigorous heat of youth, led by the suggestions
of his idle companions, he supposed he could obtain Normandy
from the king during his lifetime.   But when William refused this,

and drove away the youth by the blustering of his terrific voice,
Robert departed indignantly, and harassed his country by perpetual
attacks. His father laughed at first, and then added, " By the
resurrection of God, this little Robin Short-hose will be a clever
fellow ;" for such was his appellation from his small stature, though
there was nothing else to find fault with, as he was neither ill-
made, nor deficient in eloquence, nor was he wanting in courage
or resources of mind. At length, however, the king was so transported with anger, that he denied him his last blessing and the
inheritance of England ; and it was with difficulty and disgrace
that he could retain even Normandy. After nine years he gave
proof of his valour in the labours of the crusade, and in many
battles it was matter of wonder that neither Christian nor pagan
could ever unhorse him. More especially was he remarkable in
the battle of Antioch, where he graced the victory by a singular
achievement. For when the Turks, as we have related, were suddenly dismayed and fled, and our party vehemently attacked them
in disorder, Corbaguath, their leader, mindful of his native valour,
checked his horse, and rallied his people; calling them base slaves,
and forgetful of their ancient conquests, in suffering themselves,
the former conquerors of the East, to be driven from their territories by a strange and almost unarmed people : at this reproach,
many, resuming their courage, wheeled round, attacked the Franks,
and compelled the nearest to give way, while Corbaguath continued
to animate his men and to assault the enemy, nobly fulfilling his
duty, both as a commander and a soldier. But now the Norman
earl and Philip the Clerk, son of Roger, earl of Montgomery, and
Warin de Taney, a castle so named in Maine, who had before made
a feint of retreating, exhorting each other with mutual spirit, turned
round their horses, and each attacking his man, threw them to the
ground. Here Corbaguath, though he knew the earl, yet estimating
him merely by his size, and thinking it inglorious to fly, paid the
penalty of his bold attack, being instantly slain. The Turks, who
had already raised a shout of victory, on seeing his fall, now lost
their lately-acquired hopes, and redoubled their flight. In this
contest Warin fell : Robert, with Philip, gained the victory. The
latter, who acquired renown by this service, but afterwards, as
they report, closed an honourable career at Jerusalem, was celebrated for his learning as well as his military prowess. Robert,
thus coming to Jerusalem, tarnished his glory by an indelible stain
in refusing a kingdom [1] offered to him, as a king's son,[2] by the
consent of all ; and this, as it is asserted, not through awe of its
dignity, but through the dread of its complicated duties. How-

[1] The original historians of the crusade make no mention of Robert by name
as refusing the crown. It is, however, to be found in Henry of Huntingdon. To
Raymond of Thoulouse is also ascribed the honour of refusing the crown. (Ville-
hardouin, No. 136.) It would seem that it was offered to and refused by all the
chiefs in succession ; but Godfrey of Bouillon was compelled by the unanimous
voice of the army to accept it. Albertus Aquens. VI. xxxiii.

[2] The crown for the same reason might also have been offered to Hugh the
Great, brother of king Philippe of France, but he had embraced an ambiguous
opportunity of returning to his own country. Guibert (pp. 518, 523) attempts to
excuse Hugh the Great.

ever, returning home, where he had reckoned on giving himself up to the full indulgence of sensual pleasure, God mercifully visited him, as I believe, for this transgression; everywhere thwarting him, and turning all his enjoyments into bitterness, as will be manifested by the sequel. His wife, the daughter of William de Conversana, whom he had married in Apulia on his return, and whose surpassing beauty all endeavours to describe are vain, he lost after a few years by disease;[1] she being misled, as it is said, by the advice of the midwife, who had ordered her breasts, when in childbed, to be bound with a tight bandage, on account of the copious flow of her milk. A great consolation, however, in this extreme distress was a son by his consort, who, called William by presage of his grandfather's name, gave hope of noble talents hereafter. The immense sum which his father-in-law had given him, under the appellation of dowry, that he might with it redeem Normandy,[2] he lavished so profusely, that, in a few days, he was penniless. He accelerated his disgrace by his ill-advised arrival in England to wrest the kingdom from his brother Henry; but, failing of the assistance of the traitors who had invited him, he easily yielded to his brother's terms of peace; which, by the agreement of the chiefs of either party, were, but only verbally, that he should receive an annual present of three thousand marks from England. The king, indeed, promised this without any design of paying it; but, aware of his brother's easiness, trifled with his soft credulity, till his warlike passion should subside. And he, too, as if contending with Fortune whether she should give or he squander most, discovering the mere wish of the queen, who silently entreated it, kindly forgave the payment of this immense sum for ever, thinking it a very great matter that female pride should condescend to ask a favour. The queen was his god-daughter, so he would not bear in mind his wrongs : moreover his disposition was to forgive faults beyond what he ought to have done : he answered all who applied to him exactly as they wished, that he might not send them away sorrowful, and promised to give what was out of his power. By this suavity of disposition, he who ought to have acquired the commendations and the love of his subjects, so excited the contempt of the Normans, that they considered him as of no consequence whatever; for then all the nobility were at variance one with another, plunder was universal, and the commonalty were pillaged. Although the inhabitants laid their injuries before the duke, they gained no kind of redress; for though incensed at first, yet his anger was soon appeased, either by a trifling present or the lapse of time. Roused, however, by the extremity of their distresses, they determined to implore the assistance of king Henry to their suffering country. He, abiding by Cæsar's axiom,[3] "That if justice is ever to be violated, it ought to be violated in favour of the citizens, but

---

[1] Sibilla duchess of Normandy died by poison, according to Ordericus Vitalis, and the Continuator of William of Jumiéges. Malmesbury's account does not appear to be supported by any contemporary testimony.

[2] Normandy was only mortgaged for ten thousand marks. See § 274, 318.

[3] Cicero de Offic. III. But Malmesbury seems to have thought it necessary to soften it; as Cæsar's axiom says, "for the sake of power."

that you must be observant of duty in other points," transported his forces several times into Normandy to succour expiring justice, and at last was successful enough to subjugate the whole country, with the exception of Rouen, Falaise, and Caen. Robert was now reduced so low, as to wander, hardly to be recognised, through these towns, obtaining a precarious subsistence from the inhabitants. Disgusted at this, the people of Caen did not long regard their fidelity, but sending messengers to the king, they closed the gates of their city with locks and bolts. Robert learning this, and wishing to escape, was hardly allowed to depart; his attendant, with the furniture of his chamber, being detained. Thence flying to Rouen, he had a conference with his lord, the king of France, and his relation, the earl of Flanders, on the subject of assistance; but obtaining none, he determined, as his last resource, to risk a general action. Fortune being unfavourable to him, he was taken prisoner, and was kept, by the laudable affection of his brother, in free custody till the day of his death; for he endured no evil but solitude, if that can be called solitude where, by the attention of his keepers, he was provided with abundance both of amusement and of food. He was confined, however, till he had survived all his companions in the crusade, nor was he liberated to the day of his death. He was so eloquent in his native tongue, that none could be a more pleasant companion; in other men's affairs no man could counsel better, in military skill equal to any, yet, through the easiness of his disposition was he ever esteemed unfit to have the management of the state. But since I have already said all that I knew of Hugh the Great, and of the counts of Blois and of Flanders, I think I may, very properly, here conclude my fourth book.

PREFACE TO BOOK V.

WE have now come in the due course of events to the times of king Henry, to transmit whose actions to posterity requires an abler hand than ours. For, were only those particulars recorded which have reached our knowledge, they would weary the most eloquent, and might overload a library. Who, then, will attempt to unfold in detail all his profound counsels, all his royal achievements? These are matters too deep for me, and require more leisure than I possess. Scarcely Cicero himself, whose eloquence is venerated by all the western world, would attempt it in prose; and in verse not even a rival of the Mantuan Bard. In addition to this, it is to be observed, that while I, who am a man of retired habits, and far from the secrets of a court, withhold my assent from doubtful relators, being ignorant of his greater achievements, I touch only on a few events. Wherefore it is to be feared, that where my information falls beneath my wishes, the hero, many of whose exploits I omit, may appear to suffer. However, for this, if it be a fault, I shall have a good excuse with him who bears in mind that I could not be acquainted with the whole of his transactions, nor ought I to relate even all that I did know : the insignificance of my condition effects the one ; the disgust of my readers would be excited by the other. This fifth book, then, will display some few of his deeds, while fame, no doubt, will blazon the rest, and lasting memory transmit them to posterity. Nor will it deviate from the design of the preceding four, but will particularise some things which happened during his time, here and elsewhere, which perchance are either unrecorded, or unknown to many; they will occupy, indeed, a considerable portion of the volume, while I must claim the usual indulgence for long digressions as well in this as in the others.

THE FIFTH BOOK OF WILLIAM OF MALMESBURY'S HISTORY OF THE KINGS OF ENGLAND.

BOOK V.

Of Henry the First.

§ 390. HENRY, the youngest son of William the Great, was born[1] in England, the third year after his father's arrival ; a child, even at that time, fondly cherished by the joint good wishes of all, as being the only one of William's sons born in royalty, and to whom the kingdom seemed to pertain. The early years of instruction he passed in liberal arts, and so thoroughly imbibed the sweets of learning that no warlike commotions, no pressure of business, could ever erase them from his noble mind. Although he neither read much openly, nor displayed his attainments except sparingly, yet his learning, (as I can affirm,) though obtained by snatches, assisted him much in the science of governing; according to that saying of Plato, "Happy would be the commonwealth, if philosophers were kings, or kings would be philosophers." Thus, not slightly imbued with philosophy, he learnt by degrees, and in process of time, how to restrain the people with lenity, and never to suffer his soldiers to act but where he saw a pressing emergency. In this manner, by learning, he trained his early years to the hope of the kingdom ; and often, in his father's hearing, made use of the proverb, that "An illiterate king is a crowned ass." They relate, too, that his father, observing his disposition, never omitted any means of cherishing his lively prudence ; and that once, when he had been ill-used by one of his brothers, and was in tears, he spirited him up by saying, "Weep not, my boy, you too will be a king."

§ 391. In the twenty-first year,[2] then, of his father's reign, when

---

[1] Henry was born in 1068, not in 1070, as stated by Ordericus Vitalis. (Annal. Burton. apud Fell. inter Rer. Anglic. Script. V. p. 246.)

[2] William the Conqueror was abroad at Pentecost in the twenty-first year of his reign, A.D. 1087. Henry undoubtedly received knighthood in the year 1806, being the twentieth year after his father's reign.

he was nineteen years of age, he was knighted by him at Westminster during Pentecost; and then accompanying him to Normandy, was, shortly after, present at his funeral; the other brothers departing whither their hopes led them, as my former [1] narrative has related. Wherefore, supported by the blessing of his father, together with his maternal inheritance and immense treasures, he paid little regard to the haughtiness of his brothers, assisting or opposing each of them according to their merits. More attached, however, to Robert, by reason of his mildness, he took every means of correcting his lenity by his own severity. Robert, on the other hand, through blameable credulity, trusting to tale-bearers, injured his innocent brother in a way which it may not be irrelevant briefly to relate.

§ 392. At the time when the nobility of England were rebelling against William the Second, while Robert was waiting a wind to sail over from Normandy, Henry had, by his command, departed into Brittany. Then, eagerly seizing the opportunity, he expended on his troops all the large sum of money, amounting to three thousand marks, which had been bequeathed to the young man by the will of his father. Henry, on his return, though perhaps indignant at this, yet observed a cautious silence on the subject. However, hearing of the restoration of peace in England, the service was ended, and they laid aside their arms. The earl retired to his own territories; Henry to those which his brother had either given or promised to give him. Indeed he placed his promises to account, retaining the tower of Rouen under fealty to Robert. But, by the accusation of some infamous persons, his fidelity proved disadvantageous to him; and, for no fault on his part, Henry was, in this very place, detained in free custody, lest he should escape the vigilance of his keepers. Released at the expiration of half-a-year, on the invitation of his brother William he offered him his services; but he, remunerating the young man no better, put him off, though in distress, with empty promises for more than a year. Wherefore, Robert, by his messengers, offering reparation for what had been done, he came to Normandy, having experienced the treachery of both his brothers. For the king, angry at his departure, had in vain commanded him to be detained; and the earl, swayed by the arts of his accusers, had changed his intention; so that, when lured to him by soothing measures, he would not easily suffer him to depart. But he, escaping every danger by the providence of God and his own cautious expedition, compelled his brother gladly to accede to peace, by seizing Avranches and some other castles. Soon after, William coming into Normandy to revenge himself on his brother Robert, Henry manifested his regard to the earl at Rouen. Finally, the king's party, coming thither in the day-time, he spiritedly expelled them, when already, through the treachery of the citizens, they had overrun the whole city, sending a message to the earl to oppose them in front, while he pressed upon their rear. In consequence of this transaction one Conan was accused of treachery to the earl, who designed

[1] See § 283.

to cast him into chains, supposing that no greater calamity could be inflicted on the wretch, than dooming him to drag out an hated existence in prison. This Conan, then, Henry requested to have committed to his care, which being granted he led him to the top of the tower at Rouen, and ordering him carefully to survey the surrounding territory from the heights of the citadel, ironically declaring it should all be his, he thrust him suddenly off the ramparts into the Seine below, protesting to his companions, who at the same time assisted him, that no respite was due to a traitor, that the injuries of a stranger might be endured in some manner or other; but that the punishment of a man who turned traitor after swearing fealty and doing homage, should never be deferred. This action weighed little with Robert, who was a man of changeable disposition, for he immediately became ungrateful, and compelled his deserving brother to retire from the city. This was the period in which, as has been before mentioned,[1] Henry, as well for his security as for his fame, made a stand against both Robert and William at Mount St. Michael. Thus, though he had been faithful and serviceable to either brother, they, vouchsafing no establishment to the young man, trained him up, as he grew in years, to greater prudence, from the scantiness of his means.

§ 393. But on the violent death of king William, as before related,[2] after the solemnization of the royal funeral, he was elected king; though some trifling dissensions had first arisen among the nobility, which were allayed chiefly through the exertions of Henry earl of Warwick, a man of unblemished integrity, with whom he had long been in the strictest intimacy. He immediately promulgated an edict[3] throughout England, annulling the illegal ordinances of his brother and of Ralph; he remitted taxes, released prisoners, drove the flagitious from court, restored the nightly use of lights within the palace, which had been omitted in his brother's time, and renewed the operation of the ancient laws, confirming them with his own oath, and that of the nobility, that they might not be eluded. A joyful day then seemed to dawn on the people, when the light of fair promise shone forth, after such repeated clouds of distress. And that nothing might be wanting to the universal joy, Ralph, that sink of iniquity, was cast into the gloom of a prison,[4] and speedy messengers were despatched to recall Anselm. Wherefore, all vying in joyous acclamation, Henry was crowned king at London, on the nones of August [Aug. 5], four days after his brother's death. These acts were the more sedulously performed, lest the nobility should be induced to repent their choice, as a rumour prevailed that Robert earl of Normandy, returning from Apulia, was just on the point of arriving. Soon after, his friends, and particularly the bishops, persuading him to give up meretricious pleasures and take a lawful wife, he married,[5] on St. Martin's-day [11 Nov.],

---

[1] See § 308.   [2] See § 333.

[3] See Thorpe's Ancient Laws and Institutes of England, i. 497. 8vo. edit.

[4] Ralph Flambard, bishop of Durham, was confined in the Tower of London on the 14th of Sept. 1100, and escaped 4th of Feb. 1101.

[5] Matilda having taken the veil, though only for a purpose, scruples were raised as to the propriety of her entering the marriage state: a synod was therefore

Matilda, daughter of Malcolm king of Scotland, to whom he had long been greatly attached, little regarding the marriage portion, provided he could possess her whom he so ardently desired. For though she was of noble descent, being grand-niece of king Edward, by his brother Edmund, yet she possessed but little fortune, being an orphan, destitute of both parents; of her there will be more ample matter of relation hereafter.

§ 394. In the meantime, Robert, arriving in Normandy, recovered his earldom without any opposition; on hearing which, almost all the nobility of this country violated the fealty they had sworn to the king : some without any cause ; some feigning slight pretences, because he would not readily give them such lands as they coveted. Robert Fitz-Haimon, and Richard de Rivers, and Roger Bigod, and Robert count of Meulan, with his brother Henry, alone declared on the side of justice. But all the others either secretly sent for Robert to make him king, or openly branded their lord with sarcasms ; calling him Godric,[1] and his consort, Godgiva. Henry heard these taunts, and, with an angry grin, deferring his anger, he repressed the contemptuous expressions cast on him by the madness of fools, by a studied silence ; a calm dissembler of hatred, but, in due season, a fierce avenger. This tempest of the times was increased by the subtlety of Ralph. For, concerting with his butler, he procured a rope to be sent him. The servant who was water-bearer, (alas! what treachery) carried him a very long one in a cask; by which he descended from the wall, no one regarding whether he strained his arms, or hurt his hands. Escaping thence to Normandy, he stimulated the earl, already indignant and ripe for war, to come to England without a moment's delay.

§ 395. In the second year, then, of Henry's reign, in the month of August, arriving at Portsmouth, he landed, and divided and posted his forces over the whole district. The king was not indolent, but collected an innumerable army over against him, with which, if necessary, to assert his dignity. For, though the nobility deserted him, yet was his party strong ; being espoused by archbishop Anselm, with his brother bishops, and all the English. In consequence, grateful to the inhabitants for their fidelity, and anxious for their safety, he frequently went through the ranks, instructing them how to elude the ferocity of the cavalry by opposing their shields, and how to return their strokes : by this he made them perfectly fearless of the Normans, and ask to be led out to battle. Men, however, of sounder counsel interfering, who observed, that the laws of natural affection must be violated should brothers meet in battle, they turned their minds to peace ; reflecting, that if one fell, the other would be the weaker, as there was no other surviving brother. Besides, a promise of three thousand marks deceived the easy credulity of the earl ; who imagined that, when he had disbanded his army, he might gratify his inclinations with

called at Lambeth by archbishop Anselm, and it was there determined that, not having voluntarily become a nun, she might marry according to the law of God. See Eadmer, pp. 56, 57.

[1] These appellations seem intended as sneers at the regular life of Henry and his queen. Godric, implies God's kingdom or government.

such an immense sum of money: which, he, anxious to gratify the queen, the very next year unhesitatingly released at her request.

§ 396. The following year Robert de Belesme, eldest son of Roger de Montgomery, rebelled, fortifying the castles of Bridgenorth and Arundel against the king; carrying thither corn from all the district round Shrewsbury, and every necessary which war requires. The castle of Shrewsbury, too, joined the rebellion, the Welsh being inclined to evil on every occasion. In consequence, the king, firm in mind and bearing down every adverse circumstance by valour, collecting an army, laid siege to Bridgenorth, whence Robert had already retired to Arundel; presuming from the plenty of provision and the courage of the soldiers, that the place was abundantly secure: but, after a few days, the townsmen, impelled by remorse of conscience and by the bravery of the king's army, surrendered: on learning which, Arundel took a humbler tone; and submitted to the king, with this remarkable condition; that its lord, without personal injury, should be suffered to retire to Normandy. Moreover, the people of Shrewsbury sent the keys of the castle to the king by Ralph, at that time abbot of Sees, and afterwards archbishop of Canterbury, as tokens of present submission, and pledges of their future obedience. Thus, this fire of dissension, which was expected to become excessive, wasted to ashes in the course of very few days; and the avidity of the revolters, perpetually panting after innovation, was repressed. Robert, with his brothers, Ernulph, who had obtained the surname of his father, and Roger the Poictevin, so called because he had married his wife from that country, abjured England for ever; but the strictness of this oath was qualified with a proviso, "unless he should satisfy the king on some future occasion, by his obedient conduct."

§ 397. The torch of war now lighted up in Normandy, receiving fresh fuel by the arrival of the traitors, blazed forth and seized every thing within its reach. Normandy, indeed, though not very wide in its extent, is a convenient and patient fosterer of the abandoned. Wherefore, for a long time, she well endures intestine broils; and on the restoration of peace, becomes more flourishing than before; at her pleasure ejecting her disturbers, who feel themselves no longer safe in the province, by the open passes into France. Whereas England does not long endure the turbulent; but when once received to her bosom, either surrenders, or puts them to death; neither, when laid waste by tumult, does she again soon recover herself. The earl of Belesme, then, arriving in Normandy, had, both at that time and afterwards, accomplices in his malignity, and lest this should seem too little, inciters also. Among others was William earl of Moretol, the son of Robert, the king's uncle. He, from a boy, had been envious of Henry's fame, and had, more especially on the arrival of the Norman, manifested his evil disposition: for not content with the two earldoms, of Moretal in Normandy and Cornwall in England, he demanded from the king the earldom of Kent, which Odo his uncle had held; so troublesome and presumptuous was he, that, with shameless arrogance, he vowed, that he would not put on his cloak till he could procure the inheritance derived to him from his uncle; for such was his expression. But even then the king, with his characteristic circumspection, beguiled him by the subtlety of an ambiguous answer. The tumult, however, being allayed and tranquillity restored, he not only refused assent to his demand, but persisted in holding what he unjustly retained; though he did it with moderation, and under cover of legal proceedings, that none of his actions might appear illegal, or contrary to equity. William, ousted by the sentence of the law, retired, indignant and furious, into Normandy. Here, in addition to his fruitless attacks upon the royal castles, he assailed Richard earl of Chester, the son of Hugh; invading, plundering, and destroying some places which formed part of his possessions: the earl himself being at that time a minor, and under the protection and guardianship of the king.

§ 398. These two persons, then, the leaders of faction and fomenters of rebellion, in conjunction with others whom I am ashamed to particularise, harassed the country far and wide with their devastations. Complaints from the suffering inhabitants on the subject of their injuries, though frequent, were lavished upon the earl in vain: he was moved by them, it is true; but fearing, on his own account, lest they should disturb his ease if offended, he dissembled his feelings.[1] King Henry, however, felt deeply for his brother's infamy, carried to the highest pitch by the sufferings of the country: aware, that it was the extreme of cruelty, and far from a good king's duty, to suffer abandoned men to riot on the property of the poor. In consequence, he once admonished his brother, whom he had sent for into England, with fair words; but afterwards, arriving in Normandy, he severely reminded him, more than once, by arms, to act the prince rather than the monk. He also despoiled William, the instigator of these troubles, of everything he had in England; razing his castles to the ground. But when the king could, even thus, make no progress towards peace, he deliberated long and anxiously, whether, regardless of fraternal affection, he should rescue the country from danger, or through blind regard suffer it to continue in jeopardy. And indeed the common weal, and sense of right, would have yielded to motives of private affection, had not pope Paschal, as it is said,[2] urged him, when hesitating, to the business by his letters: averring, with his powerful eloquence, that it would not be a civil war, but a signal benefit to a noble country. In consequence, passing over,[3] he, in

---

[1] Compare Malm. de Gestis Pontific. p. 227. Edit. Francof. 1601.'

[2] There is no vestige of this exhortation in any letter of pope Paschal to king Henry now known. Indeed Paschal, writing to archbishop Anselm, enjoins him to effect a reconciliation between the king and his brother. He writes: "Significamus dilectioni tuæ, Normanorum comitem questum apud nos esse adversus Anglorum regem, quia et, fracto sacramento quod ei pro eodem regno acquirendo fecerat, regnum invaserit. Et nosti quia eidem comiti debemus auxilium, pro laboribus quos in Asianæ ecclesiæ liberatione laboravit," &c. Anselmi Op. p. 382, col. 2, ed. fol. Par. 1721.

[3] Orderic. Vital. p. 815, relates a circumstance highly indicative of the troubled state of Normandy. Henry, on his arrival, was immediately welcomed by Serlo bishop of Sees; who, on conducting him into the church, pointed out the area nearly filled with boxes and packages brought thither by the inhabitants, for security from plunderers.

a short time, took, or more properly speaking, received, the whole
of Normandy; all flocking to his dominion, that he might provide,
by his transcendent power, for the good of the exhausted province.
Yet he achieved not this signal conquest without bloodshed; but
lost many of his dearest associates. Among these was Roger of
Gloucester, a tried soldier, who was struck on the head by a bolt
from a cross-bow, at the siege of Falaise; and Robert Fitz-
Haimon,[1] who receiving a blow on the temple with a lance, and
losing his faculties, survived a considerable time, almost in a state
of idiocy. They relate, that he was thus deservedly punished,
because, for the sake of liberating him, king Henry had consumed
the city of Baieux, together with the principal church, with fire.
Still, however, as we hope, they both atoned for it: for the king
munificently repaired the damage of that church: and it is not easy
to relate, how much Robert enriched, by his favour, the monastery
of Tewkesbury; where the splendour of the edifice, and the kindness of the monks, attract the eyes, and captivate the minds of the
visitors. Fortune, however, to make up for the loss of these
persons, put a finishing hand to the war, when at its height, and,
with little labour, gave his brother, when opposing him with no
despicable force, together with William earl of Moretol, and Robert
de Belesme, into his power. This battle was fought at Tenerchebrei, a
castle of the earl of Moretol's, on Saturday,[2] the Vigil of St. Michael.
It was the same day on which, about forty years before, William
had first landed at Hastings: perhaps by the wise dispensation of
God, that Normandy should be subjected to England on the same
day that the Norman power had formerly arrived to subjugate that
kingdom. Here was taken the earl of Moretol, who came thither
to fulfil his promise of strenuous assistance to the townsmen, as
well as in the hope of avenging his injuries: but, made captive,
as I have related, he passed the residue of his life in the gloom of
a prison; meriting some credit from the vivacity of his mind, and
the activity of his youth, but deserving an unhappy end, from his
perfidy. Then, too, Belesme escaped death by flight at the onset;
but when, afterwards, he had irritated the king by secrect faction,
he also was taken; and being involved in the same jeopardy with
the others, he was confined in prison as long as he lived.[3] He
was a man intolerable from the barbarity of his manners, and
inexorable to the faults of others; remarkable besides for cruelty;
and, among other instances, on account of some trifling fault of its
father, he blinded his godchild, who was his hostage, tearing out
the little wretch's eyes with his accursed nails: full of cunning and
dissimulation, he used to deceive the credulous by the serenity of
his countenance and the affability of his speech; though the same
means terrified those who were acquainted with his malignity; as

[1] His daughter Mabil became the wife of Robert earl of Gloucester, to whom
Malmesbury dedicated this work.
[2] Michaelmas-eve in 1106 fell on Friday.
[3] Robert de Belesme was seized by order of king Henry in 1112, having come
to him in Normandy as ambassador from the king of France to treat of peace.
Robert was in the following year sent over to England, and confined in Wareham
castle until his death.

there was no greater proof of impending mischief than his pretended mildness of address.

§ 399. The king, thus splendidly successful, returned triumphant to his kingdom, having established such peace in Normandy as it had never known before ; and such as even his father himself, with all his mighty pomp of words and actions, had never been able to accomplish. Rivalling his father also, in other respects, he restrained, by edict,[1] the exactions of the courtiers, thefts, and the violation of women ; commanding the delinquents to be deprived of sight, and castrated. He also displayed singular diligence against the mintmasters, commonly called moneyers; suffering no counterfeiter, who had been convicted of deluding the ignorant by the practice of his roguery, to escape, without losing his hand.

§ 400. Adopting the custom of his brother, he soothed the Scottish kings by his affability : for William made Duncan, the illegitimate son of Malcolm, a knight ; and on the death of his father, appointed him king of Scotland. When Duncan was murdered by the wickedness of his uncle Donald, he promoted Edgar to the kingdom ; the above-mentioned Donald being dispatched by the contrivance of David, the youngest brother, and the power of William. On Edgar's death, Henry bound Alexander, his successor, with the tie of affinity, giving him his illegitimate daughter in marriage, by whom he had no issue, that I know of ; and when she died, he did not much lament her loss : for there was, as they affirm, some defect about the lady, either in correctness of manners, or elegance of person. Alexander resting with his ancestors, David, the youngest of Malcolm's sons, whom the king had made an earl and honoured with the marriage of a woman of quality, ascended the throne of Scotland ;—a youth more courtly than the rest, and who, polished from a boy by intercourse and familiarity with us, had rubbed off all the rust of Scottish barbarism. Finally, when he obtained the kingdom, he released from the payment of taxes, for three years, all such of his countrymen as would pay more attention to their dwellings, dress more elegantly, and feed more nicely. No history has ever recorded three kings, and at the same time brothers, who were of equal sanctity, or savoured so much of their mother's piety; for independently of their abstemiousness, their extensive charity, and their frequency in prayer, they so completely subdued the domestic vice of kings, that no report even prevailed, that any entered their bed except their legitimate wives, or that either of them had ever been guilty of any unlawful intercourse. Edmund was the only degenerate son of Margaret, who, partaking in his uncle Donald's crime, and bargaining for half his kingdom, had been accessory to his brother's death. But being taken, and doomed to perpetual imprisonment, he sincerely repented ; and, on his near approach to death, ordered himself to be buried in his chains : confessing that he suffered deservedly for the crime of fratricide.

§ 401. The Welsh, perpetually rebelling, were subjugated in

---

[1] See his Laws in "Ancient Laws and Institutes of England," i. 497, edited by Thorpe, edit. 8vo. 1840.

repeated expeditions by king Henry, who, relying on a prudent expedient to quell their tumults, transported thither all the Flemings then resident in England. For that country contained such numbers of these people, who, in the time of his father, had come over from national relationship to his mother, that, from their numbers, they appeared burdensome to the kingdom: in consequence, he settled them, with all their property and connexions, at Ross, a Welsh province, as in a common receptacle, both for the purpose of cleansing the kingdom and repressing the brutal temerity of the enemy. Still, however, he did not neglect leading his expeditions thither, as circumstances required : in one of which being privily aimed at with an arrow from a distance, though by whose audacity is unknown, he opportunely and fortunately escaped, thanks to the good mail of his hauberk and the counsel of God, which at the same time frustrated this treachery. The man who shot the arrow was not then discovered, nor could he ever after be detected ; although the king immediately declared that it was not discharged by a Welshman, but by a subject; swearing to it by the death of our Lord, which was his customary oath, when moved either by excess of anger or the importance of the occasion ; for at that very time the army was marching cautiously and slowly upon its own ground, not in an enemy's territory, and therefore nothing less was to be expected than an hostile attack. But, nevertheless, he desisted not from his purpose, through fear of intestine danger, until the Welsh appeased his regal wrath, by giving the sons of their nobility as hostages, together with some money and much of their substance.

§ 402. By dint of gold, too, he brought the inhabitants of Brittany to his views, whom, when a young man, he had had as neighbours to his castles of Danfront and Mount St. Michael. These are a race of people, poor at home, and seeking abroad the support of a toilsome life from foreign hire : regardless of right and of affinity, they decline not even civil war, provided they are paid for it ; and, in proportion to the remuneration, are ready to enter any service that may be offered. Aware of this custom, if at any time he had need of stipendiary troops, he used to lavish money on these Bretons ; thereby hiring the faith of a faithless nation.

§ 403. In the beginning of his reign he offended Robert, earl of Flanders, from the following cause : Baldwin the Elder, the grandfather of this Robert, had powerfully assisted William, when going to England, by the wisdom of his counsels, for which he was famed, and by a supply of soldiers. William had frequently made splendid returns for this ; giving, every year, as they report, three hundred[1] marks of silver to his father-in-law, on account of his fidelity and affinity. This munificence was not diminished towards his son Baldwin ; though it was dropped through the evil disposition of Robert le Frison, as my history has already recorded.[2] Moreover, this Robert, the son of Frison, easily obtained the omitted largess from William the Second ; because the one alleged his relationship,

---

[1] It appears from two charters printed in Rymer's Fœdera, i. 6, 7, that Henry agreed to pay a pension of four hundred marks annually to Robert earl of Flanders for the service of one thousand knights.   [2] See § 257.

and the other possessed a boundless spirit in squandering money. But Henry giving the business deeper consideration, as a man who never desired to obtain money improperly, nor ever wantonly exhausted it when acquired, gave the following reply to Robert, on his return from Jerusalem, when imperiously making a demand, as it were, of three hundred marks of silver : He said, that the kings of England were not accustomed to pay tribute to the Flemings ; and that he would not tarnish the liberty of his ancestors by the stain of his cowardice ; therefore, if he would trust to his generosity, he would willingly give him, as a kinsman and as a friend, whatever circumstances would permit ; but if he thought proper to persist in his demand, he should refuse it altogether. Confuted by this reasoning, he, for a long time, cherished his indignation against Henry : but getting little or nothing by his enmity, he bent his mind to milder measures ; having discovered that the king might be wrought upon by entreaty, but not by imperious insolence. But now, the change of times had given his son, Baldwin, matter of offence against Henry : for wishing to place William, the son of Robert the Norman,[1] in his inheritance, he voluntarily busied himself in the affairs of others, and frequently made unexpected attacks upon the king's castles in Normandy : he threatened extreme trouble to the country, had the fates permitted : but engaging at Arques[2] with a larger party of soldiers than he had apprehended, he met his death ; for his helmet being battered with repeated strokes, he received an injury in his brain. They relate, that his disorder was increased from having that day eaten garlic with goose ; and that he did not even abstain from carnal intercourse at night. Here let posterity contemplate a noble specimen of royal attention : for the king sent a most skilful physician to the patient, bewailing, as we may believe, that one should perish by disease, whom, through admiration of his valour, he had rather seen survive. Charles, his successor, never annoyed the king ; and first, with a doubtful, but afterwards, a formal treaty, embraced his friendship.

§ 404. Philip, king of France, was neither friendly nor hostile to our king, being more intent on gluttony than business ; neither were his dominions situated in the vicinity of Henry's castles ; for the few which he possessed at that time in Normandy were nearer to Brittany than France. Besides, as I have said before,[3] Philip growing in years, was oppressed by lust, and, allured by the beauty of the countess of Anjou,[4] was enslaved to illicit passion for her. In consequence of his being excommunicated by the pope, no divine service could be celebrated in the town where he resided ; but on his departure the chiming of the bells resounded on all

---

[1] William, surnamed Cliton, son of Robert duke of Normandy and Sibilla do Conversano, succeeded to the earldom of Flanders upon the death of Charles le Bon, A.D. 1127.

[2] Historians differ both as to the place where Baldwin was wounded, and where he died, and even as to the time of his death ; but it seems that he passed the last ten months of his life in the monastery of St. Bertin, where he was buried. Meyerus (Ann. Fland. lib. iv. ad an. 1119), cited in Bouquet, xiii. 14, gives an account of Baldwin. [3] See § 235.

[4] Bertrade, fourth wife of Foulques IV. earl of Anjou.

sides, at which he expressed his stupid folly by laughter, saying, "You hear, my fair, how they drive us away." He was held in such contempt by all the bishops of his kingdom, that no one, except William, archbishop of Rouen,[1] would marry them : the rashness of which deed he atoned for by being many years interdicted, and was with difficulty, at last, restored to apostolical communion by archbishop Anselm. In the meanwhile, no lapse of time could give satiety to Philip's mad excess, except that in his last days, being seized with sickness, he took the monastic habit at Flory.[2] She acted with better grace and better success, as she took the veil at Fontevrault, while yet possessed of strength and health, and undiminished beauty; she soon afterwards departed this life ; God, perhaps, foreseeing that the frame of a delicate woman could not endure the austerities of a nunnery.

§ 405. Louis, the son of Philip, was very changeable ; firmly attached to neither party. At first, extremely indignant against Robert, he instigated Henry to seize Normandy ; seduced by what had been plundered from the English, and the vast wealth of the king. Not, indeed, that the one offered it, but the other invited him, exhorting him, of his own accord, not to suffer the nerves of that once most flourishing country to be crippled by his forbearance. But an enmity afterwards arose between them, on account of Thibaut, earl of Blois, son of Stephen, who fell at Ramula, by Adala, daughter of William the Great. For a considerable time messengers on the part of our king were frequently despatched, entreating that Louis would condescend to satisfy Thibaut. But he paying little regard to entreaties, caused Thibaut to be excommunicated by the pope, as arrogant and a rebel to God ; who, in addition to the austerity of his manners, which seemed intolerable to all, was represented as depriving his lord of his hereditary possessions. Their quarrel being thus of long continuance, when, each swollen with pride, neither would veil his consequence to the other, Louis entered Normandy, devastating everything with overbearing violence. These things were reported to the king, who shut himself up in Rouen until the common soldiers infested his ears by saying,—That he ought to allow Louis to be driven back ; a man who formerly kept his bed through corpulency, but was now, by Henry's forbearance, loading the very air with threats. The king, mindful of his father's example, rather preferred crushing the folly of the Frenchman by procrastination, than repelling it by force. Moreover he kindly soothed his soldiers by addressing them to the following effect, That they ought not to wonder if he avoided lavishing the blood of those whom he had proved to be faithful by repeated trials : that it would be impious in achieving power to himself, to glory in the deaths of those persons who had devoted their lives to voluntary conflicts for his safety ; that they

[1] Ordericus Vitalis attributes this act to Odo bishop of Bayeux; but pope Urban II. in his epistle to Raynald archbishop of Rheims, ascribes it to Ursio bishop of Senlis.

[2] Although king Philippe a few years before his death entertained some notion of embracing a monastic life, as is seen in the epistle written to him by Hugh abbot of Cluni, yet it appears that he never carried his design into effect.

were the adopted of his kingdom, the foster-children of his affection, wherefore he was anxious to follow the example of a good king, and by his own moderation to check the impetuosity of those whom he saw so ready to die for him. At last, when he beheld his forbearance wrongly interpreted, and denominated cowardice, insomuch that Louis burnt and plundered within four miles of Rouen; he called up the powers of his soul with greater effort, and arraying his troops, gloriously conquered, compensating his past forbearance by a sanguinary victory. But, however, soon afterwards, peace was concluded, because there is a change in all things; and money, which is capable of persuading what it lists, extenuates every injury. In consequence, William, the son of our king, did homage to the king of France for Normandy, holding that province, in future, by legal right from him. This was the period when the same youth was betrothed to, and married the daughter of Fulk, earl of Anjou; the father prudently aiming, by means of money in one quarter and affinity in the other, at securing his son from any disturbance.

§ 406. At this time, pope Calixtus, of whom I shall relate much hereafter,[1] approached the confines of Normandy; where the king of England, entering into conference[2] with him, compelled the Romans to admire and extol the ingenuity of the Normans. For he had come, as was reported, ill-disposed towards Henry, intending severely to expostulate with him, for keeping his brother, the pilgrim of the Holy Sepulchre, in confinement. But being pressed by the king's answer, which was specious, and by his plausible arguments, he had little to reply. For even common-place topics may avail much, through eloquence of speech; and, more especially that oratory cannot be despised which is seasoned with valuable presents. And that nothing might be wanting to the aggregate of glory, he provided some youths of noble family, the sons of the earl of Meulant, to dispute with the cardinals in logic. To whose inextricable sophisms, when, from the liveliness of their arguments they could make no resistance, the cardinals were not ashamed to confess that the western climes flourished with greater literary eminence than they had ever heard of or imagined, while yet in their own country. Wherefore, the issue of this conference was, that the pope declared that nothing could be more just than the king of England's cause, more conspicuous than his prudence, more copious than his eloquence.

§ 407. The father of these youths was Robert, earl of Meulant, as I observed, the son of Roger de Beaumont, who built the monastery of Preaux in Normandy, a man of primitive simplicity and sincerity, who, being frequently invited by William the First to come to England, and receive, as a recompense, whatever possessions he chose, always declined, saying that he wished to cultivate the inheritance of his forefathers, rather than covet or invade foreign possessions which did not belong to him. He had two sons, Robert, of whom we are speaking, and Henry. Henry earl of Warwick, a

---

[1] See § 432, seqq.
[2] Pope Calixtus met King Henry at Gisors, on his return from the council at Rheims, held in Oct. 1119; see Jaffé, p. 531.

man of sweet and placid disposition, passed and ended his days in occupations congenial to his habits. The other, more shrewd, and of a subtler character, in addition to his paternal inheritance in Normandy and large estates in England, purchased from the king of France a castle called Meulant, which Hugh the son of Galeran, his mother's brother, had held. Conducted gradually by budding hope towards fame in the time of the former kings, he attained to its full bloom in Henry's days, and his advice was regarded as though the oracle of God had been consulted; indeed he was deservedly esteemed to have obtained it, as he was of ripe age to counsel; the persuader of peace, the dissuader of strife, and capable by his cogent eloquence of very speedily bringing about whatever he desired. He possessed such mighty influence in England, as to change by his single example the long-established modes of dress and of diet. Finally, the custom of one meal a day is observed[1] in the palaces of all the nobility through his means, which he, adopting from Alexis, emperor of Constantinople, on the score of his health, spread, as I have observed, among the rest by his example. He is blamed, as having done, and taught others to do this, more through want of liberality than any fear of surfeit or indigestion, but undeservedly; since no one, it is said, was more lavish in entertainments to others, or more moderate in himself. In law, he was the supporter of justice; in war, the insurer of victory; urging his lord the king to enforce the rigour of the statutes; himself not only following the existing, but proposing new ones; free himself from treachery towards the king, he was the avenger of it in others.[2]

§ 408. Besides this personage, king Henry had among his counsellors, Roger[3] bishop of Salisbury, on whose advice he principally relied; for, before his accession, he had made him regulator of his household; and, on becoming king, having had proof of his abilities, first made him his chancellor, and then a bishop. The able discharge of his episcopal functions led to a hope that he might be deserving of a higher office. He therefore committed to his care the administration of the whole kingdom, whether he might be himself resident in England or absent in Normandy. The bishop would have refused to undertake so onerous an office, had not the three archbishops of Canterbury, Anselm, Ralph, and William, and, at last, the pope, enjoined him the duty of obedience. Henry was

---

[1] This practice is referred to by Henry Huntingdon, when speaking of Hardecnut, who had four repasts served up every day, "when in our times, through avarice, or as they pretend through disgust, the great set but one meal a day before their dependents."—H. Hunt. p. 209.

[2] Henry of Huntingdon, in his epistle to Walter (Anglia Sacra, pars ii. p. 695), gives a flattering character of Robert. Ordericus Vitalis places his death on the 1st of June, A.D. 1118.

[3] Roger had a church in the neighbourhood of Caen, at the time that Henry was serving under his brother William. Passing that way, he entered in, and requested the priest to say mass. Roger began suddenly, and got through his task so quickly, that the prince's attendants unanimously declared, "no man so fit for chaplain to men of their profession." And when the royal youth said, "Follow me," he adhered as closely to him, as Peter did to his heavenly Lord uttering a similar command: for Peter, leaving his vessel, followed the King of kings; he, leaving his church, followed the prince; and, appointed chaplain to himself, and his troops, became a "blind guide to the blind." See G. Neubrig. i. 6.

extremely eager to effect this, aware that Roger would faithfully perform everything for his advantage. Nor did he deceive the royal expectation; but conducted himself with so much integrity and diligence, that not a spark of envy was kindled against him. Moreover, the king was frequently detained in Normandy, sometimes for three, sometimes four years, and sometimes for a longer period; and on his return to his kingdom, he laid it to the credit of his justiciar's discretion that he found little or nothing to distress him. Amid all these affairs, he did not neglect his ecclesiastical duties, but daily diligently transacted them in the morning, that he might be more ready and undisturbed for other business. He was a prelate of a great mind, and spared no expense towards completing his designs, especially in buildings, as may be seen in many places, but more particularly at Salisbury and at Malmesbury. For there he erected extensive edifices, at vast cost, and with surpassing beauty; the courses of stone being so correctly laid, that the line of juncture escapes the eye, and leads one to imagine that the whole wall is composed of a single block. He built anew the church of Salisbury, and beautified it in such a manner that it yields to none in England, but surpasses many; so that he had just cause to say, " Lord, I have loved the glory of thy house." [Ps. xxvi. 8.]

§ 409. Murcard king of Ireland, and his successors, whose names have not reached our notice, were so devotedly attached to our Henry, that they wrote no letters, but what tended to soothe him, and did nothing but what he commanded, although it may be observed, that Murcard, from some unknown cause, acted for a short time rather superciliously towards the English; but soon after, on the suspension of navigation and of mercantile intercourse, his insolence subsided. For, of what value could Ireland be, if deprived of the merchandise of England? From poverty, or rather from the ignorance of the cultivators, the soil, unproductive of every good, engenders, without the cities, a rustic, filthy swarm of natives; but the English and French inhabit the cities in a greater degree of civilization, through their mercantile traffic. Paul earl of Orkney, though subject by hereditary right to the king of Norway, was so anxious to obtain the king's friendship, that he was perpetually sending him presents; for our king was extremely fond of the wonders of distant countries, begging with great delight, as I have observed, from foreign kings, lions, leopards, lynxes, or camels; animals which England does not produce; and he had a park called Woodstock, in which he used to foster his favourites of this kind. He had placed there also a creature called a porcupine, sent to him by William of Montpellier, of which animal Pliny the elder, in the eighth book of his Natural History, and Isiodorus, on Etymologies, relate, that there is a creature in Africa, which the inhabitants call of the urchin kind, covered with prickly bristles, which it darts at will against the dogs, when pursuing it: the bristles which I have seen are more than a span long, sharp at each extremity, like the quills of a goose where the feather ceases, but rather thicker, and speckled, as it were, with black and white.

§ 410. What more particularly distinguished Henry, was, that though frequently and long absent from his kingdom, on account of the commotions in Normandy, yet he so restrained the rebellious, by the terror of his name, that peace remained undisturbed in England; so that even foreigners willingly resorted thither, as to the only haven of secure tranquillity. Finally, Siward king of Norway, in his early years comparable to the bravest heroes, having entered on a voyage to Jerusalem, and asking the king's permission, wintered in England. After expending vast sums upon the churches, as soon as the western breeze opened the gates of spring to soothe the ocean, he rejoined his fleet, and proceeding to sea, terrified the Balearic isles, which are called Majorca and Minorca, by his arms, leaving them an easier conquest to the before-mentioned William of Montpellier. He thence proceeded to Jerusalem, with all his ships in safety, except one; she, while delaying to loose her cable from shore, was sucked into a tremendous whirlpool, which Paul[1] the historian of Lombardy describes as lying between the coasts of the Seine and Aquitaine, with such a force of water that its dashing may be heard at thirty miles' distance. Arriving at Jerusalem, he, for the advancement of the Christian cause, laid siege to, battered, and subdued the maritime cities of Tyre and Sidon. Changing his route, and entering Constantinople, he fixed a ship, beaked with golden dragons, as a trophy, on the church of Sancta Sophia. His men dying in numbers in this city, he discovered a remedy for the disorder, by making the survivors drink wine more sparingly, and diluted with water: and this with singular sagacity; for pouring wine on the liver of a hog, and finding that it presently was dissolved by the acridity of the liquor, he immediately conjectured that the same effect took place in men; and afterwards, on the dissection of a dead body, he had ocular proof of it. Wherefore the emperor, contemplating his sagacity and courage, which promised something great, was inclined to detain him : but he adroitly deluded the expectation in which he was already devouring the Norwegian gold; for obtaining permission to go to a neighbouring city, he deposited with him the chests of his treasures, filled with lead and sealed up, as pledges of a very speedy return; by which contrivance the emperor was deceived, and the other returned home by land.

§ 411. But that my narrative may return to Henry; he was active in providing what would be beneficial to his empire;[2] firm in defending it; abstinent from war, as far as he could with honour; but, when he had determined no longer to forbear, a most severe

---

[1] Malmesbury seems to imply that the vessel was lost in the Mediterranean; but if so, he misunderstood Paulus Diaconus, who is speaking of the Race of Alderney. V. Paul. Diac. i. 6, ap. Muratori. Rer. Ital. Script. i.

[2] Of Henry's prudent accommodation to the times, a curious anecdote is related by Ordericus Vitalis, p. 815. When Serlo bishop of Sees met him, on his arrival in Normandy, he made a long harangue on the enormities of the times, one of which was, the bushiness of men's beards, which resembled Saracens rather than Christians, and which he supposes they would not clip, lest the stumps should prick their mistresses' faces : another was their long locks. Henry immediately, to show his submission and repentance, submits his bushy honours to the bishop, who, taking a pair of shears from his trunk, trims his majesty, and several of the principal nobility, with his own hands.

requiter of injuries, dissipating every opposing danger by the energy of his courage; constant in enmity, or in affection towards all, giving too much indulgence to the tide of anger in the one, gratifying his royal magnanimity in the other; for he depressed his enemies even to ruin, and exalted his friends and dependents to an enviable condition : for philosophy propounds this to be the first or greatest concern of a good king,

"To spare the suppliant, but depress the proud." [1]

Inflexible in the administration of justice, he ruled the people with moderation, the nobility with condescension. Seeking after robbers and counterfeiters with the greatest diligence, and punishing them when discovered ; neither was he by any means negligent in matters of less importance. When he heard that the tradesmen refused broken money,[2] though of good silver, he commanded the whole of it to be broken or cut in pieces. The measure of his own arm was applied to correct the false ell of the traders, and he made that the standard throughout England. He made a regulation for the followers of his court, at whichever of his possessions he might be resident, stating what they should accept without payment from the country folks, and how much, and at what price, they should purchase, punishing the transgressors by a heavy pecuniary fine, or loss of life. In the beginning of his reign, that he might awe the delinquents by the terror of example, he was more inclined to punish by deprivation of limb, afterwards by fines. Thus, in consequence of the rectitude of his conduct, as is natural to man, he was feared by the nobility and beloved by the common people. If at any time the better sort, regardless of their plighted oath, wandered from the path of fidelity, he immediately recalled them to the straight road, by the wisdom of his plans, and his unceasing exertions, bringing back the refractory to reason by the wounds he inflicted on their bodies. Nor can I easily describe what perpetual labour he employed on such persons, while suffering nothing to go unpunished which the delinquents had committed repugnant to his dignity. Normandy, as I have said before, was the chief source of his wars, in which though principally resident, yet he took especial care for England; none daring to rebel, from the consideration of his courage and of his prudence. Nor indeed was he ever singled out for the attack of treachery, by reason of the rebellion of any of his nobles, through means of his attendants, except once, the author of which was a certain chamberlain, born of a plebeian father, but of distinguished consequence, as being keeper of the king's treasures ; but, detected, and readily confessing his crime, he paid the severe penalty of his perfidy.[3] With this exception,

---

[1] Virg. Æn. vi. 853.

[2] Whilst endeavouring to distinguish good coin from counterfeits, the silver penny was frequently broken, and then refused. Henry's order, therefore, that all should be broken, enabled any one immediately to ascertain the quality, and at the same time left no pretext for refusing it, on account of its being broken money. See Edmer, Hist. Novor. p. 94.

[3] Suger relates that Henry was so terrified by a conspiracy among his chamberlains, that he frequently changed his bed, increased his guards, and caused a shield and a sword to be constantly placed near him at night : and that the person here mentioned, who had been favoured and promoted in an especial manner by

secure during his whole life, the minds of all were restrained by
fear, their conversation by regard for him.

§ 412. He was of middle stature, exceeding the diminutive, but
exceeded by the very tall ; his hair was black, and set back on the
forehead; his eyes mildly bright; his chest brawny; his body fleshy.
He was facetious in proper season, nor did multiplicity of business
cause him to be less pleasant when he mixed in society. Not pug-
nacious, he verified the saying of Scipio Africanus, " My mother
bore me a commander, not a soldier ;" wherefore, inferior in wisdom to no king of modern time, and, as I may almost say, clearly
surpassing all his predecessors in England, he preferred contending
by counsel rather than by the sword : if he could, he conquered
without bloodshed ; if it was unavoidable, with as little as possible.
Throughout his life he was wholly free from impure desires, for, as
we have learnt from those who were well informed, he partook of
female blandishments, not for the gratification of incontinency, but
for the sake of issue ; nor condescended to casual intercourse,
unless where it might produce that effect : in this respect the
master of his natural inclinations, not the passive slave of lust.
He was plain in his diet, rather satisfying the calls of hunger,
than surfeiting himself by variety of delicacies. He never drank
but to allay thirst, execrating the least departure from temperance,.
both in himself and in those about him. His sleep was heavy,.
and interrupted by frequent snoring. His eloquence was rather un-
premeditated than laboured ; not rapid, but deliberate.

§ 413. Of laudable piety towards God, he built monasteries in
England and in Normandy ; but as he has not yet completed them,
I, in the meantime, should suspend my judgment, did not my
affection for the brotherhood at Reading forbid my silence. He
built this monastery between the rivers Kennet and Thames, in a
spot calculated for the reception of almost all who might have
occasion to travel to the more populous cities of England, where
he placed monks of the Cluniac order, who are at this day a noble
pattern of holiness, and an example of unwearied and delightful
hospitality.. Here may be seen what is peculiar to this place ; for
guests arriving every hour, consume more than the inmates themselves. Perhaps some person may call me overhasty and a flatterer,
for so signally celebrating a congregation yet in its infancy, uncon-
scious what future times may produce ; but they, (as I hope,) will
endeavour, by the grace of God, to continue in virtue ; I blush not
at commending men of holiness, and admiring that excellence in
others which I possess not myself. He yielded up the investiture[1]
of the churches to God and St. Peter, after much controversy

the king, was, on his detection, mercifully adjudged to lose only his eyes and his
manhood, when he justly deserved hanging. Vit. Lud. Grossi, ap. Duchesne, iv. 308.

[1] The ceremony of giving possession of lands or offices, was, by the feudal law,
accompanied with the delivery of certain symbols. In conformity to this practice,
princes conferred bishoprics and abbies by the delivery of a crozier and a ring,
which was called their investiture : and as consecration could not take place till
after investiture, this, in fact, implied their appointment also. The popes at length
finding how much such a practice tended to render the clergy dependent on the
temporal power, inhibited their receiving investiture from laymen by the staff
and ring, which were emblems of their spiritual office. The compromise of

between him and archbishop Anselm, scarcely induced, even at last, to consent, through the manifold grace of God, by an inglorious victory over his brother. The tenor of these disputes Edmer has recorded at great length; I, to give a completer knowledge of the matter, shall subjoin the letters of the so-often-mentioned pope Paschal on the subject.

§ 414. "Paschal the bishop to king Henry, greeting. From your letters lately transmitted to us by your servant, our beloved son, William the clerk, we have been certified both of the safety of your person, and of those prosperous successes which the divine favour hath granted you in the subjugation of the adversaries of your kingdom. We have heard, too, that you have had the male issue you so much desired by your noble and religious consort. As we have derived pleasure from this, we think it a good opportunity to impress the commands and will of God more strongly upon you, at a time when you perceive yourself indebted to his kindness for such ample favours. We also are desirous of associating our kindness with the benefits of God towards you; but it is distressing that you should seem to require what we cannot possibly grant. For if we consent, or suffer, that investitures be conferred by your excellence, no doubt it will be to the great detriment both of ourselves and of you. In this matter we wish you to consider, what you lose by not performing, or gain by performing: for we, by such a prohibition, obtain no increase of influence, or patronage, over the churches; nor do we endeavour to take away anything from your just power and right; but only that God's anger may be diminished towards you, and thus every prosperity attend you. God, indeed, hath said, 'Those that honour me, I will honour; and those that despise me shall be lightly esteemed.' [1 Sam. ii. 30.] You will say then, 'It is my right.' No, truly, it is neither an imperial nor royal, but a divine right; it is his only, who has said, 'I am the door.' Wherefore, I entreat for his sake, whose due it is, that you would restore and concede it to Him, to whose goodness you owe what you possess. But why should we oppose your pleasure, or run counter to your good-will, unless we were aware that in consenting to this matter we should oppose the will of God and lose his favour? Why should we deny you anything which might be granted to any man living, when we should receive greater favours from you in return? Consider, my dearest son, whether it be an honour or a disgrace that Anselm, the wisest, and most religious of the Gallican bishops, on this account, fears to dwell with you or to continue in your kingdom. What will those persons think who have hitherto had such favourable accounts of you? What will they say when this gets noised abroad? The very people who, before your face, commend your excess, will, when out of your presence, be the first more loudly to denounce the transaction. Return then to your understanding, my dearest son, we entreat

Henry with Paschal enacted, that in future the king would not confer bishoprics by the staff and ring; but that the bishops should perform the ceremony of homage, in token of submission for their temporals; the election by this means, remaining, nominally, in the chapter, or monastery.

you, for the mercy of God and the love of his Only-begotten Son : recal your pastor, recal your father; and supposing, what we do not imagine, he hath in anything conducted himself harshly towards you, if you will give up the investitures, we will mediate according to your pleasure, as far as God permits; but nevertheless, remove from your person and your kingdom the infamy of such an expulsion. If you do this, even although you should ask very difficult matters of us; still if, with God's permission, we can grant them, you shall certainly obtain them; and we will be careful to entreat the Lord for you, Himself assisting, and will grant indulgence and absolution, as well to your sins as to those of your consort, through the merits of the holy apostles. Moreover, we will, together with you, cherish the son whom you have begotten on your exemplary and noble consort; and who is, as we have heard, named after your excellent father, William, with such anxious care, that whosoever shall injure either you or him, shall be regarded as having done injury to the church of Rome. Given at the palace of Lateran, the ninth of the kalends of December." [Nov. 23, 1103.]

§ 415. "Paschal to Anselm. We have received those most gratifying letters of your affection, written with the pen of charity. In these we recognise the fervency of your devotion; and, considering the strength of your faith, and the earnestness of your pious care, we rejoice; because, by the grace of God, promises neither elevate, nor threats depress you. We lament, however, that after having kindly received our brothers the bishops, ambassadors of the king of England, they should, on their return home, report what we never uttered, or even thought of. For we have heard, that they said, if the king conducted himself well in other respects, we should neither prohibit the investiture of the churches, nor anathematize them when conferred; but that we were unwilling thus to write, lest from this precedent other princes should make demands upon us. Wherefore we call Jesus, who trieth the hearts and reins, as witness to our soul, if ever such an horrid crime even entered our imagination, since we assumed the care of this holy see." And again further on. "If, therefore, a lay hand present the staff, the sign of the shepherd's office, or the ring, the emblem of faith, what have the bishops to do in the church? Moreover, those bishops who have changed the truth into a lie, that truth, which is God, being the criterion, we separate from the favour of St. Peter and our society, until they have made satisfaction to the church of Rome. Such, therefore, as have received investiture,[1] or consecration during the aforesaid truce,[2] we regard as aliens to our communion and to the church." [Dec. 12, 1102.]

§ 416. "Paschal to Anselm. Since the condescension of Almighty God hath inclined the heart of the king of England to

---

[1] The printed copy, as well as such manuscripts as have been consulted, read, "investituras consecrationum:" evidently wrong; the true reading, as appears from Edmer, p. 72, where the whole instrument is inserted, being "investituram vel consecrationem."

[2] On Anselm's return, shortly after Henry's accession, it was agreed that all matters should remain in abeyance, until both parties should have sent messengers to the pope, for his decision on the subject of investitures. See Edmer, p. 56.

obedience to the papal see, we give thanks to the same God of mercies, in whose hand are the hearts of kings. We believe it indeed to have been effected through favour to your charity, and the earnestness of your prayers, that, in this respect, the heavenly mercy hath regarded the people over whom your watchfulness presides. But whereas we so greatly condescend to the king, and those who seem culpable, you must know, that this has been done from kindness and compassion, that we may lift up those that are down. And you, also, reverend and dearest brother in Christ, we release from the prohibition, or as you conceive, excommunication, which, you understand, was denounced against investitures or homage, by our predecessor of holy memory, pope Urban. But do you, by the assistance of God, accept those persons who either have received investitures, or consecrated such as have received them, or have done homage, on making that satisfaction, which we signify to you by our common legates William and Baldwin, faithful and true men, and absolve them by virtue of our authority. These, either consecrate yourself, or command them to be consecrated by such as you choose; unless, perchance, you should discover somewhat in them, on account of which they ought to be deprived of their sacred honours. And if any, hereafter, in addition to the investitures of the churches, shall have accepted prelacies, even though they have done homage to the king, yet let them not, on this account, be denied the office of consecration, until by the grace of Almighty God the heart of the king may be softened, by the dew of your preaching, to omit this. Moreover, against the bishops, who have brought, as you know, a false report of us, our heart is more vehemently moved, because they have not only injured us, but have led astray the minds of many simple people, and impelled the king to set himself in opposition to the benevolence of the papal see: wherefore, by the help of God, we suffer not their crime to pass unpunished; but since the earnestness of our son the king unceasingly intreats for them, you will not deny, even to them, the participation of your communion. Indeed, you will, according to our promise, absolve from their transgressions and from penance the king and his consort, and those nobles, who for this business, together with the king, have by our command been under sentence, whose names you will learn from the information of the aforesaid William. We commit the cause of the bishop of Rouen to your consideration, and we grant to him whatsoever you may allow." [March 23, 1106.]

§ 417. In this manner acted Paschal the supreme pope, anxious for the liberty of the churches of God. The bishops, whom he accuses of falsehood, were Girard, archbishop of York, and Herbert of Norwich; whose errors were discovered by the more veracious legates, William, afterwards bishop of Exeter, and Baldwin, monk of Bec. Anselm [1] the archbishop, was now again, in the time of this king, an exile at Lyons, resident with Hugh, archbishop of that city, when the first letter which I have inserted was despatched; for

---

[1] He had been recalled on the king's accession, but afterwards quitted the kingdom again.

he himself possessed no desire to return, nor did the king, through the multitude of sycophants, suffer his animosity to be appeased. He deferred, therefore, for a long time, recalling him, or complying with the papal admonition; not from desire of power, but through the advice of the nobility; and particularly of the earl of Meulant, who, in this affair, erroneously regarding ancient custom more than a sense of right, alleged that the king's majesty would be much diminished, if, disregarding the usage of his predecessors, he ceased to invest the elected person with the staff and ring. The king, however, considering more attentively what the clear reasoning of the epistles, and the bountiful gift of divine favours plentifully showered down upon him admonished, yielded up the investiture of the ring and staff for ever: retaining only the prerogatives of election and of the first-fruits. A great council, therefore, of bishops, nobles, and abbots, being assembled at London, many points of ecclesiastical and secular business were settled: many differences adjusted. And not long after, five bishops were ordained in Kent on the same day, by archbishop Anselm: William to the see of Winchester: Roger to Salisbury: William to Exeter: Reinald to Hereford: Urban to Glamorgan. In this manner a controversy, agitated by perpetual dissensions, and the cause of many a journey to and from Rome by Anselm, met with a commendable termination.

§ 418. Henry's queen, Matilda, descended from an ancient and illustrious race of kings, daughter of the king of Scotland, as I have said[1] before, had also given her attention to literature, being educated from her infancy among the nuns at Wilton and Romsey. Wherefore, in order to have a colour for refusing an ignoble alliance, which was more than once offered by her father, she wore the garb indicative of the holy profession. This, when the king was about to advance her to his bed, became matter of controversy; nor could the archbishop be induced to consent to her marriage, but by the production of lawful witnesses, who swore that she had worn the veil on account of her suitors, but had never made her vow. Satisfied with a child of either sex, she ceased having issue, and enduring with complacency, when the king was elsewhere employed, the absence of the court, she continued many years at Westminster: yet was no part of royal magnificence wanting to her; but at all times crowds of visitants and news-bearers were, in endless multitudes, entering and departing from her superb dwelling: for this the king's liberality commanded; this her own kindness and affability attracted. She was singularly holy; by no means despicable in point of beauty; a rival of her mother's piety; never committing any impropriety, as far as herself was concerned; and, with the exception of the king's bed, completely chaste and uncontaminated even by suspicion. Clad in hair cloth beneath her royal habit, she was accustomed, in Lent, to visit the churches barefoot: nor was she disgusted at washing the feet of the diseased; handling their ulcers dripping with corruption, and, finally, pressing their hands for a long time together to her lips, and decking their table.

She had a singular pleasure in hearing the service of God ; and on this account was thoughtlessly prodigal towards clerks of melodious voice; addressed them kindly, gave to them liberally, and promised still more abundantly. Her generosity becoming universally known, crowds of scholars, equally famed for verse and for singing, came over ; and happy did he account himself, who could attract the queen's notice by the novelty of his song. Nor on these only did she lavish money, but on all sorts of men, especially foreigners ; that through her presents they might proclaim her celebrity abroad: for the desire of fame is so rooted in the human mind, that scarcely is any one contented with the precious fruits of a good conscience, but is fondly anxious, if he does anything laudable, to have it generally known. Hence, it was justly observed, the disposition crept upon the queen to reward all the foreigners she could, while the others were kept in suspense, sometimes with effectual, but oftener with empty promises. Hence, too, it arose, that she fell into the error of prodigal givers ; bringing many claims on her tenantry, exposing them to injuries, and taking away their property: but, obtaining the credit of a liberal benefactress, she little regarded the sarcasms of her own people. But a correct judgment will impute this to the designs of her servants ; who, harpy-like, conveyed everything they could gripe into their purses, or wasted it in riotous living : her ears being infected with the base insinuations of these people, she induced this stain on her noble mind ; holy and meritorious in every other respect. Amid these concerns, she was snatched away from her country, to the great loss of the people, but to her own advantage [May 1, 1118] : for her funeral being splendidly celebrated at Westminster, she entered into rest; and her spirit manifested, by no trivial indications, that she was a resident in heaven. She died, willingly leaving the throne, after a reign of seventeen years and six months ; experiencing the fate of her family, who almost all departed in the flower of their age. To her bed, but not immediately, succeeded [A.D. 1121] Adala, daughter of the duke of Louvaine, which is the principal town of Lorrain.

§ 419. By Matilda king Henry had a son named William, educated and destined to the succession, with the fondest hope and surpassing care. For to him, when scarcely twelve years of age, all the free men of England and Normandy, of every rank and condition, and under fealty to whatever lord, were obliged to submit themselves by homage and by oath. When a boy, too, he was betrothed to, and received in wedlock, the daughter of Fulk earl of Anjou, who was herself scarcely marriageable [A.D. 1119]; his father-in-law bestowing on him the county of Maine as her dower : moreover, Fulk, proceeding to Jerusalem, committed his earldom to the king, to be restored, should he return, but otherwise, to go to his son-in-law. Many provinces, then, looked forward to the government of this boy: for it was supposed that the prediction of king Edward would be verified in him ; and it was said, that now might it be expected, that the hopes of England, like the tree [1] cut down, would, through this youth, again blossom and bring forth fruit, and

[1] See § 226.

thus put an end to her sufferings : but God saw otherwise ; for this illusion vanished into air, as an early day was hastening him to his fate. Indeed, by the exertions of his father-in-law, and of Thibaut the son of Stephen, and of his aunt Adala, Louis king of France conceded the legal possession of Normandy to the lad, on his doing him homage. The prudence of his truly careful father so arranged and contrived, that the homage which he, from the extent of his empire, disdained to perform, should not be refused by his son, a youth of delicate habit, and not very likely to live. In discussing and peaceably settling these matters, the king spent the space of four years ; continuing the whole of that time in Normandy. Nevertheless, the calm of this brilliant and carefully concerted peace, this anxious, universal hope, was destroyed in an instant by the vicissitudes of human estate. For, giving orders for returning to England, the king set sail from Barfleur just before twilight on the seventh of the kalends of December [Nov. 25, 1120] ; and the breeze which filled his sails conducted him safely to his kingdom and extensive fortunes. But the young man, who was now somewhat more than seventeen years of age, and, by his father's indulgence, possessed everything but the name of king, commanded another vessel to be prepared for himself ; almost all the young nobility flocking around him, from similarity of youthful pursuits. The sailors, too, immoderately filled with wine, with that seaman's hilarity which their cups excited, exclaimed, that those who were now ahead, must soon be left astern ; for the ship was of the best construction, and recently fitted with new materials. When, therefore, it was now dark night, these imprudent youths, overwhelmed with liquor, launched the vessel from the shore. She flew swifter than the winged arrow, sweeping the rippling surface of the deep : but the carelessness of the intoxicated crew drove her on a rock, which rose above the waves not far from shore. In the greatest consternation, they immediately ran on deck, and with loud outcry got ready their boathooks, endeavouring for a considerable time to force the vessel off : but fate was against them, and frustrated, every exertion. The oars, too, dashing, horribly crashed against the rock,[1] and her battered prow hung immovably fixed. Now, too, the water washed some of the crew overboard, and, entering the chinks, drowned others ; when the boat having been launched, the young prince was received into it, and might certainly have been saved by reaching the shore, had not his illegitimate sister, the countess of Perche, now struggling with death in the larger vessel, implored her brother's assistance ; shrieking out, that he should not abandon her so barbarously. Touched with pity, he ordered the boat to return to the ship, that he might rescue his sister ; and thus the unhappy youth met his death through excess of affection : for the skiff, overcharged by the multitudes who leaped into her, sunk, and buried all indiscriminately in the deep. One rustic[2] alone escaped ; who, floating all night upon the mast,

[1] Virgil. Æneid. v. 206.
[2] He is called a butcher by Orderic. Vitalis, p. 867, who has many particulars of this event.

related in the morning the dismal catastrophe. No ship was ever productive of so much misery to England; none ever so widely celebrated throughout the world. Here also perished with William, Richard, another of the king's sons, whom a woman of no rank had borne him, before his accession; a brave youth, and dear to his father from his obedience: Richard earl of Chester, and his brother Otuell, the tutor and preceptor of the king's son: the countess of Perche, the king's daughter, and his niece the countess of Chester, sister to Thibaut: and indeed almost every person of consequence about court, whether knight, or chaplain, or young nobleman, training up to arms. For, as I have said, they eagerly hastened from all quarters, expecting no small addition to their reputation, if they could either amuse, or show their devotion to the young prince. The calamity was augmented by the difficulty of finding the bodies, which could not be discovered by the various persons who sought them along the shore; but delicate as they were, they became food for the monsters of the deep. The death of this youth being known, produced a wonderful change in existing circumstances. His father renounced the celibacy he had cherished since Matilda's death, anxious for furture heirs by a new consort: his father-in-law, returning home from Jerusalem, faithlessly espoused the party of William, the son of Robert earl of Normandy; giving him his other daughter in marriage, and the county of Maine; his indignation being excited against the king, by his daughter's dowry being detained in England after the death of the prince.

§ 420. His daughter Matilda, by Matilda, king Henry gave in marriage to Henry emperor of Germany, son of that Henry mentioned in the third book. Henry was the fifth emperor of the Germans of this name; who, although he had been extremely incensed at his father for his outrages against the holy see, yet, in his own time, was the rigid follower of, and stickler for, the same sentiments. For when Paschal, a man possessed of every virtue, had succeeded pope Urban, the question again arose concerning the investiture of the churches, together with all the former contentions and animosities; as neither party would give way. The emperor had in his favour all the bishops and abbots of his kingdoms situate on this side the mountains; because Charles the Great, to keep in check the ferocity of those nations, had conferred almost all the country on the churches: most wisely considering, that the clergy would not so soon cast off their fidelity to their lord, as the laity; and, besides, if the laity were to rebel, they might be restrained by the authority of their excommunication, and the weight of their power. The pope had brought over to his side the churches beyond the mountains, and the cities of Italy scarcely acknowledged the dominion of Henry; thinking themselves exonerated from servitude after the death of his brother Conrad, who, being left by his father as king of Lombardy, had died at Arezzo. But Henry, rivalling the ancient Cæsar in every noble quality, after tranquillizing his German empire, extended his thoughts to his Italian kingdom; purposing to quell the revolt of the cities, and decide the question of investitures according to his own pleasure.

This progress to Rome, accomplished by great exertion of mind, and much painful labour of body, hath been described by David bishop of Bangor, a Scot; though far more partially to the king than becomes an historian. Indeed he commends highly even his unheard-of violence in taking the pope captive, though he held him in free custody; citing the example of Jacob's holding the angel fast till he extorted a blessing. Moreover, he labours to establish, that the saying of the apostle, "No servant of God embroils himself in worldly business" [2 Tim. ii. 4], is not repugnant to the desires of those bishops who are invested by the laity, because the doing homage to a layman, by a clergyman, is not a secular business. How frivolous such arguments are, any person's consideration may decide. In the meantime, that I may not seem to bear hard on a good man by my judgment, I determine to make allowances for him, since he has not written an history, but a panegyric. I will now therefore faithfully insert the grant[1] and agreement extorted from the pope, by a forcible detention of three weeks; and I shall subjoin, in what manner they were soon after made of none effect, by an holier council.

§ 421. "The sovereign pope Paschal will not molest the sovereign king, nor his empire nor kingdom, on account of the investiture of bishoprics and abbeys, nor concerning the injury suffered by himself and his party in person and in goods; nor will he return evil to him, or any other person, on this account; neither, on any consideration, will he publish an anathema against the person of king Henry: nor will the sovereign pope delay to crown him, according to the ritual; and he will assist him, as far as possible, by the aid of his office, to retain his kingdom and empire. And this the sovereign pope will fulfil without fraud or evil design." These are the names of the bishops and cardinals, who, at the command of the sovereign pope Paschal, confirmed by oath the grant to and friendship with the sovereign emperor Henry: Peter, bishop of Portus: Centius, bishop of Sabina: Robert, cardinal of St. Eusebius: Boniface, cardinal of St. Mark: Anastasius, cardinal of St. Clement: Gregory, cardinal of the apostles Peter and Paul: also Gregory, cardinal of St. Chrysogonus: John, cardinal of St. Potentiana: Risus, cardinal of St. Lawrence: Reinerus, cardinal of Saints Marcellinus and Peter: Vitalis, cardinal of St. Balbina: Teuzo, cardinal of St. Mark: Theobald, cardinal of John and Paul: John, dean in the Greek School:[2] Leo, dean of St. Vitalis: Albo, dean of Sergius and Bachus.

§ 422. The king also made oath as follows. "I Henry the king will, on the fourth or fifth day of the ensuing week, set at liberty the sovereign pope, and the bishops and cardinals, and all the captives and hostages, who were taken for him, or with him; and I will cause them to be conducted safely within the gates of the city beyond the Tiber;[3] nor will I hereafter seize, or suffer to be

---

[1] This treaty may be referred to April 8, A.D. 1111.
[2] The church of St. Maria in Scuola Græca is so called from a tradition that St. Augustine, before his conversion, there taught rhetoric. See Lumisden, p. 318.
[3] Trastevere, that part in which St. Peter's is situate.

seized, such as remain under fealty to the lord pope Paschal: and with the Roman people, and the city beyond the Tiber, I will, as well by myself as by my people, preserve peace and security to such persons as shall keep peace with me. I will faithfully assist the sovereign pope, in retaining his papacy, quietly and securely. I will restore the patrimony and possessions of the Roman church which I have taken away; and I will aid him in recovering and keeping everything which he ought to have, after the manner of his predecessors, with true faith, and without fraud or evil design: and I will obey the sovereign pope, saving the honour of my kingdom and empire, as Catholic emperors ought to obey Catholic Roman pontiffs." And they who swore on the part of the king are these: Frederic, archbishop of Cologne: Godebard, bishop of Trent: Bruno, bishop of Spires: count Berengar: Albert the chancellor: count Herman: Frederic, count palatine: the marquis Boniface: Albert, count of Blandriac: count Frederic: count Godfrid: and the marquis Warner.

§ 423. This treaty being settled, and confirmed by the oath of the aforesaid bishops and cardinals, and mutual embraces exchanged, the sovereign pope, on the fourth of the ides of April [April 13, 1111], being Quasimodo Sunday, celebrated mass; in which, after his own communion and that of the ministers at the altar, he gave the Body and Blood of our Lord to the emperor with these words: "This Body of the Lord, which the truly holy church retains, born of the Virgin Mary, exalted on the cross for the redemption of mankind, we give to thee, dearest son, for the remission of thy sins, and for the preservation of the peace and true friendship to be confirmed between me and thee, the empire and the priesthood." Again, on the next day, the pope and the king met at the columns [1] which are in the Forum, guards being stationed wherever it was deemed necessary, that the consecration of the king might not be impeded. And at the Silver [2] gate he was received by the bishops and cardinals, and all the Roman clergy; and the prayer being begun, as contained in the ritual, by the bishop of Ostia, (as the bishop of Albano, by whom it ought to have been said had he been present, was absent,) he was conducted to the middle of the Rota, [3] and there received the second prayer from the bishop of Portus, as the Roman ritual enjoins. After this they led him, with litanies, to the confessionary of the Apostles, [4] and there the bishop of Ostia anointed him between the shoulders, and on the right arm. This being done, he was conducted by the sovereign pontiff to the altar of the aforesaid apostles, and there the crown being placed on his head by the pope himself, he was consecrated emperor. After putting on the crown, the mass of the Resurrection of the Lord was celebrated, during which, before the communion, the sovereign pope, with his own hand, gave to the emperor the grant in which he conceded to

[1] Three beautiful columns, supposed to be remains of the temple of Jupiter Stator.

[2] The principal entrance to St. Peter's church, so called by way of pre-eminence.

[3] The Rota, which seems to have been a part of St. Peter's church, is not enumerated by Fontana, de Basilica Vaticana.

[4] The chapel, in which the tombs of the apostles are said to be placed.

him, and his kingdom, what is under-written; and in the same place confirmed it by the sanction of a curse.

§ 424. "Paschal the bishop, servant of the servants of God, sendeth greeting and his apostolical benediction, to his dearest son in Christ, Henry, by the grace of Almighty God, august emperor of the Romans. The Divine disposal hath ordained, that your kingdom shall unite with the holy Roman church, since your predecessors, through valour and surpassing prudence, have obtained the crown and sovereignty of the Roman city; to the dignity of which crown and empire, the Divine majesty, by the ministry of our priesthood, hath advanced your person, my dearest son Henry. That pre-eminence of dignity, then, which our predecessors have granted to yours, the Catholic emperors, and have confirmed in the volume of grants, we also concede to your affection, and in the scroll of this present grant confirm also, that you may confer the investiture of the staff and ring on the bishops or abbots of your kingdom freely elected without violence or simony: but, after their investiture, let them receive canonical consecration from the bishop to whom it pertains. But if any person shall be elected, either by the clergy or the people, against your consent, unless he be invested by you, let him be consecrated by no one; excepting such, indeed, as are accustomed to be at the disposal of the archbishops, or of the Roman pontiff. Moreover, let the archbishops or bishops have permission canonically to consecrate bishops or abbots invested by you. Your predecessors, indeed, so largely endowed the churches of their kingdom with their royalties, that it is fitting that kingdom should be especially strengthened by the power of bishops or abbots; and that popular dissensions, which often happen in all elections, should be checked by royal majesty. Wherefore, your prudence and authority ought to take more especial care, to preserve the grandeur of the Roman church, and the safety of the rest, through God's assistance, by your gifts and services. Therefore, if any ecclesiastical or secular person, knowing this document of our concession, shall rashly dare oppose it, let him be anathematized, unless he recant, and let him run the risk of losing his honour and dignity: but may God's mercy preserve such as keep it, and may He grant your person and authority to reign happily to his honour and glory." [April 12, 1111.]

§ 425. The whole ceremony of the consecration being completed, the pope and the emperor, joining their right hands, went with much state to the chamber which fronts the confessionary of St. Gregory, that the pope might there put off his pontifical, and the emperor his regal vestments. As the emperor retired from the chamber divested of his royal insignia, the Roman patricians met him with a golden circle, which they placed upon his head, and by it gave him the supreme Patriciate[1] of the Roman city, with common consent and universal approbation.

§ 426. All this parade of grants and consecration I have taken

---

[1] The patrician of Rome appears to have been its chief magistrate, derived from the office of præfect or patrician under the emperors of Constantinople.

literally from the narrative of the aforesaid David, written, as I have said, with too great partiality towards the king. In the following year, however, a council was assembled at Rome, rather by the connivance than the command of the pope, and the grant was nullified. The authors of its reversal were the archbishop of Vienne, who was afterwards pope, and Girard, bishop of Angoulesme, who stimulated their brother bishops to make these concessions of none effect. The proceedings of that council were as follows :—

§ 427. In the year of our Lord's incarnation one thousand one hundred and twelve, the fifth of the indiction, in the thirteenth year of the pontificate of our Lord the pope Paschal the second, in the month of March, on the fifteenth of the kalends of April [18 March], a council was held at Rome, at the Lateran, in the church of Constantine ;[1] where, when pope Paschal, together with the archbishops, bishops, and cardinals, and a mixed company of clergy and laity, had, on the last day of the council, taken his seat, making public profession of the Catholic faith, lest any one should doubt his orthodoxy, he said, " I embrace all the Holy Scripture of the Old and New Testament, the law written by Moses and by the holy prophets; I embrace the four Gospels, the seven canonical Epistles, the Epistles of the glorious preacher St. Paul the apostle, the holy Canons of the apostles, the four Universal councils, to wit, the Nicene, Ephesian, Constantinopolitan, Chalcedonian, in the same manner as I do the four Gospels ; moreover the council of Antioch and the decrees of the holy fathers, the Roman pontiffs ; and, more especially, the decrees of my lords pope Gregory the seventh, and pope Urban of blessed memory. What they have approved, I approve; what they held, I hold ; what they have confirmed, I confirm ; what they have condemned, I condemn ; what they have opposed, I oppose ; what they have interdicted, I interdict ; what they have prohibited, I prohibit : I will persevere in the same in everything and through everything." This being ended, Girard, bishop of Angoulesme, legate in Aquitaine, rose up for all, and by the unanimous consent of pope Paschal and of all the council, read the following writing :—

§ 428. " That grant which is no grant, but ought more properly to be called an abomination,[2] for the liberation of captives and of the church, extorted from the sovereign pope Paschal by the violence of king Henry, all of us in this holy council assembled, with the sovereign pope, condemn by canonical censure and ecclesiastical authority, by the judgment of the Holy Spirit ; and we adjudge it to be void and altogether nullify it ; and that it may have neither force nor efficacy we interdict it altogether. And it is condemned on this account, because in that abomination it is asserted, that a person canonically elected by the clergy and the people, shall not be consecrated by any one, unless first invested by the king, which is contrary to the Holy Spirit and to canonical institution."

---

[1] The church of St. Saviour, or St. John Lateran, built by Constantine the Great.
[2] MSS. C. D. E. L 2. "pravilegium;" a play on the words "privilegium" and "pravilegium.".

This writing being read, the whole council, and all present, unanimously cried out, " Amen, Amen : So be it, So be it."

§ 429. The archbishops there present with their suffragans were these : John, patriarch of Venice; Semies of Capua ; Landulf of Benevento ; those of Amalfi, Reggio, Otranto, Brindisi, Capsa, Gerenza ; and the Greeks, Rosanus, and the archbishop of St. Severina. The bishops were: Censius of Sabina ; Peter of Portus ; Leo of Ostia; Cono of Preneste; Girard of Angoulesme; Galo of Leon, legate for Berri ; and the archbishop of Vienne, Roger of Volterra ; Geoffrey of Sienna ; Roland of Populonia ; Gregory of Terracina; William of Troy; William of Syracuse, legate for all the Sicilians; and near an hundred other bishops. Siwin, and John bishop of Tusculum, though at Rome, were not present on that day of the council ; but they, afterwards, on the reading of the condemnation of the grant, assented to, and approved of it.

§ 430. These things gaining publicity, all France made no scruple of considering the emperor as accursed by the power of ecclesiastical zeal hurled against him. Roused at this, in the seventeenth year of pope Paschal, he proceeded to Rome to inflict signal vengeance on him. But he, by a blessed departure,[1] had avoided all earthly molestation, and from his place of repose on high, laughed at the threats of the angry emperor, who, having heard of his death, quickened his journey, in order that, ejecting John of Gaeta, chancellor to the late pope, who had been already elected and called Gelasius, he might intrude Maurice, bishop of Braga, surnamed Burdin, on the see ; but the following epistle of Gelasius will explain the business more fully :—

" Gelasius, servant of the servants of God, to the archbishops, bishops, abbots, clergy, princes, and other faithful people throughout Gaul, sends greeting. As you are members of the church of Rome, we are anxious to signify to your affection what has there lately taken place. Shortly after our election, then, the sovereign emperor coming by stealth and with unexpected haste to Rome, compelled us to depart from the city. He afterwards demanded peace by threats and intimidation, saying he would do all he might be able, unless we assured him of peace by oath. To which we replied thus : ' Concerning the controversy which exists between the church and the empire, we willingly agree to a meeting or to legal discussion, at proper time and place, that is to say, either at Milan or Cremona, on the next feast of St. Luke, at the discretion of our brethren, who, by God, are constituted judges in the church, and without whom this matter cannot be treated of. And since the sovereign emperor demands security from us, we promise such to him, by word and by writing, unless in the interim he himself shall violate it ; for otherwise to give security is dishonourable to the church and contrary to custom.' He, immediately, on the forty-fourth day after our election, intruded into the mother church the bishop of Braga, who, the preceding year, had been excommunicated by our predecessor pope Paschal, in a council at Benevento, and who had also, when he formerly received the pall from our

[1] Paschal died in January 1118; see Pagi ad an. § 1.

hands, sworn fidelity to the same pontiff and his catholic successors, of whom I am the first. In this prodigious crime, however,
thanks be to God, the sovereign emperor had no single Roman associate, only the Guibertines, Romanus of St. Marcellus, Centius,
who was called of St. Chrysogon; Teuzo, who for a long time was
guilty of many excesses in Dacia; these alone transacted so shameless a deed. We command your wisdom, therefore, on the receipt
of these presents, that, deliberating on these matters in common,
by the grace of God, you be prepared, by his help, to avenge the
mother church, as you are aware ought to be done by your joint
assistance. Given at Gaeta on the seventeenth of the kalends of
February [16th Jan. A.D. 1119]."

§ 431. Gelasius, after his expulsion, embarking at Salerno, came
thence to Genoa, and afterwards proceeded by land to Clugny, where
he died. Then, that is, in the year of our Lord one thousand one
hundred and nineteen, the cardinals who had accompanied him, together with the whole Cisalpine church, having regard to the piety and
energy of Guido, archbishop of Vienne, elevated him with great pomp
to the papacy, and called him Calixtus, hoping, that through his
power, as he possessed great influence, they might be able to withstand the force of the emperor. Nor did he deceive their confidence; for soon after, calling a council at Rheims, he separated
from the churches such as had been, or should be, invested by the
laity, including the emperor also, unless he should recant. Thus
continuing for some time in the hither districts, to strengthen his
party, and having settled all affairs in Gaul, he came to Rome, and
was gladly received by the citizens, as the emperor had now
departed. Burdin then, deserted, fled to Sutri, determining to
nurture his power by many a pilgrim's loss; but how he was
ejected thence the following epistle explains:—

§ 432. "Calixtus, the bishop, servant of the servants of God, to
his beloved brethren and sons, the archbishops, bishops, abbots,
priors, and other faithful servants of St. Peter, clergy as well as
laity, situated throughout Gaul, sends greeting and apostolical
benediction. As the people have forsaken the law of the Lord, and
walk not in His judgments, God visits their iniquities with a rod,
and their sins with stripes; but retaining the bowels of paternal
love, He does not desert such as trust in His mercy. For a long time,
indeed, their sins so requiring, the faithful of the church have been
disturbed by Burdin, that puppet of the king of Germany; nay, some
have been taken captive, others starved to death in prison. Lately,
however, after celebrating the festival of Easter, when we could no
longer endure the complaints of the pilgrims, and of the poor, we
left the city with the faithful servants of the church, and laid siege
to Sutri, until the Divine power delivered that Burdin aforesaid,
the enemy of the church, (who had there made a nest for the
devil,) as well as the place itself, entirely into our power. We beg
your brotherly love therefore, to return thanks with us to the King
of kings, for such great benefits, and to remain most firmly in
obedience and duty to the catholic church, as you will receive from
God Almighty, through his grace, due recompence for it, both

here and hereafter. We beg, too, that these letters be made public with all due diligence. Given at Sutri on the fifth of the kalends of May."

§ 433. How exquisite and refined a piece of wit, to call the man he hated the puppet of the king of Germany! for the emperor certainly held in high estimation Maurice's skill in literature and politics. He was, as I have said, archbishop of Braga, a city of Spain; a man whom any one might highly reverence, and almost venerate, for his active and unwearied assiduity, had he not been led to make himself conspicuous by so disgraceful an act; nor would he have hesitated to purchase the holy see, if he could have found a purchaser so desperate as to buy what he was ready to sell. But being taken and made a monk, he was sent to the monastery called "The Den."[1]

§ 434. The laudable magnanimity of the pope proceeded still farther in the promotion of justice, to the end that he might repress the boundless and innate cupidity of the Romans. In his time there were no snares laid for the traveller in the neighbourhood of Rome, no assaults on him when he arrived within the city. The offerings to St. Peter, (which, through insolence, and for their lusts, the powerful used to pillage, basely injuring such preceding popes as dared even complain,) Calixtus brought back to their proper use, that is to say, for the public service of the ruler of the holy see. Neither could the desire of amassing money, nor the love of it when collected, produce in his breast anything repugnant to justice; so that he admonished the English pilgrims, on account of the length of the journey, rather to go to St. David's[2] than to Rome, allowing the benefit of the same benediction to such as went twice to that place, as resulted to those who went once to Rome. Moreover that inveterate controversy between the empire and the priesthood, concerning investiture, which for more than fifty years had created commotions, to such a degree, that, when any favourer of this heresy was cut off by disease or death, immediately, like the hydra's heads, many sprouted up afresh; this man by his diligence cut off, brought low, and rooted out, decapitating German fierceness with the vigorous stroke of the papal hatchet. This, the declaration of the emperor, and of the pope, will show to the world in the following words :—

§ 435. "I, Calixtus, bishop, servant of the servants of God, do grant unto you, my beloved son, Henry, by the grace of God, emperor of the Romans, that the election of bishops and abbots of the German empire, who pertain to the regality, shall take place in your presence without simony or any violence; so that if any discord shall arise between the parties, you may give your assent or aid to the worthier side, by the counsel or judgment of the metropolitan

---

[1] A monastery near Salerno, inaccessible, except by one passage. Here were kept such as from their conduct had become either dangerous or scandalous; they were supplied with everything necessary, according to their order, but were held in close confinement. Its name was given from the untameable disposition of its inmates. See Orderic. Vital. p. 870.

[2] MSS. A. C. D. E. L 2. "Sanctum David." By a singular blunder, Saville's text here reads "dictum."

or suffragans. But the elect shall receive the royalties from you, and do whatever, by these, he is lawfully bound to perform to you; but any one consecrated in the other parts of the empire, shall, within six months, receive his royalties from you, by your sceptre, and do whatever, by these, he is lawfully bound to perform to you; all things excepted which are known to belong to the Roman church. Moreover in those matters whereof you have complained and demanded my assistance, I will afford you aid according to the duty of my office. I grant firm peace to you, and to all who are, or were, aiding you at the time of this dispute. Farewell."

§ 436. "In the name of the Holy and Undivided Trinity, I, Henry Augustus, by the grace of God, emperor of the Romans, for the love of God, and of the holy Roman church, and of the sovereign pope Calixtus; and for the release of my soul, do give up unto God, and to God's holy apostles Peter and Paul, and to the holy catholic church, all investitures by the ring and staff, and do allow canonical election and free consecration to take place in all churches of my kingdom or empire. The possessions and prerogatives of St. Peter, which, from the beginning of this dispute to the present day, have been taken away, either in my father's or my own time, and which I now hold, I restore to the same holy Roman church; and such as I do not possess, I will faithfully assist her in recovering. And of the possessions of all other churches, princes, and others, clergy as well as lay, which have been forfeited in this contention by the advice of my princes, or by course of law, such as I have I will restore, and such as I do not possess I will faithfully assist in recovering. And I grant firm peace to the sovereign pope Calixtus, and to the holy Roman church, and to all who are, or have been, on her side; and I will faithfully assist the holy Roman church in everything in which she requires assistance; and will afford her due justice in such matters whereof she shall have complained." All these affairs were transacted by the consent and counsel of the nobility, whose names are subscribed: Albert, archbishop of Mentz; Frederic, archbishop of Cologne; the bishop of Ratisbon; the bishop of Bamburg; Bruno, bishop of Spires; the bishop of Augsburg; the bishop of Utrecht; the bishop of Constance; the abbot of Fulda; duke Herman; duke Frederic; Boniface the marquis; Thibaut the marquis; Ernulf count palatine; Otbert count palatine; and count Berengar.

§ 437. The long-standing malady which had disturbed the church being thus cured, every true Christian greatly rejoiced, that this emperor, who, in military glory, trod fast upon the footsteps of Charles the Great, neither degenerated from his devotion to God: for, in addition to nobly quelling the rebellions of his German empire, he subdued his Italian dominions in such wise as none had done before. Entering Italy thrice, within the space of ten years, he restrained the pride of the cities: at his first coming he exterminated by fire, Novara, Placentia, and Arezzo: at the second and third, Cremona and Mantua: and quieted the sedition at Ravenna, by a siege of a few days' continuance; for the Pisans and Pavians, with the people of Milan, embraced his friendship, rather than encounter his enmity. The daughter of the king of England, who, as I said before,[1] was married to him, resembled her father in fortitude, and her mother in sanctity: piety and assiduity vied with each other in her character, nor was it easy to discern which of her good qualities was most commendable.

§ 438. At that time lived William earl of Poictiers; a giddy unsettled kind of man; who after[2] he returned from Jerusalem, as the preceding book[3] relates, wallowed as completely in the stye of vice, as though he had believed that all things were governed by chance, and not by Providence. Moreover, he rendered his absurdities pleasant by a show of wit; exciting the loud laughter of his hearers. Finally, erecting, near a castle called Niort, certain buildings after the form of a little monastery, he used to talk idly about placing therein an abbey of prostitutes, naming several of the most abandoned courtesans, one as abbess, another as prioress; and declaring that he would fill up the rest of the offices in like manner. Repudiating his lawful consort, he carried off the wife of a certain viscount, of whom he was so desperately enamoured, that he placed on his shield the figure of this woman; affirming, that he was desirous of bearing her in battle, in the same manner as she bore him at another time. Being reproved and excommunicated for this by Girard bishop of Angoulesme, and ordered to renounce this illicit amour,—" You shall curl with a comb," said he, "the hair that has forsaken your forehead, ere I repudiate the viscountess;" thus taunting a man, whose scanty hair required no comb. Nor did he less when Peter bishop of Poictou, a man of noted sanctity, rebuked him still more freely; and, when contumacious, began to excommunicate him publicly: for becoming furious, he seized the prelate by the hair, and flourishing his drawn sword,—" You shall die this instant," said he, " unless you give me absolution." The bishop, then, counterfeiting alarm, and asking leave to speak, boldly completed the remainder of the form of excommunication; suspending the earl so entirely from all Christian intercourse, that he should neither dare to associate nor speak with any one, unless he speedily recanted. Thus fulfilling his duty, as it appeared to him, and thirsting for the honour of martyrdom, he stretched out his neck, saying, " Strike, strike." But William, becoming somewhat softened, regained his usual pleasantry, and said, "Certainly I hate you so cordially, that I will not dignify you by the effects of my anger, nor shall you ever enter heaven by the agency of my hand." After a short time, however, tainted by the infectious insinuations of this abandoned woman, he drove the rebuker of his incest into banishment; who there, making a happy end, manifested to the world, by great and frequent miracles, how gloriously he survives in heaven. On hearing this, the earl abstained not from his inconsiderate speeches, openly declaring, that he was sorry he had not dispatched him before; that, so, his pure

---

[1] See § 420.
[2] Guibert of Nogent excuses himself from commemorating the valour of many of the crusaders, because, after their return, they had run headlong into every kind of enormity. Opera, p. 431. [3] See § 383.

soul might chiefly have to thank him, through whose violence he had acquired eternal happiness. The following verses are a tribute of applause to the life and death of Peter. It was said of him when alive,—

> Coarse food, his body ; and the poor, his store
> Consumed ; while study morals gave, and lore.
> Virtues he rear'd, check'd faults, encouraged right,
> And law : while peace, not tumult, did delight.
> Help to the wretch, to sinners pardon gives,
> And, for his friend, his ardour ever lives.
> Busy for man was Martha; Mary's heart,
> Intent on God, assumed the better part ;
> So 'twas in him ; for God his soul possess'd,
> Unmix'd : his friendless neighbour had the rest.
> Rachel he loved ; nor Leah's hopes deprived
> Of joy; another Jacob, doubly-wived;
> Dotes on the one, for beauty's matchless grace ;
> Regards the other, for her numerous race.

And when dead, it was said of him,—

> Poor and confined, and exiled from his see,
> The virtuous prelate bore each injury :
> Now rich, free, fix'd, his suff'rings are made even,
> For Christ he follows, and inherits heaven.
> His life, religion ; and a judgment sound,
> His mind, adorn'd : his works his fame resound,
> Reading his knowledge, and a golden mean
> His words, arranged ; in his decisions seen
> Was law : severity his justice arm'd,
> And graceful beauty in his person charm'd :
> His breast was piety's perpetual stand,
> The pastor's crosier well became his hand :
> The pope promotes him, but the earl deprives :
> Through Christ to joy eternal he survives.

§ 439. The contemporaries and associates in religion of this Peter, were Robert de Arbreisil,[1] and Bernard abbot of Tiron, the first of whom was the most celebrated and eloquent preacher of these times. So much did he excel, not in frothy, but honeyed diction, that from the gifts of persons vying with each other in making presents, he founded that noble monastery of nuns at Font-Evraud, in which every secular pleasure being extirpated, no other place possesses such multitudes of devout women, fervent in their obedience to God : for in addition to the rejection of other allurements, how great is this, that they never speak but in the chapter; the rule of constant silence being enjoined by the superior, because, when this is broken, women are prone to vain talk. The other, a noted admirer of poverty, leaving a most opulent monastery, retired with a few followers into a woody and sequestered place, and there, as the light could not be hidden under a bushel, vast numbers flocking to him, he founded a monastery, more celebrated for the piety and number of the monks, than for the splendour and extent of its riches.

§ 440. And, that England may not be supposed destitute of virtue, who can pass by Serlo, abbot of Gloucester, who advanced that place, almost from meanness and insignificance, to a glorious pitch ? All England is acquainted with the considerate rule professed at Gloucester, which the weak may embrace, and the strong

---

[1] Robert de Arbrisil died A.D. 1117.

cannot despise. Their leader Serlo's axiom was, "Moderation in all things." Although mild to the good, he was fierce and terrific to the haughty; to corroborate which, I shall insert the verses of Godfrey the prior concerning him :—

> The church's bulwark fell, when Serlo died,
> Virtue's sharp sword, and justice's fond pride :
> Speaker of truth, no vain discourse he loved,
> And pleased the very princes he reproved :
> A hasty judgment, or disorder'd state
> Of life, or morals, were his utter hate.
> The third of March was the propitious day,
> When Serlo wing'd, through death, to life his way.

§ 441. Who can in silence pass Lanzo, who flourished at that time, equal to any in sanctity? A monk of Clugny, and prior of St. Pancras [1] in England; who, by his worth, so ennobled that place with the grace of monastic reverence, that it might be justly declared the peculiar habitation of virtue. As nothing I can say will equal the merits of his life, I shall merely subjoin, in the language I found it, an account of his death; that it may plainly appear, how gloriously he had lived, who died so highly favoured.

§ 442. " The affectionate Lord, who scourges every son whom He receives ; who promises the just, that, as of his sufferings, so shall they be partakers of his consolation ; permitted Lanzo to approach his death by such bitter sickness, during three days, that if any spot, from earthly intercourse, had adhered to his pure soul, it must, no doubt, have been wiped away by that suffering. For, as that great apostle, who reclined on the breast of our Lord, says, ' If we say that we have no sin, we deceive ourselves, and the truth is not in us ' [1 John i. 8]; and, since Christ will judge every sin, either lightly here, or more severely hereafter, He was unwilling that any offence should be in the way of him after death, whom He knew to have loved Him with all his heart ; wherefore, if there was anything which He thought worthy of reproof in Lanzo, He was desirous of exterminating it in his life-time. To this assertion his confidence in death bore witness. For when, in full health, on the fifth day of the week, before the passion of our Lord, having read the psalter, according to the daily custom of Lent, and being about to celebrate mass at the third hour, he had robed himself to the chasuble,[2] and had proceeded in the service till mass was on the eve of beginning, he was suddenly seized with such an acute disorder, that he himself laying aside the garments he had put on, left them not even folded up :[3] and, departing from the oratory, he was afflicted for two days, without intermission, that is, till the Saturday, having no rest, either sitting, walking, standing, lying, or sleeping. During the nights, however, he never spoke to his brethren, though entreating him to break silence : but to this he did not consent, beseeching them not to sully the purity of his vow ; for, since he had assumed the monastic habit, whenever he had gone out from complines, he had never spoken till the primes of the ensuing day.

---

[1] At Lewes in Sussex.
[2] The uppermost garment of the priest, covering the rest entirely.
[3] Those who officiated were enjoined to fold up their garments.

But on the Saturday, though so convulsed as to expect dissolution every moment, he commanded the brethren, now rising for mattins, to come and anoint him; and when he was anxious to kiss them, after being anointed, as is the custom, through excess of love, he saluted them, not lying or sitting, but, though agonized to death, standing, supported in their arms. At dawn, being conducted to the chapter-house,[1] when he had taken his seat, he asked all the brethren to come before him, and giving them the paternal benediction and absolution, he entreated the like from them. He then instructed them what they were to do, in case he died: and so, returning whence he came, he passed the rest of the day, with the succeeding Sunday, rather more tranquilly: but, behold, after this, that is, after Sunday, signs of approaching death were discovered; and having his hands washed, and his hair combed, he entered the oratory to hear mass; and receiving the Body and Blood of the Lord, retired to his bed. After a short time he became speechless, gave his benediction to the brethren, singly, as they came before him, and, in like manner, to the whole society. But lifting his eyes to heaven, he attempted with both hands to bless the abbot, with all committed to his charge. Being entreated by the fraternity to be mindful of them, with the Lord, to whom he was going, he most kindly assented, by an inclination of his head. After he had done this and other similar things, he beckoned for the cross to be presented to him, which, adoring with his head, and indeed the whole of his body, and embracing with his hands, he appeared to salute with joyful lips, and to kiss with fond affection, when he distressed the standers-by with signs of departing, and being caught up in their arms, was carried, yet alive, into the presbytery, before the altar of St. Pancras. Here, surviving yet a time, and pleasing from the rosy hue of his countenance, he departed to Christ, pure, and freed eternally from every evil, at the same hour of the day on which, for his purification, he had been stricken with disease. And behold how wonderfully all things corresponded; the passion of the servant, with the passion of the Lord; the hour of approaching sickness, with the hour of approaching eternal happiness; the five days of illness, which he endured for purifying the five senses of the body, through which none can avoid sin. Moreover, from his dying ere the completion of the fifth day, we think it is signified, that he had never sinned in the last sense, which is called the touch. And what else can the third hour of the day, in which he fell sick, and by dying entered into eternal life, signify, than that the same grace of the Holy Spirit, by which we know his whole life was regulated, was evidently present to him, both in his sickness and his death? Besides, we cannot doubt but that he equalled our fathers Odo and Odilo,[2] both in virtue and in its reward, as a remarkable circumstance granted to them, was allowed to him also. For as the Lord permitted them to die on the octaves of those festivals which they loved beyond all other, (for St. Odo chiefly loved the feast of St. Martin, and

[1] It was customary to hold a short chapter immediately after primes.
[2] Odo was founder of the Cluniac Rule, in the tenth century. Odilo was also abbot of Cluny, in the same century.

St. Odilo the nativity of our Lord, and each died on the octaves of these tides ;) so to Lanzo, who, beyond all of this age, observed the rule of St. Benedict, and venerated the holy mother of God and her solemnities with singular regard, it happened that as, according to his usual custom, both on the demise of St. Benedict, and on the festival of St. Mary, which is called the Annunciation, he celebrated high mass in the convent ; so, on the eighth day from the aforesaid anniversary of St. Benedict, being stricken with sickness, he also, on the eighth day from the Annunciation, departed to Christ. Wherefore, he who is unacquainted with the life of Lanzo, may learn from his death, how pleasing it was to God ; and will believe with us, that these things, which I have mentioned, did not happen after the common course of dying persons, as he was a man surpassed by none, in the present times, for the gift of the Holy Spirit."

§ 443. Nor ought the memory of Godfrey, prior of Winchester, to decay, who was celebrated in these times for his learning and his piety. His learning is attested by many works and epistles, composed in his familiar and pleasing style ; but principally by his epigrams, written after the manner of satires, and his verses in celebration of the chief personages of England.[1] Indeed he restored every divine office to its native grace, from the manner in which he treated it ; though before it had become obsolete from antiquity. The laws of religion and of hospitality, already happily traced out, he strongly impressed on the monks, who, to this day, so closely follow the footsteps of the prior in both, that they deserve all, or nearly all, possible commendation : indeed in this house, there is a place of entertainment to any extent, for travellers of every description, by sea or land, with boundless expense and ceaseless attention. Among other things, this holy man was noted for his humility; so that nothing but what savoured of modesty and sweetness proceeded from this singular depository of philosophy. How great indeed must this commendation seem ! for there is hardly any one, even the least tinctured with learning, who does not appear to consider others beneath his dignity, by his haughty gestures and proud gait proclaiming the consciousness of his own erudition. However, that no perfection might be wanting to his pure soul, he kept his lowly bed for many years, equally consuming his vitals and his transgressions in the furnace of lasting sickness.

§ 444. But why should I enlarge on such characters ? there were indeed, at that time, in England, many persons illustrious both for learning and for piety; whose virtue was the more commendable in proportion to its constancy and vigour in these degenerate times. By a blameless life, therefore, they gave credibility to ancient histories, and freed them from any suspicion of falsehood; as they produced modern example of the possibility of doing what was there recorded. Moreover, were there any prelates

---

[1] Godfrey was prior of Winchester from A.D. 1082 to 1107. His verses, in commendation of the chief personages of England, are in the manner of those already inserted on Serlo abbot of Gloucester. Many of his epigrams have very considerable merit.

apparently degenerating from the sanctity of ancient times, that is to say, skilled in secular, indolent in spiritual matters ; if there were such, I say, they endeavoured to shade their failings by costly ornaments for their cathedrals. Each of them erected new churches, and adorned the bodies of their saints with silver and gold ; lavish of expense, to secure the good opinion of the beholders. Among these is Ranulph[1] before-mentioned, who, being made bishop of Durham, purchased some glory for his name, by new buildings for the monks, and by regard to St. Cuthbert. His fame is exalted by his translation of the holy body, which, when taken from its resting-place, he exhibited to all who wished to behold it. Radulf, at that time abbot of Sees, and afterwards archbishop of Canterbury, with fortunate temerity, handled and displayed the uncorrupted body ; for it had become matter of doubt with certain persons, whether the miracle of the incorruption of the corpse, which had formerly been reported, still continued. About the same time, in the monastery of Ely, under abbot Richard, the virgin relics of St. Etheldritha, subjects of amaze and reverence to the beholders, were seen entire. This monastery, lately changed by king Henry into a bishopric, had Hervey for its first prelate ; who, from the scantiness of its revenues, had deserted Bangor, where he had been enthroned. And that the bishop of Lincoln might not complain of the mutilation of his diocese, the king made up his loss out of the possessions of Ely, and satisfied his claim. Indeed, whatever, in his time, was unjustly purloined, or violently taken, from the primacy of the two metropolitans of Canterbury and York, I will relate in its proper place. For having now ended the series of the kings, it seems incumbent on me to speak of that of the bishops of all England ; and here I wish I had abundant matter for relation, in order that such splendid luminaries of the country might no longer be lost in obscurity. Moreover, there will perhaps be many in different parts of England, who may say, that they have heard and read some things differently related from the mode in which I have recorded them ; but, if they judge candidly, they will not, on this account, brand me with censure ; since, following the strict laws of history, I have asserted nothing but what I have learnt either from relators, or writers of veracity. But be these matters as they may, I especially congratulate myself as being, through Christ's assistance, the only person, or at least the first, who, since Beda, has arranged a continuous history of the English. Should any one, therefore, as I already hear it intimated, undertake, after me, a work of a similar nature, he may be indebted to me for having collected materials, though the selection from them must depend upon himself.[2]

§ 445. Thus much then, my venerated lord, I have had to relate, concerning the history of the English, from their first arrival in this country, till the twenty-eighth year of your father's most happy reign ; the remainder will occupy a separate volume, if you

---

[1] See § 314.

[2] He probably has Henry Huntingdon in view, who wrote an History of England, shortly after him.

condescend a kind regard to these. For when I had finished this
work, after contemplating many characters, I determined that it
ought more especially to be dedicated to you. When I examine
others, I observe nobility in one; in another military science; in
a third learning; justice in a fourth; but munificence in few indeed:
I admire some things in one, some in another; but in you the
aggregate of all. For, if ever any man was truly noble, you certainly excel in that quality, being descended from the most glorious
kings and earls, and resembling them in your disposition. From
the Normans, therefore, you derive your military skill; from the
Flemings your personal elegance; from the French your surpassing
munificence. Of your activity in war, who can doubt, when your
most excellent father himself looks up to it? For whenever any
tumults are reported in Normandy, he despatches you before him,
in order that they may be dispelled by your valour, and that wavering peace may be restored by your sagacity. When he returns to
his kingdom, he brings you with him, as a safeguard to him abroad,
a delight at home, and an ornament everywhere.

§ 446. So devoted are you to literature, that though distracted
by such a mass of business, you yet snatch some hours to yourself,
for the purpose either of reading, or of hearing others read. Justly
do you regulate, indeed, your exalted rank in life, neither omitting
the toils of war for literature, nor contemning literature, as some
do, for military service. Here, also, the excess of your learning
appears; for, whilst you love books, you manifest how deeply you
have drunk of the stream. For many things, indeed, are eagerly
desired when not possessed; but no person will love philosophy
who shall not have imbibed it thoroughly.

§ 447. The fame of your justice reaches even our parts; for a
false sentence has never been extorted from you, either by eleva-
tion of rank or by scantiness of fortune. The person who wishes
to subvert justice, finds in your breast nothing conducive to his
design, either by the offering of presents, or by the charm of
favour.

§ 448. Your munificence and disregard of money is amply
shown by the monastery of Tewkesbury; from which, as I hear,
you not only do not extort presents, but even return its voluntary
offerings. You must be well aware how noble such a proceeding
is, more especially at the present time; how much it redounds to
your glory among men, how productive of the favour of God.
Happy, then, according to Plato, is the republic whose ruler is a
philosopher, whose sovereign delights not in gifts. More could I
add on such subjects, did not the suspicion of flattery on my part,
and commendable modesty on yours, restrain my tongue. In
truth my design was not to pass by in silence the things I have
uttered, in order that, by my agency, your worth might reach
posterity, and that it may continue to proceed from virtue to virtue.
Moreover, it was long since my intention, at the instance of certain
persons, to subjoin to this work whatever I may deem of importance, according to the successive years; but it appears advisable
rather to form another volume of such matters, than to be perpe-

tually adding to that already completed. Nor can any one say, that I engage in a superfluous work, if I record the transactions of the most celebrated among the kings of his time. Indeed my lowly condition is much indebted to his greatness, and will be still more so, were it for nothing else than his being able to pride himself on such a son.[1] For, when he had most auspiciously begotten, he first commanded you to be instructed, not superficially, as plainly appears at the present day, in science; he next made you master of a most princely fortune; and, at this moment he reposes his paternal regards upon you. Let this volume then, whatever be its merits or defects, be altogether dedicated to your fame; in the next my life and my history will terminate together. Farther, kindly accept this my offering, that I, whose judgment has not erred in its choice, may be gratified by the good wishes of my patron.

PREFACE TO THE HISTORY OF HIS OWN TIMES.

Addressed to Robert, Earl of Gloucester.

To his most loving lord, Robert, son of king Henry, and earl of Gloucester, William, the Librarian of Malmesbury, wishes, after completing his victorious course on earth, eternal triumph in heaven. Many of the transactions of your father, of glorious memory, I have not omitted to record, both in the fifth book of my Regal History, and in those three smaller volumes, which I have intituled Chronicles.[2] Your highness is now desirous that those events which, through the miraculous power of God, have taken place in recent times, in England, should be transmitted to posterity; truly, like all your other desires, a most noble one. For what more concerns the advancement of virtue, what more conduces to justice, than to recognise the Divine favour towards good men, and his vengeance upon the wicked? What, too, more grateful, than to commit to the page of history the exploits of brave men, by whose example others may shake off their indolence, and take up arms in defence of their country? As this task is committed to my pen, I think the narrative will proceed with exacter order, if, going back a little, I trace the series of years from the return of the empress into England, after the death of her husband. First, therefore, invoking the help of God, as is fitting, and purposing to write the truth, without listening to enmity, or sacrificing to favour, I shall begin as follows.

---

[1] Terentii Andria, i. 1.
[2] What these were is unknown, as it is believed that there is no MS. of them now to be met with.

WILLIAM OF MALMESBURY'S HISTORY OF HIS OWN TIMES.

BOOK I.

§ 1. In the twenty-sixth year of Henry king of England, which was in the year of our Lord one thousand one hundred and twenty-six, Henry emperor of Germany, to whom Matilda, the aforesaid king's daughter, had been married, died[1] in the very bloom of his life and of his conquests. Our king was, at that time, residing in Normandy, to quell whatever tumults might arise in those parts. As soon as he heard of the death of his son-in-law, he recalled his daughter, by honourable messengers despatched for that purpose. The empress, as they say, returned with reluctance, as she had become habituated to the country which was her dowry, and had large possessions there. It is well known, that several princes of Lorrain and Lombardy came, during succeeding years, repeatedly into England, to ask her in marriage; but they lost the fruit of their labours, the king designing by the marriage of his daughter, to procure peace between himself and the earl of Anjou. He was certainly, in an extraordinary degree, the greatest of all kings in the memory either of ourselves, or of our fathers : and yet, nevertheless, he ever, in some measure, dreaded the power of the earls of Anjou. Hence it arose, that he broke off and annulled the espousals[2] which William, his nephew, afterwards earl of Flanders, was said to be about to contract with the daughter of Fulk, earl of Anjou, who was afterwards king of Jerusalem. Hence, too, it arose, that he united a daughter of the same earl to his son William, while yet a stripling; and hence it was, that he married his daughter (of whom we began to speak), after her imperial match, to a son of the same Fulk, as my ensuing narrative will show.

§ 2. In the twenty-seventh year of his reign, in the month of September, king Henry came to England, bringing his daughter with him. But, at the ensuing Christmas, convening a great number of the clergy and nobility at London, he gave the county of Salop to his wife, the daughter of the earl of Louvain, whom he had married after the death of Matilda. Distressed that this lady had no issue, and fearing lest she should be perpetually childless, with well-founded anxiety, he turned his thoughts on a successor to the kingdom. On which subject, having held much previous and long-continued deliberation, he now at this council compelled all the nobility of England, as well as the bishops and abbots, to make oath, that, if he should die without male issue, they would, without delay or hesitation, accept his daughter Matilda, the late empress, as their sovereign; observing, how prejudicially to the country, fate

---

[1] The emperor Henry V. died 23d of May A.D. 1125; and in Sept. 1126, king Henry returned from Normandy with his daughter, the empress.

[2] See History of the Kings, § 419.

had snatched away his son William, to whom the kingdom by right had pertained; and that his daughter still survived, to whom alone the legitimate succession belonged, from her grandfather, uncle, and father, who were kings, as well as from her maternal descent for many ages back: inasmuch as from Egbert, king of the West Saxons, who first subdued or expelled the other kings of the island, in the year of the Incarnation eight hundred, through a line of fourteen kings, down to the year one thousand and forty-three, in which king Edward, who lies at Westminster, was elevated to the throne, the line of royal blood did never fail nor falter in the succession.[1] Moreover, Edward, the last, and at the same time the most noble of that stock, had united[2] Margaret, his grand-niece by his brother Edmund Ironside, to Malcolm king of Scotland, whose daughter Matilda, as was well known, was the empress's mother.

§ 3. All, therefore, in this council, who were considered as persons of any note, took the oath: and first of all, William, archbishop of Canterbury; next, the other bishops, and the abbots in like manner. The first of the laity who swore was David, king of Scotland, uncle of the empress; then Stephen, earl of Moriton and Boulogne, nephew of king Henry by his sister Adala; then Robert, the king's son, who was born to him before he came to the throne, and whom he had created earl of Gloucester, bestowing[3] on him in marriage Mabel, a noble and excellent woman; a lady as devoted to her husband as blessed in a numerous and beautiful offspring.   There was a singular dispute, as they relate, between Robert and Stephen, contending, with laudable emulation, which of them should take the oath first; one alleging the privilege of a son, the other the dignity of a nephew.   Thus all being bound by fealty and by oath, they, at that time, departed to their homes.   But after Pentecost, the king sent his daughter into Normandy, ordering her to be betrothed, by the archbishop of Rouen, to the son of Fulk aforesaid, a youth of high nobility and noted courage; nor did he himself delay setting sail for Normandy, for the purpose of uniting them in wedlock. Which being completed, all declared prophetically, as it were, that, after his death, they would break their plighted oath.   I have frequently heard Roger bishop of Salisbury say, that he was freed from the oath he had taken to the empress; for that he had sworn conditionally, that the king should not marry his daughter to any one out of the kingdom, without his consent and that of the rest of the nobility: that none of them advised the match, or indeed knew of it, except Robert earl of Gloucester, Brian the earl's son, and the bishop of Lisieux.   Nor do I relate this merely because I believe the assertion of a man who knew how to accommodate himself to every change of time and fortune; but, as an historian of veracity, I write the general belief of the people.

§ 4. The remaining years of the life and reign of Henry, I must review briefly, in order that posterity may neither be defrauded of

---

[1] This must be understood with the exception of Cnut and his sons, between Edmund Ironside and Edward the Confessor.
[2] Here seems a mistake. Margaret was given to Malcolm by her brother Edgar Atheling, while in exile in Scotland, A.D. 1067. See Saxon Chronicle.
[3] MSS. E. inserts from "bestowing" to "offspring."

a knowledge of these events; nor that I may seem to dwell on topics little relevant to this history. In his twenty-eighth year the king returned from Normandy; in his twenty-ninth a circumstance occurred in England which may seem surprising to our long-haired gallants, who, forgetting what they were born, transform themselves into the fashion of females, by the length of their locks. A certain English knight, who prided himself on the luxuriance of his tresses, being stung by conscience on the subject, seemed to feel, in a dream, as though some person strangled him with his ringlets. Awaking in a fright, he immediately cut off all his superfluous hair. The example spread throughout England, and, as recent punishment is apt to affect the mind, almost all military men allowed their hair to be cropped in a proper manner without reluctance. But this decency was not of long continuance, for scarcely had a year expired, ere all who thought themselves courtly, relapsed into their former vice ; they vied with women in length of locks, and wherever they were defective, put on false tresses, forgetful, or rather ignorant, of the saying of the apostle, " If a man nurture his hair, it is a shame to him." [1 Cor. xi. 14.][1] In his thirtieth year [A.D. 1130], king Henry went into Normandy. Pope Honorius dying in this year, the church of Rome was agitated by great contentions about electing his successor. There were, at that time, in the city, two very celebrated cardinals, Gregory, deacon of St. Angelo, and Peter, cardinal-priest, son of Leo, prince of the Romans, both noted for learning and activity, nor could the people easily discern which of them more justly ought to be elected by the clergy. The party, however, which favoured Gregory took the lead, and ordaining him pope, called him Innocent. Moreover a rumour was disseminated among the people, that Honorius was still just alive, and had commanded this to be done. The promoters of this choice were, William, bishop of Preneste, Matthew of Albano, Conrad of Sabina, John of Ostia, Peter of Crema, cardinal of St. Chrysogonus, and Haimeric the chancellor. But the other party, after Honorius was buried, at the instigation of Peter's brothers, who were the most opulent and powerful of the Romans, having elected and consecrated him, gave him the name of Anaclet. The chief adviser and instigator to this ordination, was Peter, bishop of Portus, whose letter, if I subjoin it, will disclose the whole controversy, although it incline rather to Anaclet.

§ 5. " Peter, bishop of Portus, to the four bishops, William of Preneste, Matthew of Albano, Conrad of Sabina, and John of Ostia. How great is the tribulation of my heart for you, He only knows who knows all things ; indeed you would have already been acquainted with it, in part, by my letters, did not the sentence and the common authority of the church prohibit. Of the praise or

---

[1] It is very remarkable what excessive pains were employed to prevail on the young men to part with their locks. In the council held at London by archbishop Anselm, A.D. 1102, it is enacted, that those who had long hair should be cropped, so as to show part of the ear, and the eyes. From the apparently strange manner in which this fashion is coupled in Edmer, p. 81, one might be led to suspect it was something more than mere spleen which caused this enactment. See also Orderic. Vitalis

dispraise of those persons, concerning whom so many different
opinions are at present given, it is not of this world to judge:
there is One who may seek and judge. But if any be ready to
accuse, one will be ready, and who is also bound to reply; more
especially when both in your and my sight, and in that of the
whole church, each of them has lived discreetly and honestly, and
has hitherto executed his office impartially. It rather concerns you
to abstain from idle language and the words of haste; if the
question be of report, the business is far different from what your
letters to me declare. In addition to this; if you regard the
accounts you have published, and the order of proceeding, (with
due reverence to you be it spoken,) by what boldness, by what
assurance, do you presume to call that usurpation of yours an
election? Why do you call that man of yours ordained, when
there was no order whatever in his case? Is it thus that you have
learnt to elect a pope? In a corner, in an hidden place, in darkness, and in the shadow of death? If you were desirous that a
living should succeed to a dead pope, why would you give out that
the deceased was still alive? It were much better, surely, to pay
the last sad offices to the dead, and in this manner provide for the
succour of the living; but, behold, while you seek succour for the
living from the dead, you destroy both the living and the dead at
the same time. Lastly, it was neither your office nor mine to
elect; but rather to refuse or to approve the person elected by the
brethren. Since, therefore, in neglect of the ritual, contempt of
the canon, and disregard of the very anathema framed by yourselves, without consulting me your superior, or your elder brethren
and superiors, or even summoning or waiting for them; when you
were inexperienced, and but very few in number, you have pre-
sumed to do this; you must be sensible, from your own estimation
of the case, that it must be considered void and of no avail whatever. The Lord, however, quickly came to our assistance, and
pointed out a method whereby to obviate your error: for your
brethren the cardinals, (who possess the chief voice in elections,)
together with the whole clergy, at the request of the people, and
with the consent of the nobility, openly, in the light of day, have
unanimously and heartily elected the noble cardinal Peter, as
Roman pontiff, by the name of Anaclet. I was present at this
election, which was made according to the canons, and have confirmed it by the authority of God. The church accepts and vene-
rates him, and by the grace of God the bishops and abbots, chief
princes and barons, some by themselves and others by their dele-
gates, acknowledge him in our presence. The robbery and cruelty
you mention I do not perceive: whoever goes to him for consulta-
tion, or on business, is kindly received, and still more kindly dismissed. Return then, return to your understanding; do not
make a schism in the church; do not persist in this perdition of
souls; let the fear of God possess you, not worldly shame. Does
any sleep, will he not add that he must rise again? Cease now
from lies, in which the wicked put their hope. The lord Tiburtius
hath testified by oath in writing, that I have deemed the deacon of

St. Angelo the only fit person for the office of pope ; let him look to what he hath said ; I have spoken nothing in secret ; no person hath ever heard such a word as this from my mouth. My opinion always was, that till the pope was buried no mention should be made of his successor. I have held, and will hold, the unity of the church ; I will be careful to adhere to truth and justice, confidently hoping that truth and justice will set me free." After this manner wrote the aforesaid Peter, bishop of Porto, rather partial to Peter the son of Leo. Nor did the other party at all give way; but called Peter himself, a lion's whelp,[1] and his partisans, the leaders of a faction. And they, indeed, acted variously among themselves under these doubtful circumstances. Innocent, however, excluded from Rome, passed the Alps and went into France. Here he was immediately received by all the Cisalpine churches.; and moreover, even king Henry, who did not easily change his opinion, willingly acknowledged him at Chartres ; and at Rouen condescended to honour him, not only with presents from himself, but also from the nobility, and even the Jews. Yet Innocent, though greatly assisted by the kings of England and France, and the emperor of Germany, could never enjoy peace, because Anaclet occupied the see of Rome. However, Anaclet himself dying in the eighth year of his usurped papacy, as it was called, Innocent enjoys the papal dignity unmolested to the present time.[2]

§ 6. [A.D. 1131.] In the thirty-first year of his reign, king Henry returned to England. The empress, too, in the same year, arrived on her native soil, and a full meeting of the nobility being held at Northampton, the oath of fidelity to her was renewed by such as had already sworn, and also taken by such as hitherto had not. In the same year, Louis, king of France, growing aged and unwieldy through extreme corpulency, commanded his son to be crowned as successor to the kingdom ; but being killed soon after by the fall of his horse, Louis caused another of his sons to be consecrated king, by the hands of the Roman pontiff. He, they say, does not degenerate from the ancient valour of the French, and has also acquired Aquitain as the marriage portion of his wife, which, it is well known, the kings of France have never held in their own right, since Louis, son of Charles the Great.

§ 7. [A.D. 1132.] In the thirty-first[3] year of king Henry, a dreadful murrain among domestic animals extended over the whole of England : entire herds of swine suddenly perished ; whole stalls of oxen were swept off in a moment ; the same contagion continued in the following years, so that no village throughout the kingdom was free from this calamity, or able to exult at the losses of its neighbours. At this time, too, the contention between Bernard, bishop of St. David's, and Urban of Llandaff, on the rights of their dioceses, which Urban had illegally usurped, was finally put to rest. For after being agitated by so many appeals to the court of Rome,

---

[1] An allusion to his name, which signifies a lion.

[2] Pope Innocent died 24 Sept. A.D. 1143.

[3] So both printed copy and the MSS. which have been consulted; but it should be 1132.

so many expensive journeys, so many debates of lawyers for a number of years, it was at last terminated, or rather cut short, by the death of Urban at Rome; the pope also, weighing the equity of the case, did justice to the piety and right of the bishop of St. David's by a suitable judgment.   In the same year, William archbishop of Canterbury personally obtained the legation of England through the indulgence of the see of Rome.

§ 8. The day before the thirty-second[1] year of his reign was completed, Henry, on the nones of August, (the very day on which he had formerly been crowned at Westminster,) set sail for Normandy. This was the last, the fatal voyage of his reign. The providence of God, at that time, bore reference in a wonderful manner to human affairs; for instance, that he should embark, never to return alive, on that day on which he had originally been crowned so long and prosperously to reign.   It was then, as I have said, the nones of August; and on the fourth day of the week,[2] the elements manifested their sorrow at this great man's last departure. For the sun on that day, at the sixth hour, shrouded his glorious face, as the poets say, in hideous darkness, agitating the hearts of men by an eclipse; and on the sixth day of the week, early in the morning, there was so great an earthquake that the ground appeared absolutely to sink down, a horrid sound being first heard from beneath the surface.   During the eclipse I saw stars around the sun; and, at the time of the earthquake the wall of the house in which I was sitting was lifted up by two shocks, and settled again with a third. The king, therefore, continued in Normandy for the space of three[3] whole years, and so much longer as from the nones of August, on which day, as has been said, he crossed the sea, to the kalends of December, on which night he died.   Doubtless, he performed many things worthy of record while in Normandy, but it was my design to omit whatever did not come authenticated to my knowledge.   Divers expectations of his return to England were all frustrated by some adverse fate, or by the will of God.   He reigned, then, thirty-five years, and from the nones of August to the kalends of December, that is, four months wanting four days.   Engaged in hunting at Liuns, he was taken suddenly ill. His malady increasing, he summoned to him Hugh, whom, from prior of Lewes, he had made abbot of Reading, and afterwards archbishop of Rouen, who was justly indebted to him and his heirs for such great favours. The report of his sickness quickly gathered the nobility around him. Robert, too, his son, the earl of Gloucester, was present, who, from his unblemished fidelity and matchless virtue, has deserved to be especially signalized throughout all ages.   Being interrogated by these persons as to his successor, he awarded all his territories, on either side of the sea, to his daughter, in legitimate and perpetual

---

[1] Malmesbury seems to have committed two oversights here. Henry went to Normandy for the last time on the third of the nones of August (that is, third, instead of fifth) A. D. 1133. This is evident from the eclipse he mentions, which took place on that day, as well as from the testimony of the continuator of Florence of Worcester, a contemporary writer.

[2] Wednesday, 2d August, 1133.

[3] From what has been said above this should be two.

succession, being somewhat displeased with her husband, as he had
irritated him both by threats and by certain injuries. Having passed
the seventh day of his sickness, he died about midnight. I waive
describing his magnanimous character in this place, as I have been
diffuse upon it in the fifth book of my Regal History. In how
Christian a manner he departed, the following epistle of the aforesaid archbishop of Rouen will testify.

§ 9. "To his Lord and Father, pope Innocent, his servant,
Hugh, priest of Rouen, sends his humble duty. I have deemed it
proper, to write to your fatherly affection concerning the king my
master, never to be remembered but with grief; for, being seized
with sudden sickness, he wished for me to console his sufferings,
and sent messengers as soon as possible for that purpose. I went
and passed three melancholy days with him. Agreeably to my
suggestion, he confessed his sins, he beat his breast, and he laid
aside all his animosities. Through the grace of God, and through
our advice and that of the bishops, he promised to attend to the
amendment of his life. Under this promise, according to our
office, on the third day, and three days successively, we gave him
absolution. He devoutly adored the cross of our Lord, and received his Body and Blood; bestowed his alms thus, saying, ' Let
my debts be paid, let the wages[1] and stipends which I owe be discharged, let the remainder be distributed to the poor. I wish they
who held and do hold his treasures had done thus. At last, I
earnestly stated to him our duty concerning the unction of the
sick, which the church adopted from the apostle St. James; and, at
his own devout request, I anointed him with holy oil. Thus he
rested in peace, and may God grant him the peace he loved."

§ 10. These circumstances relating to the faith of king Henry
when dying, were truly attested by the aforesaid archbishop of
Rouen. The body, royally attended, and borne by the nobility in
turn, was brought to Rouen, where, in a certain retired part of the
principal church, it was disembowelled, lest, becoming putrid, it
should offend the senses of those who approached it. The intestines were buried in the monastery of St. Mary des Prees, near the
city, which, as I hear, he had honoured with no mean presents, as
it had been begun by his mother. His body was kept at Caen till
the season, which was then very boisterous, became more tranquil.

§ 11. In the meantime, Stephen, earl of Mortain and Boulogne,
nephew of king Henry (as I have before said) who, after the king
of Scotland, was the first layman that had sworn fidelity to the
empress, hastened his return into England by way of Whitsand.
The empress, from certain causes, as well as her brother, Robert
earl of Gloucester, and almost all the nobility, delayed returning to
the kingdom. However, some castles in Normandy, the principal
of which was Danfront, espoused the party of the heiress. Moreover, it is well known, that on the day on which Stephen disem-

---

[1] "Liberationes," signifies, sometimes, what we now call liveries, that is, garments; sometimes money at stated periods, or, as we should say, wages: it is
here rendered in the latter sense, as being distinct from "solidatæ," pay or
stipends. Perhaps it was intended to distinguish two orders of persons by this
bequest; servants and soldiers: otherwise it may mean garments and wages.

barked in England, there was, very early in the morning, contrary
to the nature of winter in these countries, a terrible peal of thunder,
with most dreadful lightning, so that the world seemed well-nigh
about to be dissolved. After being acknowledged as king by the
people of London and of Winchester, he gained over also Roger
bishop of Salisbury, and William de Pont de l'Arche, the keepers
of the royal treasures. Yet, not to conceal the truth from posterity,
all his attempts would have been vain, had not his brother, Henry
bishop of Winchester, who is now legate of the papal see in
England, granted him his entire support; allured, indeed, by the
fullest expectation that Stephen would follow the example of his
grandfather William in the management of the kingdom, and more
especially in the strictness of ecclesiastical discipline. In consequence, when Stephen was bound by the rigorous oath which
William archbishop of Canterbury required from him, concerning
restoring and preserving the liberty of the church, the bishop of
Winchester became his pledge and surety. The written tenor of
this oath I shall be careful hereafter to insert in its proper place.

§ 12. Stephen, therefore, was crowned king of England on
Sunday, the eleventh of the kalends of January [Dec. 22], the
twenty-second day after the decease of his uncle, in the year of
our Lord's incarnation, one thousand one hundred and thirty-five ;
in the presence of three bishops, that is, the archbishop, and those
of Winchester and Salisbury; but there were no abbots and scarcely
any of the nobility. He was a man of activity, but imprudent ;
strenuous in war ; of great mind in attempting works of difficulty ;
mild and compassionate to his enemies, and affable to all ; kind
as far as promise went, but sure to disappoint in its truth and
execution : whence he soon afterwards neglected the advice of his
brother, befriended by whose assistance, as I have said, he had
supplanted his adversaries and obtained the kingdom.

§ 13. In the year of our Lord one thousand one hundred and
thirty-six, the wind being now favourable, the body of king Henry
was, immediately after Christmas, put on ship-board, and brought
to England; and, in the presence of his successor in the kingdom,
was buried at the monastery of Reading, which he had liberally
endowed, and filled with an order of monks of singular piety.
Shortly afterwards, a little before Lent, king Stephen went into
Northumberland, that he might have a conference with David,
king of Scotland, who was said to entertain hostile sentiments
towards him. From David he readily obtained what he wished,
because, being softened by the natural gentleness of his manners,
or by the approach of old age, he willingly embraced the tranquillity
of peace, real or pretended.

§ 14. In the same year, after Easter, Robert earl of Gloucester,
of whose prudence Stephen chiefly stood in awe, came to England.
While he was yet resident in Normandy, he had most earnestly
considered what line of conduct he should determine upon in the
present state of affairs. If he became subject to Stephen, it seemed
contrary to the oath he had sworn to his sister ; if he opposed him,
he saw that such conduct could nothing benefit her or his nephews,

but would certainly most grievously injure himself. For the king, as I said before, had an immense treasure, which his uncle had been accumulating for many years. His coin, and that of the best quality,[1] was estimated at an hundred thousand pounds; besides which there were vessels of gold and silver, of great weight and inestimable value, collected by the magnificence of preceding kings, and chiefly by Henry.[2] A man possessed of such boundless treasures could not want supporters, more especially as he was profuse, and, what by no means becomes a prince, even prodigal. Soldiers of all kinds, and light-armed troops, were flocking to him, chiefly from Flanders and Brittany. These were a most rapacious and violent race of men; who made no scruple to violate churchyards[3] or rob a church: moreover, not only would they drag men of religious order from their horses, but also make them captive; and this was done not merely by foreigners, but even by the native soldiers, who had abhorred the tranquillity of king Henry's time, because it subjected them to a life of poverty. All these most readily resorted to the prince whom they could easily incline to their purposes, pushing their fortune at the expense of the people. Stephen, indeed, before he came to the throne, from his complacency of manners, and readiness to joke, and sit, and regale, even with low people, had gained so much on their affections as is hardly to be conceived; and already had all the nobility of England willingly acknowledged him. This most prudent earl, therefore, was extremely desirous to convince them of their misconduct, and recal them to wiser sentiments by his presence; for, to oppose Stephen's power, he was unable, from the causes aforesaid: indeed, he had not the liberty of coming to England, unless, appearing as a partaker of their revolt, he dissembled for a time his secret intentions. He did homage to the king, therefore, under a certain condition; namely, so long as he should preserve his rank entire, and maintain his engagements to him; for having long since scrutinized Stephen's disposition, he foresaw the instability of his faith.

§ 15. In the same year, soon after the earl's arrival, the bishops swore fidelity to the king, so long as he should maintain the liberty of the church and the vigour of its discipline. He himself also swore according to the tenor of the following instrument:—

" I, Stephen, by the grace of God, elected king of England by the consent of the clergy and of the people, and consecrated by the lord William, archbishop of Canterbury and legate of the holy Roman church, and afterwards confirmed by Innocent, pope of the holy Roman see, through respect and love towards God, do grant the holy church to be free, and confirm to it all due reverence. I pro-

---

[1] There was a great difference in the money of this period: it was often so debased, that payments were made by weight, or by assay, and not by tale.

[2] The progress of some of Henry's treasure is curious. Theobald, earl of Blois, gave many jewels, which had been bestowed on him by Stephen his brother, to certain abbeys, and these again sold them for four hundred pounds to Suger, abbot of St. Denis. Henry, Suger observes, used to have them set in most magnificent drinking vessels. Suger, ap. Duchesne, iv. 345.

[3] Church-yards were, by the canons, privileged, so that persons in turbulent times conveyed their property thither for security.

mise that I will neither do anything simoniacally, nor permit it to be done, in the church, or in matters ecclesiastical. The jurisdiction and power over beneficed clergy, and over all persons in orders, and their property, and the distribution of effects of ecclesiastics, I admit to be in the hands of the bishops, and confirm it so to be. I grant and appoint, that the immunities of the churches, confirmed by their charters, and their customs observed from ancient usage, do remain inviolate. All the possessions of the churches, and the tenures which they.held at the death of my grandfather king William, I grant to them free, and discharged from the claim of all parties : but if the church shall hereafter claim anything as held or possessed before the death of the king, of which it is now deprived, I reserve such matter for discussion, or restitution at my will and pleasure. Moreover, whatever, since that king's death, has been obtained by the liberality of kings, or the gift of princes ; by offerings, or purchase, or by any exchange of the faithful, I confirm. I pledge myself to keep peace, and do justice to all, and to preserve them to my utmost ability. I reserve to myself the forests which king William, my grandfather, and William the Second, my uncle, have made and possessed : all the rest which king Henry added, I give and grant, without molestation, to the churches and the kingdom. And if any bishop or abbot, or other ecclesiastical person, shall have properly distributed[1] his property before his death, or appointed such distribution, I allow it to remain good ; but if he shall have been suddenly seized by death, before making a disposition, let the said distribution be made, at the discretion of the church, for the repose of his soul. Moreover, when the sees shall be vacant, let both them and their whole possessions be committed into the hands and custody of the clergy, or of lawful men of the same church, until a pastor be canonically appointed. I entirely do away all exactions, mischeningas,[2] and injustices, whether illegally introduced by the sheriffs, or any one else. I will observe the good and ancient laws and just customs, in murders, pleas, and other causes, and I command and appoint them to be so observed. Done at Oxford, in the year of our Lord, one thousand one hundred and thirty-six, in the first year of my reign."

§ 16. The names of the witnesses, who were numerous, I disdain to particularise, because he as basely perverted almost everything, as if he had sworn only that he might manifest himself a violator of his oath to the whole kingdom. This easy man must pardon me for speaking the truth ; who, had he entered on the sovereignty lawfully, and not given a ready ear to the insinuations of the malevolent in the administration of it, would have wanted little in any

---

[1] It had been the practice to seize, to the king's use, whatever property ecclesiastics left behind them. Henry Huntingdon relates, that on the death of Gilbert Universalis, bishop of London, who was remarkable for his avarice, all his effects, and among the rest, his boots crammed with gold and silver, were conveyed to the Exchequer. Anglia Sacra, ii. 698. Sometimes, even what has been distributed on a death-bed, was reclaimed for the king. Vide G. Neub. iii. 5.

[2] It seems to have been a vexatious fine imposed on litigants when, in their pleadings, they varied from their declaration.—Murder is sometimes taken in its present acceptation ; sometimes it means a certain fine levied on the inhabitants where murder had been committed.

princely quality. Under him, therefore, the treasures of several churches were pillaged, and their landed possessions given to laymen ; the churches of the clergy were sold to foreigners ; the bishops made captive, or forced to alienate their property ; the abbeys given to improper persons, either through the influence of friendship or for the discharge of debts. Still I think such transactions are not so much to be ascribed to him as to his advisers, who persuaded him that he ought never to want money so long as the monasteries were stored with treasure.

§ 17. [A.D. 1137.] In the year of our Lord one thousand one hundred and thirty-seven, in the beginning of Lent, the king crossed the sea. The earl, too, having thoroughly sounded, and discovered the inclinations of such as he knew to be tenacious of their plighted oath, and arranged what he conceived proper to be done afterwards, himself embarked on Easter-day, and prosperously reached the continent. Not long after, he had very nearly experienced the malignity of adverse fortune ; for the king endeavoured to intercept him by treachery, at the instigation of one William de Ipres. The earl, however, informed of it by one of the accomplices, avoided the snare prepared for him, and absented himself from the palace, whither he was repeatedly invited, for several days. The king, troubled at having succeeded so little by his artifices, and thinking to effect his design by cunning, endeavoured, by a serene countenance and gratuitous confession, to extenuate the enormity of his crime. He swore, in words framed at the earl's pleasure, never again to give countenance to such an outrage ; and still more to recover his good graces, he confirmed his oath, by Hugh, archbishop of Rouen, giving his hand to Robert. This he did, it is true ; but he never bestowed his unreserved friendship on that man, of whose power he was ever apprehensive. Thus, in his presence, he would pleasantly and affably call him " earl ;" when he was absent, he would vilify him, and would deprive him of such portions of his estates as he was able. Robert, too, artfully eluding his duplicity, disguised his feelings, and allowing the king to depart peaceably to his kingdom, continued in Normandy, intent on his own concerns. Wherefore while Stephen, perplexed by many commotions in England, and first attacking one, and then another, justly verified what was said of Ishmael, that the hands of all were against him, and his hand against all, Robert passed that whole year in Normandy in perfect quiet. The king pointedly, as it is reported, used frequently to say of his rebellious subjects, " Since they have elected me king, why do they desert me ? By the birth of God, I will never be called a fallen king !" Robert, placed as it were on an eminence, watched the event of circumstances, and earnestly revolved how he might escape, before God and man, the imputation of falsifying the oath he had sworn to his sister.

§ 18. [A.D. 1138.] In the year of our Lord one thousand one hundred and thirty-eight, England was shaken with intestine commotions. For many persons, emboldened to illegal acts, either by nobility of descent or by ambition, or rather by the unbridled heat of youth, were not ashamed, some to demand castles, others estates, and indeed whatever came into their fancy, from the king: and when he delayed complying with their requests, alleging the dismemberment of his kingdom, or that others would make similar claims, or were already in possession of them; they, becoming enraged immediately, fortified their castles against him, and drove away large booties from his lands. Nor, indeed, was his spirit at all broken by the revolt of any, but attacking them suddenly in different places, he always concluded matters more to his own disadvantage than to theirs; for, after many great but fruitless labours, he gained from them, by the grant of honours or castles, a feigned and temporary peace. He created likewise many earls,[1] where there had been none before, appropriating to them possessions and rents, which rightfully belonged to the crown. They were the more greedy in asking, and he the more profuse in giving, because a rumour was pervading England, that Robert earl of Gloucester, who was in Normandy, would shortly espouse the cause of his sister, after first renouncing his fealty to the king. This report was in fact well founded: for shortly after Pentecost, despatching some of his people to Stephen, from Normandy, he, according to ancient usage, renounced his fealty and friendship, and annulled his homage; assigning as a just reason for so doing, that the king had illegally aspired to the kingdom, and neglected his plighted faith to him, not to say absolutely belied it: and, moreover, that he himself had acted contrary to law; who, after the oath sworn to his sister, had not blushed to do homage to another during her lifetime. Doubtless also his mind was biassed by the answers of many ecclesiastics, whom he had consulted upon the subject; who declared that he could by no means pass the present life without ignominy, nor deserve the happiness of the next, if he violated the oath made to paternal affection. In addition to this, he contemplated the tenor of the papal decree, commanding obedience to the oath taken in the presence of his father; a copy of which decree I shall be careful to give in my next book. Robert, who had imbibed knowledge by a copious draught from the fount of science, was aware that these things would be of great advantage to him hereafter. But the king, indignant at the spirit of the earl, deprived him, as far as he was able, of all his possessions in England, and levelled some of his castles to the ground. Bristol alone remained, which not only expelled the enemy, but even harassed the king by frequent incursions. But as it may suffice to have brought the first book of the history of our own times from the return of the empress to her father (after the death of her husband), down to this period, I shall now begin the second, from the year in which this heroine came to England, to assert her right against Stephen.

[1] Earls, till this time, had apparently been official; each having charge of a county, and receiving certain emoluments therefrom: but these created by Stephen seem to have been often merely titulary, with endowments out of the demesnes of the crown. Rob. Montensis calls these persons Pseudo-Comites, imaginary earls, and observes that Stephen had completely impoverished the crown by his liberalities to them. Henry the Second, however, on being firmly seated on the throne, recalled their grants of crown lands, and expelled them from the kingdom.

THE SECOND BOOK OF WILLIAM OF MALMESBURY'S HISTORY OF HIS OWN TIMES.

BOOK II.

§ 91. [A.D. 1139.] In the year of our Lord's incarnation, one thousand one hundred and thirty-nine, the venom of malice, which had long been nurtured in the breast of Stephen, at length openly burst forth. Rumours were prevalent in England, that earl Robert was on the very eve of coming from Normandy with his sister; and when, under such an expectation, many persons revolted from the king, not only in inclination but in deed, he avenged himself for this injury at the cost of numbers. He also, to his disgrace as a king, seized many when at court, through mere suspicion of hostility to him, and obliged them to surrender their castles, and accede to any conditions he prescribed. There were at that time two very powerful bishops in England, Roger of Salisbury, and his fraternal nephew, Alexander of Lincoln. Alexander had built the castle of Newark, as he said, for the defence and dignity of the bishopric. Roger, who wished to manifest his magnificence by building, had erected extensive castles at Shireburn, and more especially at Devizes. At Malmesbury, even in the churchyard, and scarcely a stone's throw from the principal church, he had begun a castle. He had gotten into his custody the castle of Salisbury, which, being royal property, he had obtained from king Henry, and surrounded with a wall. Some powerful laymen, hurt at the probability of being surpassed by the clergy in extent of riches and magnitude of their towns, took offence at this, and fostered the latent wound of envy in their bosoms. Wherefore they poured forth their imagined grievances to the king; observing that the bishops, regardless of their order, were mad for erecting castles: that none could doubt but that they were designed for the overthrow of the king; for as soon as the empress should arrive, they would, induced doubtless by the recollection of her father's kindness to them, immediately greet their sovereign with the surrender of their fortresses: that therefore they ought to be prevented, and compelled to give up their strongholds; otherwise the king would repent too late, when he saw in the power of the enemy that which, had he been wise, he might have applied to his own purpose. Such were the frequent insinuations of the nobility. The king, though far too partial to them, for some time pretended not to listen to what gratified his ear so much; assuaging the bitterness of delay, either by his respect for the piety of the bishops, or, as I rather think, from apprehension of the odium he might incur by seizing their castles. Finally, he only postponed the execution of what the nobles had urged him to, till an opportunity presented itself for his purpose; which was as follows:

§ 20. A great assembly of the nobles being held at Oxford about the eighth of the kalends of July [June 24], the prelates above-mentioned also repaired thither. The bishop of Salisbury set out on this expedition with great reluctance; for I heard him speaking to the following purport: " By my Lady St. Mary, I know not why, but my heart revolts at this journey; this I am sure of, that I shall be of much the same service at court as a foal is in battle :" thus did his mind forbode future evils. Here, as though fortune would seem subservient to the king's wishes, a quarrel arose between the servants of the bishops and those of Alan, earl of Brittany, about a right to quarters, which had a melancholy termination; as the bishop of Salisbury's retainers, then sitting at table, left their meal unfinished and rushed to the contest. At first, they contended with reproaches, afterwards with swords. The domestics of Alan were put to flight, and his nephew nearly killed : nor was the victory gained without bloodshed on the bishops' side; for many were wounded, and one knight[1] even slain. The king, eagerly seizing the opportunity, ordered the bishops to be convened by his old instigators, that they might make satisfaction to his court, as their people had infringed his peace : and that this satisfaction should be, the delivery of the keys of their castles, as pledges of their fidelity. Though prepared to make compensation, they hesitated at the surrender of their fortresses; and in consequence, lest they should depart, he ordered them into close confinement. So he took bishop Roger unfettered, but the chancellor, the nephew, (or as it was reported, more than the nephew,) of the bishop, in chains, to Devizes; intending, if he could, to get possession of the castle, which was erected at great and almost incalculable expense, not, as the prelate himself used to say, for the ornament, but as the real fact is, to the detriment of the church. At the first summons, the castles of Salisbury, Shireburn, and Malmesbury, were yielded to the king; Devizes also surrendered at the end of three days, after the bishop had voluntarily enjoined himself abstinence from all food, that by his personal sufferings he might work upon the mind of the bishop of Ely, who had taken possession of it.[2] Nor did Alexander bishop of Lincoln act more perseveringly; for he purchased his liberty by the surrender of his castles of Newark and Sleaford.[3]

§ 21. This transaction on the part of the king gave rise to the expression of many different opinions. Some observed that the bishops were justly dispossessed of their castles, as they had built them in opposition to the injunction of the canons; they ought to be preachers of peace, not builders of houses which might be a refuge for evil-doers. Such was the doctrine enforced, with ampler reasons

---

[1] The term "miles" is very ambiguous : sometimes it is a knight; sometimes a trooper; sometimes a soldier generally. In later times it signified almost always a knight; but in Malmesbury it seems mostly a horseman, probably of the higher order.

[2] The author of the "Gesta Stephani" says, the king ordered both bishops to be kept without food, and threatened, moreover, to hang the son of bishop Roger. Gest. Stephani, 944. The continuator of Flor. Wigorn. adds, that one was confined in the crib of an ox-lodge, the other in a vile hovel, A.D. 1138.

[3] Castellorum, Newarke, et Esleford, MS. E.

and discourses, by Hugh archbishop of Rouen; as far as his eloquence extended, the strenuous champion of the king. Others took
the opposite side of the question; among whom was Henry bishop
of Winchester, legate of England from the papal see, and brother to
king Stephen, as I have said before, whom neither fraternal affection nor fear of danger could turn aside from the path of truth. He
spake to this effect: " If the bishops had in anything overpassed
the bounds of justice, the judging them did not pertain to the king,
but to the ecclesiastical canons; that they ought not to be deprived
of any possession but by a public and ecclesiastical council; that
the king had not acted from zealous regard to right, but with a view
to his own advantage; as he had not restored the castles to the
churches, at whose expense, and on whose land, they were built, but
had delivered them to laymen, and those by no means of religious
character." Though the legate made these declarations, not only
privately, but publicly also before the king, and urged him to the
liberation and restitution of the bishops, yet being entirely disregarded, he lost his labour. In consequence, deeming it proper to
resort to canonical power, he summoned his brother, without delay,
to be present at a council he intended to hold at Winchester, on
the fourth of the kalends of September [Aug. 29].

§ 22. On the appointed day, almost all the bishops of England,
with Theobald archbishop of Canterbury, who had succeeded
William, came to Winchester. Turstin, archbishop of York, excused himself, on account of the malady with which he was afflicted:
for he was so enfeebled as to be hardly able to guide his steps: the
others apologized for their absence, by letter, by reason of the war.
The bull of pope Innocent was first read in the council, whereby, even
from the kalends of March, if I rightly remember, he had enjoined the
administration of his anxious charge to the lord bishop of Winchester, as legate in England. This was received with much good-
will, as the bishop had shown his forbearance, by the lapse of time,
and had not proclaimed himself legate with precipitate vanity. Next
followed, in the council, his address, in the Latin tongue, directed
to the learned, on the disgraceful detention of the bishops; of whom
the bishop of Salisbury had been seized in a chamber of the palace,
Lincoln in his lodgings, and Ely, fearing a similar treatment, had
escaped the calamity by a hasty retreat to Devizes: he observed, that it was a dreadful crime, that the king should be so
led away by sinister persons, as to have ordered violent hands to be
laid on his subjects, more especially bishops, in the security of his
court; that, to the king's disgrace, was to be added the offence
against God, in despoiling the churches of their possessions, under
pretext of the criminality of the prelates; that the king's outrage against the law of God was matter of such pain to him, that
he had rather himself suffer grievous injury, both in person and
property, than have the episcopal dignity so basely humiliated;
moreover, that the king, being repeatedly admonished to amend his
fault, had at last not refused that the council should be summoned:
that, therefore, the archbishop and the rest should deliberate what
was proper to be done; and he would not be wanting to execute

the sentence of the council, either through regard to the friendship of the king, who was his brother, or loss of property, or even danger of life.

§ 23. When he had gradually expatiated on these matters, the king, not distrusting his cause, sent certain earls[1] into the council, to demand wherefore he was summoned. The legate briefly replied: That, when he recollected he was in subjection to the faith of Christ, he ought not to be displeased, if, when guilty of a crime such as the present age had never witnessed, he was required, by the ministers of Christ, to make satisfaction; that it was the act of heathen nations to imprison bishops, and divest them of their possessions; that they should tell his brother, therefore, that if he would deign a patient assent to his advice, he would give him such, by the authority of God, as neither the church of Rome, nor the French king's court, nor even earl Theobald, their common brother, a man of surpassing sense and piety, could reasonably oppose; but such as they ought favourably to embrace; that, at present, the king would act advisedly, if he would either account for his conduct, or submit to canonical judgment; it was, moreover, a debt he owed, to favour the church, by whose fostering care, not by military force, he had been promoted to the kingdom. The earls retiring after this speech, returned shortly with an answer prepared. They were accompanied by one Alberic de Ver, a man deeply versed in legal affairs. He reported the king's answer, and aggravated as much as possible the case of bishop Roger, for bishop Alexander, whom he supported, had departed; but this he did with moderation and without using opprobrious language, though some of the earls, standing by, repeatedly interrupted his harangue, by casting reproaches on the bishop.

§ 24. The sum of what Alberic had to allege, was as follows: That bishop Roger had greatly injured king Stephen; that he seldom came to court but his people, presuming on his power, excited tumults; that they had frequently at other places, and very lately at Oxford, attacked the attendants, and even the nephew of earl Alan, as well as the servants of Hervy de Liuns, a man of such high nobility, and so extremely haughty, that he had never deigned to visit England, though king Henry had invited him; that the injury, therefore, of such violence having been offered him, doubly recoiled on king Stephen, through respect to whom he had come hither; that the bishop of Lincoln had been the author of the tumult excited by his followers, from ancient enmity to Alan; that the bishop of Salisbury secretly favoured the king's enemies, though he disguised his subtlety for the moment; that the king had discovered this beyond all doubt, from many circumstances; more especially, however, from the said bishop having refused permission to Roger de Mortimer, with the king's soldiers whom he was conducting, when under the greatest apprehensions from the garrison of Bristol, to continue even a single night at Malmesbury; that it was in every

---

[1] It has before been related that Stephen made many earls, where there had been none before; these seem the persons intended by Malmesbury in many places, when speaking of some of the king's adherents.

person's mouth, that as soon as the empress should arrive, he would join her party, with his nephews and his castles; that Roger, in consequence, was made captive, not as a bishop, but as the king's servant, who had administered his affairs and received his wages; that the king had not taken their castles by violence, but that both bishops had surrendered them voluntarily, to escape the punishment due to the disturbance they had excited in the court; that the king had found some trifling sums of money in the castles, which must lawfully belong to himself, as bishop Roger had collected it from the revenues of the exchequer, in the times of his uncle and predecessor, king Henry; that the bishop had readily relinquished this money, as well as the castles, through consciousness of his offences, of which the king did not want witnesses; that, therefore, it was his will that the conditions entered into by himself and the bishops should remain in force.

§ 25. It was rejoined, by bishop Roger, in opposition to the speech of Alberic, that he had never been the minister of king Stephen, nor had he received his wages. This spirited man, too, who blushed at being cast down by adversity, threatened, that if he could not have justice from that council, for the property which had been wrested from him, he would seek it in the audience of an higher court. The legate, mildly, as usual, observed, that every allegation against the bishops ought to be made, and the truth of it inquired into, in an ecclesiastical court, before passing sentence, contrary to the canons, on innocent persons; that the king ought, therefore, to do as was incumbent in civil courts, that is, re-invest the bishops with their own property, otherwise, being disseized, by the law of nations they would not plead.

§ 26. Many arguments of this kind being used on both sides, the cause, at the king's request, was adjourned to the next day; then, on the morrow, prolonged still a day farther, till the arrival of the archbishop of Rouen. When he came, while all were anxious to hear what he had to allege, he said he was willing to allow the bishops their castles, if they could prove by the canons that they ought justly to possess them; but as they were not able to do this, it was the height of impudence to contend against the canons. "And admitting," said he, "that it be just for them to possess castles, yet most assuredly, as the times are eventful, all chiefs, after the custom of other nations, ought to deliver up the keys of their fortifications to the will of the king, who is bound to wage war for the common security." Thus the whole plea of the bishops was shaken: for, either according to the decrees of the canons, it was unjust for them to have castles; or, if that were allowed by the king's indulgence, they ought to yield to the emergency of the times, and give up the keys.

§ 27. To this the aforesaid pleader, Alberic, added, that, it had been signified to the king, that the bishops murmured among themselves, and had even made preparation for some of their party to proceed to Rome against him. "And this," said he, "the king advises that none of you presume to do; for if any person shall go from England to any place, in opposition to him and to the dignity of his kingdom, perhaps his return may not be so easy. Moreover, he, as he sees himself aggrieved, of his own accord summons you to Rome."

§ 28. When the king had sent such a message, partly advising, and partly threatening, it was perceived what was his design. In consequence, the council broke up, as he would not submit to canonical censure, and the bishops deemed it unadvisable to enforce it against him for two reasons; first, because it was a rash act to excommunicate the king without the knowledge of the pope; secondly, because they understood, or some of them even saw, that swords were unsheathed around them. It was no longer a joking matter, but a struggle for life and death. The legate and the arch-bishop, still, however, were anxiously observant of their duty. They humbly prostrated themselves before the king in his chamber, entreating him to take pity on the church, and to consider his soul and his reputation; and that he would not suffer a schism to be made between the empire and the priesthood. Although he, in some measure, removed the odium of his former conduct, by con-descendingly rising to them, yet, prevented by ill advice, he carried none of his fair promises into effect.

§ 29. The council broke up on the kalends of September [Sept. 1]; and on the day previous to the kalends of October [Sept. 30], earl Robert, having at length surmounted every cause of delay, arrived with the empress, his sister, in England, relying on the pro-tection of God and the observance of his lawful oath; but with a much smaller military force than any other person would have required for so perilous an enterprise; for he had not with him, at that time, more than one hundred and forty horsemen. My assertion is supported by persons of veracity; and did it not look like flattery, I would say that he was not inferior to Julius Cæsar, at least in resolution, whom Livy[1] relates to have had but five cohorts, when he began the civil war, and with which he attacked the world. But the comparison between Julius and Robert is in-vidious; for Julius, an alien to the true faith, reposed his hope on his good fortune, as he used to say, and the valour of his legions; Robert, celebrated for Christian piety, relied only on the assistance of the Holy Spirit, and the Lady St. Mary. The former had par-tisans in Gaul, in parts of Germany, and Brittany; and had attached to him, by means of presents, all the Roman people, with the ex-ception of the senate; the latter, with the exception of a very few who regarded their plighted oath, found the nobility in England either opposing or affording him no assistance. He landed, then, at Arundel, and, for a time, delivered his sister into the safe keeping, as he supposed, of her mother-in-law, whom Henry, as I have before related, had married on the death of the empress's mother. He himself proceeded through the hostile country to Bristol, accompanied, as I have heard, by scarcely twelve horse-men, and was joined in the midst of his journey by Brian the earl's son from Wallingford. Nor was it long ere he learnt that his sister had quitted Arundel; for her mother-in-law, through female

[1] It would seem from this passage, that he had seen Livy's work entire.

inconstancy, had broken the faith she had repeatedly pledged by messengers sent into Normandy. The king, therefore, placed the empress under the care of Henry bishop of Winchester, and Waleran earl of Meulan for safe-conduct; a favour never denied to the most inveterate enemy by honourable soldiers. Waleran, indeed, declined going farther than Calne; but the bishop continued his route. The earl, therefore, quickly collecting his troops, came to the boundary appointed by the king, and placed his sister in safer quarters at Bristol. She was afterwards received into Gloucester by Milo, who held the castle of that city under the earl in the time of king Henry, doing him homage and swearing fidelity to him; for this is the chief city of his county.

§ 30. On the nones of October [Oct. 7] one Robert Fitz-Hubert, a savage barbarian, by night clandestinely entering the castle of Malmesbury, which bishop Roger had inauspiciously founded, and burning the town, boasted of the deed, as though he had gained a great triumph. But, within a fortnight, his joy was at an end, being put to flight by the king. Stephen, in the meantime, commanded possession to be kept of the castle, until, on the restoration of peace, it might be destroyed. The king, moreover, before he came to Malmesbury, had occupied and placed a garrison in a small fortress called Cerney, belonging to the aforesaid Milo. In consequence, thinking that he should be equally successful elsewhere as at that place and at Malmesbury, he assailed a castle called Trowbridge, belonging to Humphrey de Bohun, who was on the side of the empress, but he departed without success.

§ 31. The whole country, then, around Gloucester, to the extremity of Wales, partly by force, and partly by favour, in the course of the remaining months of that year, gradually espoused the side of the empress. The owners of certain castles, securing themselves within their fastnesses, waited the issue of events. The city of Hereford was taken without difficulty; the few soldiers, who, determining on resistance, had thrown themselves into the castle, being blockaded therein. The king drew nigh, if possible, to devise means for their assistance; but, frustrated in his attempt, he retired with disgrace. He also approached Bristol, and going beyond it, burnt the neighbourhood around Dunstore, leaving nothing, as far as he was able, which could afford sustenance for his enemies, or advantage to any one.

§ 32. On the third of the ides of December [Dec. 11], death kindly relieved Roger bishop of Salisbury from the quartan ague which had long afflicted him. They assert that his sickness was brought upon him through grief at the severe and repeated injuries he had received from king Stephen. To me it appears that God exhibited him to the wealthy as an example of the mutability of fortune, in order that they should not trust in uncertain riches, which, as the apostle[1] says, "while some have coveted, they have made shipwreck of their faith." He first ingratiated himself with prince Henry, who became afterwards king, by his prudence in the management of domestic matters, and by restraining the excesses

[1] 1 Tim. i. 19.

of his household. For, before his accession, Henry had been careful
and economical in his expenses, compelled thereto by the scantiness
of his resources, and the illiberal treatment of his brothers, William
and Robert. Knowing his disposition in this way, Roger had deserved so well of him in his time of need, that, when he came to the
throne, he denied him scarcely anything he thought proper to ask; he
gave him estates, churches, prebends, entire abbeys of monks; and,
lastly, committed even the kingdom to his fidelity: he made him
chancellor in the beginning of his reign, and not long after, bishop
of Salisbury.   Roger, therefore, decided causes; he regulated the
expenditure; he had charge of the treasury. Such were his occupations when the king was in England; such, without associate or
inspector, when he resided in Normandy, which took place repeatedly, and for a long time together. And not only the king, but
the nobility, even those who were secretly stung with envy at his
good fortune, and more especially the ministers and debtors of the
king, gave him almost whatever he could fancy. If there was anything contiguous to his property which might be advantageous to
him, he would directly extort it, either by entreaty or purchase; or,
if that failed, by force. With unrivalled magnificence in their construction, as our times may recollect, he erected splendid mansions
on all his estates; in merely maintaining which, the labour of his
successors shall toil in vain. His cathedral he dignified to the
utmost with matchless ornaments, and buildings on which no
expense was spared. It was truly wonderful to behold in this man
what abundant power attended him in every kind of dignity, and
flowed, as it were, to his hand. How great was the glory, (indeed,
what could exceed it?) that he should have made his two nephews—
by virtue of the education which he bestowed upon them, men of
noted learning and industry—bishops; and not of mean sees, but
of Lincoln and Ely, than which I know not whether there be more
opulent in England! He was sensible of his power, and, somewhat
more harshly than became such a character, abused the favours of
Heaven. Lastly, as the poet observes of some rich man,[1]

"He builds, destroys, and changes square for round,"

so Roger attempted to turn abbeys into bishoprics, and bishoprics
into abbeys. The most ancient monasteries of Malmesbury and
Abbotsbury, he annexed, as far as he was able, to his see; he
changed the priory of Shireburn, which is subject to the bishop of
Salisbury, into an abbey; and the abbey of Hortun was forthwith
dissolved and united to it. These events took place in the time of
king Henry, under whom, as I have observed, his prosperity reached
its zenith; for under Stephen, as I have before related, it began to
decline; except that in the beginning of his reign, he obtained for
one of his nephews the chancellorship; for the other the office of
treasurer; and for himself the town of Malmesbury; the king repeating often to his companions, "By the birth of God, I would
give him half England, if he asked for it; till the time be ripe, he
shall tire of asking, ere I tire of giving." But fortune, who, in

[1] Horat. Epist. I. i. 100.

former times, had flattered him so long and so transcendently, at last cruelly pierced him with her scorpion-sting. Such was that instance, when he saw those whom he dearly regarded, wounded, and his most favoured knight killed before his face; the next day, himself, as I said before, and his nephews, very powerful bishops, the first compelled to fly, the second detained, and the third, a young man to whom he was greatly attached, bound with chains; on the surrender of his castles, his treasures pillaged, and himself afterwards, in the council, loaded with the most disgraceful reproaches: finally, when he was on his death-bed at Salisbury, the residue of his money and utensils, which he had placed upon the altar for the purpose of completing the church, were carried off against his will. The height of his calamity was, I think, a circumstance which even I cannot help commiserating; that, though he appeared wretched to many, yet there were very few who pitied him; so much envy and hatred had his excessive power drawn on him, and undeservedly, too, from some of those very persons whom he had advanced to honour.

§ 33. In the year of the Incarnate Word one thousand one hundred and forty, the monks of those abbeys, which Roger had unjustifiably usurped, waiting on the king, were permitted to enjoy their ancient privileges, and abbots, as formerly. John, a monk of that place, a man highly celebrated for the affability of his manners and the liberality of his mind, was elected abbot of Malmesbury by the monks, according to the tenur of the privilege which St. Aldhelm had obtained from pope Sergius four hundred and sixty-six years before, and had caused to be confirmed by the kings, Ina of the West Saxons, and Ethelred of the Mercians. The legate approved the claim, but disapproved of the person; for he could not be induced to believe that the king had consented to the election but by a gift in money. And, indeed, a small sum had been promised, on the score of liberating the church, not for the election of the person. Wherefore, John, though removed by a premature death within the year, still left a lasting and laudable memory of himself to all succeeding ages. For no monk of that place, I confess the truth, would have pursued a task of such difficulty, had not John begun it. Wherefore let his successors be praised, if they shall preserve the liberty of that church; he certainly rescued it from thraldom.

§ 34. The whole of this year was embittered by the horrors of war. There were many castles throughout England, each defending, or more properly speaking, laying waste, its neighbourhood. The garrisons drove off from the fields, both sheep and cattle, sparing neither churches nor churchyards. Seizing[1] such of the vavassours[2] and country-people as were reputed to be possessed of money, they compelled them, by extreme torture, to promise whatever they thought fit. Plundering the houses of the wretched husbandmen, even to their very beds, they cast them into prison;

---

[1] MS. E. adds from "seizing" to "thought fit."

[2] The meaning of "vavassour" is very various; here it seems to imply what we call a yeoman.

nor did they liberate them, but on their giving everything they possessed, or could by any means scrape together, for their release. Many calmly expired in the midst of torments inflicted to compel them to ransom themselves, bewailing, which was all they could do, their miseries to God. At the instance of the earl, indeed, the legate, with the bishops, repeatedly excommunicated all violators of churchyards and plunderers of churches, and those who laid violent hands on men in holy or monastic orders, or their servants; but this his attention profited but little. It was distressing, therefore, to see England, once the fondest cherisher of peace and the signal home of tranquillity, reduced to such a pitch of misery, that not even the bishops or monks could pass in safety from one town to another. Under king Henry, many foreigners, who had been driven from home by the commotions of their native land, were accustomed to resort to England, and rest in quiet under his fostering protection; in Stephen's time, numbers of freebooters from Flanders and Brittany flocked to England, in expectation of rich pillage. Meanwhile, the earl of Gloucester conducted himself with caution, and his most earnest endeavours were directed to gaining conquests with the smallest loss to his adherents. Such of the English nobility as he could not prevail upon to regard the obligation of their oath, he held it sufficient if he could so restrain, that, if they did not assist, they would not injure the cause; being willing, according to the saying of the comic writer, to do what he could, when he could not do what he would. But when he saw the opportunity present itself, he strenuously performed the duty both of soldier and of general; more especially he valiantly subdued those strongholds, which were of signal detriment to the cause he had espoused; that[1] is to say, Harpetrey, which king Stephen had taken from certain soldiers of the earl before he came to England, and many others; Sudley, Cerney, which the king had garrisoned, as I have said; and the castle which Stephen had fortified over against Wallingford he levelled to the ground. He also, in these difficult times, created his brother Rainald, earl of Cornwall. Nor, indeed, did the king show less spirit in performing the duties of his station; for he omitted no occasion of repeatedly beating off his adversaries, and defending his own possessions. But he failed of success, and his affairs grew worse for lack of justice. Dearth of provisions, too, increased by degrees; and the scarcity of good money was so great, from being counterfeited, that sometimes, out of ten or more shillings, hardly a dozen pence would be received. The king himself was reported to have ordered the weight of the penny, as established in king Henry's time, to be reduced, because, having exhausted the vast treasures of his predecessor, he was unable to provide for the expense of so many soldiers. All things, then, became venal in England; and churches and abbeys were no longer secretly, but even publicly, exposed to sale.

§ 35. During this year, in Lent, on the thirteenth of the kalends of April [March 20], at the ninth hour of the fourth day of the week,

---

[1] MS. E. inserts from "that" to "the ground."

there was an eclipse, throughout England, as I have heard. With us, indeed, and with all our neighbours, the obscuration of the sun was so remarkable, that persons sitting at table, as it then happened almost everywhere, (for it was Lent,[1]) at first feared that chaos was come again; afterwards learning its cause, they went out, and beheld the stars around the sun. It was thought and said by many, not untruly, that the king would not continue a year in the government.

§ 36. In the following week, that is, during the time of the Passion, on the seventh of the kalends of April [March 26], the fore-mentioned barbarian,[2] Robert Fitz-Hubert, a character well calculated for the stratagems of war, surprised the castle of Devizes.[3] He was a man by far the most cruel of any within the circle of this age's memory; and blasphemous, also, towards God: he used voluntarily to boast of having been present at a place where twenty-four monks were burnt, together with the church; declaring, that he, too, would frequently do the like in England, and grieve God, by the plunder of the church of Wilton, and the destruction of Malmesbury, with the slaughter of all its monks; that he would return them this good office, because they had admitted the king, to his disadvantage; for of this he accused them, though without foundation. I myself have heard, when, at any time, which was extremely rare indeed, he liberated his captives without torture, and they thanked him for it, on the part of God, I have heard him, I say, reply; "Never let God owe me any thanks." He used to expose his prisoners, naked and rubbed with honey, to the burning heat of the sun; thereby exciting flies, and other insects of that kind, to sting them. But, having now got possession of Devizes, he hesitated not to boast, that he should gain, by means of this castle, the whole district from Winchester to London; and that he would send to Flanders for soldiers to defend him. While meditating, however, such a scheme, Divine vengeance overtook him, through the agency of John Fitz-Gilbert, a man of surprising subtlety, who held the castle at Marlborough: for being thrown into chains by him, because he refused to surrender Devizes to his sovereign, the empress, he was hanged, like a common thief. Wonderful was the judgment of God on this sacrilegious wretch, that he should meet with such an ignominious end, not from the king, to whom he was inimical, but from the very persons he appeared to favour. The authors of his death ought worthily to be extolled, for having freed the country from such a pest, and justly dispatched an intestine enemy.

§ 37. In the same year, during Pentecost [May 26], the king resided at London, in the Tower, attended only by the bishop of Sees, for the others disdained, or feared, to come thither. Some little time after, by the mediation of the legate, a conference was appointed between the empress and the king, that, if possible, by God's help, peace might be restored. The conference was held near

---

[1] The passage within brackets occurs only in E.   [2] See § 30, p. 400.
[3] This he effected by means of scaling ladders, made of thongs of leather. Gest. Stephani, 951.

Bath; on the part of the empress were sent her brother Robert, and others of her friends; on the king's, the legate, the archbishop, and also the queen. But they wasted words and time, to no purpose, and departed without being able to conclude a peace. Nor was the ground of separation equal on both sides, as the empress, more inclined to justice, had declared, that she was not averse to the decision of the church; but the king's party were averse to this, so long as they could make their ascendency over him answer their own purposes. In September following, the legate, who knew that it was the especial duty of his office to restore peace, undertaking the toil of a foreign voyage for its accomplishment, hastened to sail over to France. After a long and anxious discussion, for tranquillizing England, had taken place, between the king of France, count Thibaut, and many of the clergy, he returned, nearly at the end of November, bringing back counsels wholesome for the country, could they have been carried into effect. And indeed the empress and the earl assented to them immediately, but the king delayed from day to day, and finally rejected them altogether. Upon this, at last, the legate discontinued his exertions, waiting, like the rest, for the issue of events: for what avails it to swim against the stream? and, as some one observes, " To seek odium only by one's labours is the height of madness."

PREFACE TO BOOK III.

I NOW attempt[1] to give a clue to the mazy labyrinth of events and transactions which occurred in England, during the year one thousand one hundred and forty-one,[2] lest posterity, through my neglect, should be unacquainted with them; as it is of service, to know the volubility of fortune, and the mutability of human estate, God only permitting or ordaining them. And, as the moderns greatly and deservedly blame our predecessors, for having left no memorial of themselves or their transactions, since the days of Beda, I think I ought to be very favourably regarded by my readers, if they judge rightly, for determining to remove this reproach from our times.

THE THIRD BOOK OF WILLIAM OF MALMESBURY'S HISTORY OF HIS OWN TIMES.

BOOK III.

§ 38. KING STEPHEN had peaceably departed from the county of Lincoln before Christmas, and had augmented the honours of the earl of Chester, and of his brother; of whom the earl, long since, in the time of king Henry, had been married to the daughter of the

---

[1] Here the MSS. fluctuate as to the commencement of the third book, of which, in some, this is called the prologue.

[2] Several MSS. (D. E 2. L 2.), as well as Saville's printed copy, read 1142, but one (E 1.) has 1141, which is right.

earl of Gloucester. In the meanwhile, the citizens of Lincoln, who wished to acquire great favour with the king, certified him by a message, when resident in London, that the two brothers had taken up their abode in security, in the castle of that city ; and that, suspecting nothing less than the arrival of the king, they might be very easily surprised, while they themselves would provide that he should get possession of the castle as secretly as possible. As Stephen never wished to neglect any opportunity of augmenting his power, he gladly repaired thither. In consequence, the brothers were surprised, and besieged, even in the Christmas holidays. This step appeared unjustifiable to many, because, as I have observed, he had left them before the festival, without any suspicion of enmity; nor had he, even now, after ancient usage, abjured his friendship with them, which they call " defying." However, the earl of Chester, though surrounded with imminent dangers, adroitly escaped from the castle. By what management this was accomplished, I know not; whether through consent of some of the besiegers, or whether because valour, when taken by surprise, frequently tries a variety of methods, and often discovers a remedy for its emergencies. Not content with his own escape, he earnestly deliberated, how to devise the safety of his brother and of his wife, whom he had left in the fortress. The more prudent mode seemed to be, to request assistance from his father-in-law, although he had long since offended him, on many accounts ; but principally because he appeared staunch to neither party. He sent messengers, therefore, promising eternal fidelity to the empress, if, induced more by affectionate regard than any desert of his, he would rescue those from danger, who were already in the very jaws of captivity.

§ 39. Unable to endure this indignity, the earl of Gloucester readily assented. Weary of delay, too, as the fairest country was harassed with intestine rapine and slaughter for the sake of two persons, he preferred bringing the matter to an issue at once, would God permit. He hoped also for the Divine assistance on his undertaking, as the king had molested his son-in-law, without any fault on his part ; was at that moment besieging his daughter ; and had castellated the church of the holy mother of God, in Lincoln. How much ought these things to weigh in the mind of a prince ? Would it not be better to die, and fall with honour, than endure so marked a disgrace ? For the sake then of avenging God, and his sister, and liberating his relations, he entered on this perilous undertaking. The supporters of his party readily accompanied him ; the major part of whom being deprived of their inheritances, were instigated to hostility by rage at their losses, and the consciousness of their valour. However, during the whole extended march from Gloucester to Lincoln, he studiously concealed his intention, leaving all the army, with the exception of a very few, in suspense, by his mysterious conduct.

§ 40. At length, on the day of the Purification of the blessed Mary [Feb. 2], they arrived at the river flowing between the two armies, called the Trent, which, from its springs, together with floods of rain, had risen so high, that it could not possibly be forded. Here, at last, disclosing his intention to his son-in-law, who had joined him with a strong force, and to those he had brought with him, he added, that he had long since made up his mind, never to be induced to fly, be the emergency what it might; if they could not conquer, they must die, or be taken. All encouraged him to hope the best; and wonderful to hear, though on the eve of hazarding a battle, he swam over the rapid river I have mentioned, with the whole of his party. So great was the earl's ardour to put an end to calamity, that he preferred risking extremities, to prolonging the sufferings of the country. The king, too, with many earls, and an active body of cavalry, abandoning the siege, courageously presented himself for battle. The royalists began the prelude to the fight, which they call the "joust,"[1] as they were skilled in that exercise; but when they saw that the consular party, if they may be so called, did not attack from a distance, with lances, but at close-quarters, with swords, and broke the king's ranks with violent and determined onset, the earls, to a man,[2] (for six of them had entered the conflict together with the king,) consulted their safety by flight. A few barons of laudable fidelity and valour, who would not desert him, even in his necessity, were made captive. The king, though he by no means wanted spirit to defend himself, being at last attacked on every side by the earl of Gloucester's soldiers, fell to the ground by a blow from a stone; but who was the author of this deed is uncertain. Thus, when all around him were either taken or dispersed, he was compelled to yield to circumstances and become a captive. On which the truly noble earl of Gloucester commanded the king to be preserved uninjured, not suffering him to be molested, even with a reproach; and the person, whom he had just before fiercely attacked when dignified with the sovereignty, he now calmly protected when subdued; that, the tumults of anger and of joy being quieted, he might show kindness to his relation, and respect the dignity of the diadem in the captive. The citizens of Lincoln were slaughtered on all sides by the just indignation of the victors, and without commiseration on the part of the conquered, as they had been the origin and fomenters of this calamity.

§ 41. The king, according to the custom of such as are called captives, was presented to the empress, at Gloucester, by her brother, and afterwards conducted to Bristol. Here at first he was kept with every mark of honour, except the liberty of going at large: but in succeeding time, through the presumption of certain persons, who said openly and contumeliously, that it did not behove the earl to treat the king otherwise than they chose; and also, because it was reported, that, having either eluded or bribed his keepers, he had been found, more than once, beyond the appointed limits, more especially in the night time, he was confined with fetters.

§ 42. In the meanwhile, both the empress and the earl dealt by messengers with the legate his brother, that he should forthwith

---

[1] The joust signifies a contest between two persons, on horseback, with lances; each singling out his opponent.

[2] The passage here within brackets occurs only in E.

receive her into the church,[1] and to the kingdom, as the daughter of king Henry, to whom all England and Normandy had sworn allegiance. This year, the first Sunday in Lent happened on the fourteenth of the kalends of March [Feb. 16]. By means of negotiators on both sides, the business was so far forwarded, that they agreed to meet in conference, on an open plain on this side of Winchester. They assembled, therefore, on the third Sunday in Lent [March 2], a day dark and rainy, as though the fates would portend a woful change in this affair. The empress swore, and pledged her faith to the bishop, that all matters of importance in England, and especially the bestowing of bishoprics and abbeys, should be under his control, if he, with the holy church, would receive her as sovereign, and observe perpetual fidelity towards her. Her brother, Robert, earl of Gloucester, swore as she did, and pledged his faith for her, as did also Brian Fitz-Count, lord Marcher[2] of Wallingford, and Milo of Gloucester, afterwards earl of Hereford, with some others. Nor did the bishop hesitate to receive the empress as sovereign of England, and, together with certain of his party, to pledge his faith, that so long as she did not infringe the covenant, he would observe his fidelity to her. On the morrow, which was the fifth of the nones of March [March 3], a splendid procession being formed, she was received in the cathedral of Winchester; the bishop-legate conducting her on the right side, and Bernard bishop of St. David's on the left. There were present also, Alexander bishop of Lincoln, Robert of Hereford, Nigel of Ely, Robert of Bath: the abbots, Ingulf of Abingdon, Edward of Reading, Peter of Malmesbury, Gilbert of Gloucester, Roger of Tewkesbury, and some others. In a few days, Theobald, archbishop of Canterbury, came to the empress at Winchester, by invitation of the legate: but he deferred swearing fealty to her, deeming it beneath his reputation and character to change sides, till he had consulted the king. In consequence, he, and many other prelates, with some few of the laity, were allowed to visit Stephen and converse with him; and, graciously obtaining leave to submit to the exigency of the times, they embraced the sentiments of the legate. The empress passed Easter, which happened on the third of the kalends of April [March 30], at Oxford; the rest returned to their respective homes.

§ 43. On the second day after the octaves of Easter [April 7], a council began, with great parade, at Winchester, consisting of Theobald archbishop of Canterbury, all the bishops of England, and many abbots; the legate presiding. Such as were absent, accounted for it by messengers and letters. As I was present at the holding of this council, I will not deny posterity a true account of its proceedings: I perfectly remember that, on the same day, after the letters were read by which some excused their absence, the legate called the bishops apart, and discoursed with them in secret of his

---

[1] That is, as appears after, to acknowledge her publicly as their sovereign.

[2] Marchio. This latterly signified marquis in the sense we now use it; but in Malmesbury's time, and long after, it denoted a guardian of the borders: hence the lords marchers on the confines of Scotland and Wales; though it does not appear very clearly how this should apply to Wallingford.

design; then the abbots, and, lastly, the archdeacons were sum-moned. Of his intention nothing transpired publicly, though what was to be done engrossed the minds and conversation of all.

§ 44. On the third day of the week [April 8], the speech of the legate ran nearly to this effect: "That, by the condescension of the pope, he acted as his vicegerent in England: wherefore, by his authority, the clergy of England were assembled at this council, to deliberate on the peace of the country, which was exposed to immi-nent danger : that, in the time of king Henry, his uncle, England had been the peculiar abode of peace; so that, by the activity, and spirit, and care of that most excellent man, not only the natives, of whatever power or dignity, dared make no disturbance; but, by his example, each neighbouring king and prince, also, yielded to peace, and either persuaded, or compelled, his subjects to do the like ; moreover, that this king, some years before his death, had caused the whole realm of England, as well as the duchy of Normandy, to be engaged, by the oaths of all the bishops and barons, to his daughter, late the empress, (who was his only surviving issue by his former consort,) if he should fail of male offspring by the wife he had espoused from Lorrain : and adverse fortune," said he, "was envious of my most excellent uncle, and suffered him to die in Normandy without male issue. Therefore, as it seemed long to wait for a sovereign who delayed coming to England, (for she resided in Normandy,) we provided for the peace of the country, and my brother was allowed to reign. And although I gave myself as surety between him and God, that he would honour and advance the holy church, and uphold good, but abrogate evil laws : yet it grieves me to remember, it shames me to say, how he conducted himself in the kingdom; how justice ceased to be exerted against the daring; how all peace was annihilated, almost within the year : the bishops made captive, and compelled to give up their posses-sions ; the abbeys sold ; the churches robbed of their treasures ; the counsels of the abandoned regarded, while those of the virtuous were postponed, or totally despised. You know how often I addressed him, both by myself, and the bishops, more especially in the council held last year for that purpose, and that I gained by it nothing but odium. Every one who shall think rightly must be aware, that I ought to love my mortal brother, but that I should still more regard the cause of my immortal Father. Wherefore, since God has exercised his judgment on my brother, by permitting him, without my knowledge, to fall into the hands of the powerful, I have invited you all here to assemble by virtue of my legation, lest the kingdom should fall to decay through want of a sovereign. The case was yesterday agitated in private, before the major part of the English clergy, to whose right it principally pertains to elect the sovereign, and also to crown him. First, then, as is fitting, invoking God's assistance, we elect the daughter of that peaceful, that glorious, that rich, that good, that, in our times, incomparable king, as sovereign of England and Normandy, and promise her fidelity and support."

§ 45. When all present had either becomingly applauded his

sentiments, or by their silence assented thereto, he added : ." We
have despatched messengers for the Londoners, (who, from the importance of their city in England, are nobles, as it were,) to meet
us on this business : and have sent them a safe-conduct : and I
trust they will not delay their arrival beyond to-morrow : wherefore
let us give them indulgence till that time."

. § 46. On the fourth day of the week [April 9], the Londoners
came ; and being introduced to the council, urged their cause, so
far as to say, that, they were sent from the fraternity, as they call it,
of London, not to contend, but to entreat that their lord the king
might be liberated from captivity ; that all the barons who had long
since been admitted to their fellowship, most earnestly solicited
this of the lord legate and the archbishop, as well as of all the
clergy who were present. The legate answered them copiously and
eloquently : and, that their request might be the less complied with,
the speech of the preceding day was repeated, with the addition, that
it did not become the Londoners, who were considered, as the chief
people of England, in the light of nobles, to side with those persons
who had deserted their lord in battle ; by whose advice, the king
had dishonoured the holy church ; and who, in fact, only appeared to favour the Londoners, that they might drain them of
their money.

. § 47. In the meantime, a certain person, whose name, if I
rightly remember, was Christian, a clerk belonging to the queen, as
I heard, rose up, and held forth a paper to the legate. He, having
silently perused it, exalted his voice to the highest pitch, and said,
that it was informal, and improper to be recited in so great an
assembly, especially of dignified and religious persons. For, among
other offensive and singular points, the signature of a person was
affixed to it, who, in the preceding year, at a similar council, had
attacked the venerable bishops with opprobrious language. The
legate thus baffling him, the clerk was not wanting to his mission,
but, with notable confidence, read the letter in their hearing ; of
which this was the purport :—" The queen earnestly entreated the
whole clergy assembled, and especially the bishop of Winchester,
the brother of her lord, to restore the said lord to his kingdom,
whom abandoned persons, and even such as were under homage to
him, had cast into chains." To this suggestion, the legate answered
to the same effect as to the Londoners. These conferring together,
declared, that they would relate the decree of the council to their
townsmen, and give it their support, as far as they were able. On
the fifth day of the week the council broke up, many of the royal
party having been first excommunicated ; more especially William
Martel, who had formerly been cup-bearer to king Henry, and was
at that time butler to Stephen ; for he had sorely exasperated the
legate, by intercepting and pilfering much of his property.

. § 48. It was now a work of great difficulty to soothe the minds
of the Londoners ; for, though these matters, as I have said, were
agitated immediately after Easter, yet was it only a few days before
the Nativity of St. John [June 24] that they would receive the
empress. At that time, great part of England readily submitted to

her government; her brother Robert was assiduously employed in promoting her dignity by every becoming method; kindly addressing the nobility, making many promises, and intimidating the adverse party, or even, by messengers, exhorting them to peace; and, already, restoring justice and the law of the land, and tranquillity, throughout every district which favoured the empress : and it is sufficiently notorious, that if his party had trusted to Robert's moderation and wisdom, it would not afterwards have experienced so melancholy a reverse. The lord legate, too, appeared of laudable fidelity, in furthering the interests of the empress. But, behold! at the very moment when she imagined she should get immediate possession of all England, everything was changed. The Londoners, ever suspicious and murmuring among themselves, now burst out into open expressions of hatred; and, as it is reported, even laid wait for their sovereign and her nobles. Aware of, and escaping, this plot, they gradually retired from the city, without tumult, and in a certain military order. The empress was accompanied by the legate, and David king of Scotland, the heroine's uncle, together with her brother Robert, who then, as at every other time, shared her fortune; and, in short, all her partisans, to a man, escaped in safety. The Londoners learning their departure, flew to their residence, and plundered everything which they had left in their haste.

§ 49. Not many days after, a misunderstanding arose between the legate and the empress, which may be justly considered as the melancholy cause of every subsequent evil in England. How this happened, I will explain. King Stephen had a son named Eustace, begotten on the daughter of Eustace earl of Boulogne. For king Henry, the father of the empress, (that I may go back somewhat, to acquaint posterity with the truth of these transactions,) had given Mary, the sister of his wife, the mother of this lady, in marriage to the aforesaid earl, as he was of noble descent, and equally renowned for prudence and for valour. By Mary, Eustace had no issue except a daughter, called Matilda. When she became marriageable, after the death of her father, the same truly magnificent king gave her in wedlock to his nephew Stephen, and also procured, by his care, the county of Boulogne for him, as he had before conferred on him that of Moritol in Normandy. The legate had justly proposed that these counties should be bestowed on his nephew Eustace, whom I mentioned, so long as his father should remain in captivity. This the empress altogether opposed, and it is doubtful whether she had not even promised them to others. Offended at the repulse, he kept from her court many days; and though repeatedly sent for, persisted in refusing to go thither. In the meanwhile, he held a friendly conference with the queen, his brother's wife, at Guildford, and being wrought upon by her tears and concessions, bent his mind to the liberation of Stephen : he also absolved, without consulting the bishops, all those of the king's party whom he had excommunicated in the council. His complaints against the empress were disseminated through England : that she wished to seize his person; that she observed nothing which she had sworn to him; that all the barons of England had performed their engagements towards her, but that she had violated hers, as she knew not how to use her prosperity with moderation.

§ 50. To allay, if possible, these commotions, the earl of Gloucester, with a small retinue, proceeded to Winchester; but failing in his endeavours, he returned to Oxford, where his sister had for some time established her residence. She, therefore, understanding, as well from what she was continually hearing, as from what she then learnt from her brother, that the legate had no friendly dispositions towards her, proceeded to Winchester with such forces as she could muster. Being immediately admitted into the royal castle, she sent messengers to the bishop, probably with good intentions, requesting that, as she was upon the spot, he would come to her without delay. He, not thinking it safe to go, deceived the messengers by an evasive answer; merely saying, "I will prepare myself:" and immediately he sent for all such as he knew were well-disposed to the king. In consequence, almost all the earls of England came; for they were full of youth and levity, and preferred military enterprise to peace. Besides, many of them were ashamed at having deserted the king in battle, as has been said before; and thought to wipe off the ignominy of having fled, by attending this meeting. Few, however, attended the empress: there were, David king of Scotland, Robert earl of Gloucester, Milo of Hereford, and some barons: for Ranulph earl of Chester came late, and to no purpose. To comprise, therefore, a long series of events within narrow limits: the roads on every side of Winchester were watched by the queen and the earls who had come with her, lest supplies should be brought in to those who had sworn fidelity to the empress. The town of Andover, also, was burnt. On the west, therefore, necessaries were procured but scantily, and with difficulty; some persons found on the road being intercepted, and either killed or maimed: while on the east, every avenue towards London was crowded with supplies destined for the bishop and his party; Geoffrey[1] de Mandeville, who had now again revolted to them, (for formerly, after the capture of the king, he had sworn fidelity to the empress,) and the Londoners, lending every possible assistance, and omitting no circumstance which might distress the empress. The people of Winchester were, though secretly, inclined to her side; regarding the faith they had before pledged to her, although they had been, in some degree, compelled by the bishop to such a measure. In the meanwhile combustibles were hurled from the bishop's castle on the houses of the townspeople, (who, as I have said, rather wished success to the empress than the bishop,) which caught and burnt the whole abbey of nuns, within the city; and the monastery, which is called Hide, without the walls. Here was an image of our crucified Lord, wrought with a profusion of gold and silver and precious stones, through the pious solicitude of Cnut, who was formerly king, and presented it. This being seized by the flames and thrown to the ground, was afterwards stripped of its ornaments at the command of the legate himself: more than five

[1] MS. E. adds from "Geoffrey," to "empress, and."

hundred marks of silver, and thirty of gold, which were found on it,
served for a largess to the soldiers. The abbey of nuns at Warewell
was also burnt by one William de Ipres, an abandoned character,
who feared neither God nor man, because some of the partisans of
the empress had secured themselves within it.

§ 51. In the meantime, the earl of Gloucester, though suffering,
with his followers, by daily contests with the royalists, and though
circumstances turned out far beneath his expectation, yet ever
abstained from the burning of churches, notwithstanding he resided
in the vicinity of St. Swithun's. But unable to endure any longer
the disgrace of being, together with his party, almost besieged, and
seeing fortune inclining towards the enemy, he deemed it expedient
to yield to necessity; and, having marshalled his troops, he prepared
to depart. Sending his sister, therefore, and the rest in the vanguard,
that she might proceed without interruption, he himself retreated
gently, with a chosen few, who had spirit enough not to be alarmed
at a multitude. The earls immediately pursued him, and as he
thought it disgraceful and beneath his dignity to fly, and was the
chief object of universal attack, he was made captive. The rest,
especially the chiefs, proceeded on their destined journey, and, with
the utmost precipitation, reached Devizes. Thus they departed
from Winchester on the day of the Exaltation of the Holy Cross
[Sept. 14], which at that time happened on a Sunday, having come
thither a few days before the Assumption of the holy mother of God
[Aug. 15]. It appeared to some rather miraculous, and was matter
of general conversation in England, that the king on the Sunday of
the Purification of our Lady [Feb. 2], and the earl on the Sunday
of the Exaltation of the life-imparting Cross, should each experience
a similar fate. This, however, was truly worthy of remark and
admiration, that no one, on this mischance, ever beheld the earl
of Gloucester either dispirited or dejected in countenance; for he
breathed too high a consciousness of dignity, to subject himself to
the caprice of fortune; and although he was at first invited by
soothing measures, and afterwards assailed by threats, he never
consented to treat of his liberation, except with the privity of his
sister. At last the affair was thus decided: that the king and
himself should be liberated on equal terms; no condition being
proposed, except that each might defend his party, to the utmost
of his abilities, as before. These matters, after repeated and long
discussion, from the Exaltation of the Holy Cross to the festival of
All Saints [Sept. 14—Nov. 1], then came to a suitable conclusion; and on the latter day, the king was released. On the
same day he left his queen, and son, and two of the nobility, at
Bristol, as sureties for the liberation of the earl; and came with the
utmost speed to Winchester, where the earl, now brought from
Rochester, whither he had first been taken, was at this time confined. The third day after, when the king came to Winchester, the
earl departed, leaving there on that day his son William, as a pledge,
till the queen should be released. Performing with quick despatch
the journey to Bristol, he liberated the queen, on whose return,
William, the earl's son, was set free. It is, moreover, sufficiently

notorious, that although during the whole of his captivity and of
the following months till Christmas, he was enticed, by numberless
and magnificent promises, to revolt from his sister, yet he always
deemed his fraternal affection of greater importance than any promise which could be made him : for leaving his property and his
castles, which he might have quietly enjoyed, he continued unceasingly near the empress at Oxford, where, as I have said before, she
fixed her residence and held her court.

§ 52. In the meantime, the legate, a prelate of unbounded spirit,
who was never inclined to leave incomplete what he had once purposed, summoned by his legatine authority a council at Westminster,
on the octaves of St. Andrew [Dec. 7]. I cannot relate the transactions of this council with that certainty with which I did those of the
former, as I was not present. We have heard, that a letter was then
read from the sovereign pope, in which he gently rebuked the legate
for not endeavouring to release his brother ; but that he forgave him
his former transgression, and earnestly exhorted him to attempt his
liberation by any mode, whether ecclesiastical or secular : that the
king himself entered the council, and complained to the reverend
assembly, that his own subjects had both made captive, and nearly
killed him by the indignities they inflicted on him, who had never
refused them justice.   That the legate himself, too, with great eloquence, endeavoured to extenuate the odium of his own conduct ;
saying, that, in truth, he had received the empress, not from inclination, but necessity ; for that while his brother's overthrow was yet
recent, (all the earls being either dispersed or waiting the issue of
events in suspense,) she had surrounded Winchester with her party;
that she had obstinately persevered in breaking every promise she
had made pertaining to the right of the churches ; and that he had
it from unquestionable authority, that she and her partisans had
not only had designs on his dignity, but even on his life ; that, however, God in his mercy had caused matters to fall out contrary to
her hopes, so that he himself had escaped destruction, and rescued
his brother from captivity ; that he commanded, therefore, on the
part of God and of the pope, that they should strenuously assist the
king, who had been anointed by the will of the people, and with the
approbation of the holy see : but that such as disturbed the peace,
in favour of the countess of Anjou, should be excommunicated, with
the exception of herself, who was sovereign of the Angevins.

§ 53. I do not say, that this speech was kindly received by all the
clergy, though certainly no one opposed it ; for all the clergy bridled
their tongues, either through fear or through reverence.   There was
one layman sent from the empress, who openly forbade the legate,
by the faith which he had pledged to her, to ordain anything, in
that council, repugnant to her honour ; and said, that he had made
oath to the empress not to assist his brother, unless, perchance, by
sending him twenty horsemen at the utmost ; that her coming to
England had been effected by his frequent letters ; that her taking
the king, and holding him in captivity, had been done principally
by his connivance.   The advocate affirmed these and many other
circumstances, with great harshness of language, and by no means

sparing the legate. However, he could not be prevailed upon, by any force of argument, to lay aside his animosity; for, as I have said before, he was an active perseverer in what he had once taken in hand. This year, therefore, (the misfortunes of which I have briefly related,) was fatal, and nearly destructive to England; during which, though conceiving that she might now, perhaps, experience some little respite, yet she became again involved in calamity, and, unless God's mercy shall shortly come to her relief, must there long continue.

§ 54. It seems fitting that I should commence the transactions of this year, which is the year of our Lord one thousand one hundred and forty-three, with certain events which were unnoticed in the former; and, at the same time, briefly recapitulate what has been said, in various places, of Robert earl of Gloucester, son of king Henry, and submit it, thus arranged, to the consideration of the reader. For, as he was the first to espouse the just defence of his sister, so did he persevere with unshaken constancy in her cause, without remuneration; I say, without remuneration, because some of her supporters, either, following the course of fortune, are changed with its revolutions, or, having already obtained considerable benefits, fight for justice under expectation of still further recompence: Robert alone, or nearly alone, uninfluenced by such considerations, was never swayed, as will appear hereafter, either by hope of advantage or fear of loss. Let no one, therefore, suspect me of adulation, if I relate these matters circumstantially; for I shall make no sacrifice to favour; but pure historical truth, without any stain of falsehood, shall be handed down for the information of posterity.

§ 55. It has been related of the earl, how, first[1] of all the nobility, after David king of Scotland, he confirmed by oath his fealty to his sister, the empress, for the kingdom of England and the duchy of Normandy, in the presence of his father Henry: there having been some contention, as I have said, between him and Stephen earl of Boulogne, afterwards king of England, who should swear first; Robert alleging the preference of a son, Stephen the dignity of a nephew.

§ 56. It has been recorded, too, what reasonable causes, from December, when his father died, till after the ensuing Easter, detained him, in Normandy, from coming immediately into England to avenge his sister's injuries: and when at last he did come, with what just deliberation, and with what proviso, he consented to do homage to the king; and how justly, in the following year and thenceforward, he abjured it.

§ 57. Nor has his second arrival in England from Normandy, after his father's death, with his sister, been omitted; where, relying on the favour of God and his innate courage, he ventured himself, as into a desert full of wild beasts, though scarcely accompanied by one hundred and forty horsemen. Neither has it been unnoticed, that, amid such tumult of war, while anxious watch was kept on all sides, he boldly came to Bristol with only twelve horse-

---

[1] This seems an oversight: as he had before related, more than once, that Stephen preceded Robert in taking the oath to Matilda.

men, having committed his sister to safe custody, as he supposed, at
Arundel; nor with what prudence, at that time, he received her from
the very midst of her enemies, and afterwards advanced her in all
things to the utmost of his power; ever busied on her account, and
neglecting his own interest to secure hers, while some persons,
taking advantage of his absence, plundered his possessions on every
side; and, lastly, urged by what necessity, namely, to rescue his
son-in-law, whom the king had besieged, he engaged in an hazardous
conflict, and took the king prisoner. This fortunate event, however,
was somewhat obscured by his own capture at Winchester, as I
have recorded in the transactions of the former year; though, by
the grace of God, he showed himself, not so much an object of
commiseration, as of praise, in that capture. For, when he saw
that the royalist earls were so persevering in the pursuit that the
business could not be gotten through without loss on his part, he
sent forward all those for whom he was under apprehension, and
more especially the empress. When they had proceeded far
enough to escape in safety, he followed leisurely, that the retreat
might not resemble a flight, and received the attack of the pursuers himself; thus purchasing, by his own detention, the liberty of
his friends. And now even at the moment of his capture, no one,
as I have said above, perceived him either dispirited, or humbled
in language; he seemed so far to tower above fortune, that he
compelled his persecutors, for I am loth to call them enemies, to
respect him. Wherefore the queen, though she might have
remembered that her husband had been fettered by his command,
yet never suffered fetters of any kind to be put upon him, nor pre-
sumed on her dignity to treat him dishonourably. And finally, at
Rochester, for thither he was conducted, he went freely whither he
pleased to the churches below the castle, and conversed with whom
he chose, the queen only being present: after her departure he was
held in free custody in the keep, and such forethought and sense of
security had he, that, getting money from his vassals in Kent, he
bought some valuable horses, which were both serviceable and
beneficial to him afterwards.

§ 58. The earls, and those whose business it was to speak of
such matters, at first, tried if he would allow of the king and himself being liberated on equal terms. Though his countess, Mabil,
out of solicitude for her beloved husband, would have embraced
these terms the moment she heard them, being, through conjugal
affection, bent on his liberation, yet he, in his wiser policy, refused;
asserting that a king and an earl were not of equal importance;
however, if they would allow all who had been taken with him, or
for him, to be set at liberty, to this he might consent. But the
earls and other royalists would not assent to these terms; they
were anxious, indeed, for the king's liberty, but not at their own
pecuniary loss; for earl Gilbert had taken William of Salisbury;
and William de Ipres had taken Humphry de Bohun; and others
had made such captures as they could, at Winchester, greedily
expecting large sums for their ransom.

§ 59. Next attacking the earl another way, they anxiously endeavoured to seduce him with magnificent promises. Would he go over to the king's side, and dismiss his sister, he should govern the whole country; all things should await his decision; the crown should be the only distinction between him and the king; over all others he should rule as he pleased. The earl rejected these unbounded promises, with a memorable reply, which I wish posterity to hear and to admire. "I am not my own master," said he, "but am in another's power; when I shall see myself at my own disposal, I promise to do everything which reason dictates on the matter you propound."

§ 60. Irritated and incensed at this, when they could do nothing by fair means, they began to threaten that they would send him over sea to Boulogne, and keep him in perpetual bondage till death. Still, however, with a serene countenance, dispelling their threats, he firmly and truly protested that he feared nothing less: for he relied on the spirit of the countess, his wife, and the courage of his partisans, who would immediately send the king into Ireland, if they heard of any foul deed perpetrated against himself.

§ 61. A month elapsed in these transactions; so difficult a work was it to effect the liberation of princes whom fortune had fettered with her chain. But, at length, the supporters of the empress having conferred together, entreated the earl by frequent messages, that as he could not do what he would, according to the comic writer, he would do what he could; that he should allow, therefore, the king and himself to be set at liberty on equal terms. "Otherwise," said they, "we fear lest the earls, inspirited by the consciousness of their great and most distinguished exploit in making you captive, should attack us one by one, reduce our castles, and even make an attempt upon your sister."

§ 62. Robert, wrought upon at length, assented to the proposal of the legate and archbishop, but still on condition that none of the castles, or territories, should be restored, which had come under the power of the empress, or of any of her adherents, since the capture of the king; but he could not by any means obtain the release of his friends, as he had given offence to some persons in rejecting, with a kind of superciliousness, their magnificent promises with respect to the government of the whole kingdom. And as they were extremely anxious that, for the royal dignity, the king should be first set at liberty, and then the earl; when he demurred to this, the legate and the archbishop made oath, that if the king, after his own liberation, refused to release the earl, they would forthwith deliver themselves up into Robert's power, to be conducted wherever he pleased.

§ 63. Nor did he rest here; for his sagacious mind discovered an additional security. It might fall out, that the king, as often happens, listening to evil counsel, would consider the detention of his brother and of the archbishop as of very little consequence, so that he himself were at his ease. He demanded, therefore, from them both, separately, instruments, with their seals, addressed to the pope, to the following effect : " That the sovereign pope was to understand, that they, for the liberation of the king and the peace of the kingdom, had bound themselves to the earl by this covenant, that, if the king refused to liberate him after his own release, they themselves would willingly surrender to his custody.   Should it, therefore, come to this calamitous issue, they earnestly entreated, (what it would well become the papal goodness voluntarily to per-form,) that he would release them, who were his suffragans, as well as the earl, from unjustifiable durance." There was something more to the same effect.

§ 64. These writings, received from both prelates, Robert de-posited in a place of safety, and came to Winchester with them and a great company of the barons.   The king also, as has been before observed, coming thither soon after, had a friendly interview with the earl.   But although he, and all the earls present, eagerly busied themselves in bringing over Robert to their wishes, yet, " firm as a rock amid the ocean in his resistance," he rendered their attempts abortive, or refuted them by argument.   He affirmed, that it was neither reasonable nor natural, that he should desert his sister, whose cause he had justly espoused, not for any benefit to himself, nor so much out of dislike to the king, as regard to his oath, which, they also ought to remember, it was impiety to violate; especially when he called to mind, that he had been enjoined by the pope to respect the oath he had taken to his sister in the presence of his father.   Thus failing of peace, they severally departed.

§ 65. The reason why I have not incorporated these events with the transactions of the former year, is, that I did not then know them ; for I have always dreaded to transmit anything to posterity, through my narrative, the truth of which I could not perfectly vouch for.   What, then, I have to relate of the present year, will com-mence as follows :

§ 66. The respective parties of the empress and of the king con-ducted themselves with quiet forbearance from Christmas to Lent [March 4], anxious rather to preserve their own, than to ravage the possessions of others.   The king went to a distant part of the king-dom, for the purpose of quelling some disturbances.   Lent coming on, gave all a respite from war ; in the midst of which, the empress came with her party to Devizes, where her secret designs were de-bated.   So much of them however transpired, that it was known that all her partisans had agreed to send for the earl of Anjou, who was most interested in the defence of the inheritance of his wife and children in England. Men of respectability were, therefore, despatched, and such as might fitly execute a business of such magnitude.

§ 67. Not long after, in the Easter holidays, the king, while meditating, as it is said, some harsh measures, was detained by an acute disease at Northampton ; so severe, indeed, that he was re-ported, almost throughout England, as being at the point of death.

His sickness continued till after Pentecost [June 7], when returning health gradually restored him.

§ 68. In the meantime, the messengers returning from Anjou, related the result of their mission to the empress and the princes in a second council, held at Devizes on the octaves of Pentecost [June 14]. They said, that the earl of Anjou, in some measure, favoured the mission of the nobility; but that among them all, he was only well acquainted with the earl of Gloucester, of whose prudence and fidelity, greatness of mind and industry, he had long since had proof. Were he to make a voyage to him, he would, as far as he was able, accede to his wishes; but that all other persons would expend their labour in passing and re-passing to no purpose.

§ 69. The hopes of all the assembly being thus excited, they entreated that the earl would condescend to undertake this task, on account of the inheritance of his sister and nephews. At first he excused himself, alleging the difficulty of the business; the perilous journey, beset with enemies, on either side of the sea; that it would be attended with danger to his sister; as, in his absence, those persons would be hardly able to defend her, who, distrusting even the strength of their own party, had nearly deserted her during his captivity. Yielding at length to the general desire, he demanded hostages, especially from those who were considered as the chief persons, to be taken with him into Normandy, and to be pledges, as well to the earl of Anjou, as to the empress; and that all, continuing at Oxford, should unite in defending her from injury to the utmost while he was absent. His propositions were eagerly approved, and hostages given him to be conducted into Normandy.

§ 70. Robert, therefore, bidding adieu to his sister, and taking with him his hostages and some light troops, proceeded by safe marches to Wareham, which town and castle he had, long since, entrusted to his eldest son, William. There, soon after the festival of St. John [June 24], committing himself, by the grace of God, to the ocean, with such vessels as he then possessed, he weighed anchor. When they were about mid-sea, a tempest arose, and all, except two, were dispersed; some were driven back, and some carried beyond their destination: two only, in one of which was the earl with his most faithful adherents, keeping their course, arrived in the wished for port. Proceeding thus to Caen, he sent messengers for the earl of Anjou. The earl came without reluctance, but stated his difficulties, and those not a few, to the object of the embassy, when proposed to him; among others, that he should be detained from coming into England by the rebellion of many castles in Normandy. This circumstance delayed the earl of Gloucester's return longer than he had intended: for, that he might deprive the earl of Anjou of every excuse, he assisted him in subduing ten castles in Normandy, the[1] names of which were, Tenerchebrei, Seithilaret, Bri-

---

[1] To the end of the sentence from E.

chesart, Alani, Bastonborg, Triveres, Castel de Vira, Plaseiz, Vilers, Moretoin. Yet, even by this activity, he furthered the end of his mission but little. The earl of Anjou stated fresh causes, as the former were done away, to excuse his coming into England. Indeed, as a very singular favour, he permitted his eldest son, by the empress, to accompany his uncle to England, by whose presence the chiefs might be encouraged to defend the cause of the lawful heir. The youth is named Henry, after his grandfather; may he hereafter resemble him in happiness and in power.

§ 71. In England, in the meantime, the king, seizing the opportunity of the earl's absence, came unexpectedly to Wareham, and finding it slightly garrisoned, he burnt and plundered the town, and immediately got possession of the castle also. Not content with this (as he saw fortune inclined to favour him), three days before the festival of St. Michael, by an unexpected[1] chance, he burnt the city of Oxford, and laid siege to the castle, in which was the empress with her household troops. This he did with such determined resolution, that he declared no hope of advantage or fear of loss should induce him to depart, till the castle was delivered up, and the empress surrendered to his power. Shortly after, all the nobility of the empress's party, ashamed at being absent from their sovereign in violation of their compact, assembled in large bodies at Wallingford, with the determination of attacking the king, if he would risk a battle in the open plain; but they had no intention of assailing him within the city, as the earl of Gloucester had so fortified it with ditches that it appeared impregnable, unless by fire.

§ 72. These rumours becoming prevalent in Normandy, Robert earl of Gloucester hastened his return. He embarked, therefore, somewhat more than three hundred horsemen on board fifty-two vessels; to these were added two which he took at sea on his return. God's grace so singularly favoured his pious resolution, that not one ship out of so great a number was separated, but all nearly close together, or gently proceeding one before the other, ploughed the calm bosom of the deep. Nor did the waves violently dash against the fleet, but rather seemed subserviently to further their passage; like that most beautiful appearance of the sea, when the wave, gradually approaching, gently breaks upon the shore. Thus making the port of Wareham, these favoured vessels restored the earl and all his companions to the wishes of their friends.

§ 73. He had, at first, thought of landing at Southampton, at once to wreak his vengeance, both on its inhabitants and on their lord; but this resolution was changed through the repeated entreaties of the Vituli, who were fearful that their dearest connexions, who resided at Southampton, would be involved in the general calamity. These are a kind of mariners, who are known by the name of

---

[1] The garrison having sallied out against him, he suddenly passed a ford, which was not generally known, and repelling the enemy, entered the town with them. Gesta Regis Stephani, 958.

Vituli; and as they are his faithful adherents, he thought fit to listen to their petitions, and desist from his design. Again, it appeared more dignified to return to the place whence he had departed, and to recover by force what he had lost by a similar mode. Reducing, therefore, immediately the port and town, he laid siege to the castle; which by its strength stimulated the spirit, not to call it obstinacy, of the king's choicest troops who defended it. Yet, nevertheless, soon after, the garrison, shaken in their resolution by the engines of the earl, and greatly alarmed, begged a truce, that, as is the custom of the military, they might demand assistance from the king; consenting to deliver up the castle, if he refused to come by a certain day. This, though he was possessed with the utmost impatience to become master of the fortress, was very agreeable to the earl, as it led him to suppose it might draw off Stephen from besieging his sister. We may imagine what firmness of mind this man possessed, who, with little more than three hundred horsemen, and, as yet, joined by no succours in England, could undauntedly await the king, who was reported to have more than a thousand; for many persons had joined the siege, not so much through dislike to the empress, as through the hope of plunder.

§ 74. However, when it was certified that the king refused assistance to the besieged at Wareham, the earl, pertinaciously keeping up the attack, got possession of the castle, and with the same celerity subdued the island of Portland, which they had fortified, as well as a third castle, called Lulleworth, which belonged to a certain chamberlain, called William of Glastonbury, who had lately revolted from the empress. Robert, then, at the beginning of Advent [Nov. 29], summoned the whole of Matilda's partisans to Cirencester: where, all resolving to afford their sovereign every possible assistance, they meditated a march to Oxford, courageously determining to give the king battle, unless he retreated. But as they were on their route, the pleasing account reached them, that the empress had escaped from the blockaded castle at Oxford, and was now at Wallingford in security. Turning aside thither, then, at the suggestion of their sovereign, (since the soldiers who had remained at her departure, after delivering up the castle, had gone away without molestation, and the holidays admonished them to repose awhile,) they resolved to abstain from battle, and retired to their homes.

HERE ENDS THE THIRD BOOK OF MALMESBURY'S HISTORY OF HIS OWN TIMES.

§ 75. I would very willingly subjoin the manner of the empress's liberation, did I know it to a certainty; for it is undoubtedly one of God's manifest miracles. This, however, is sufficiently notorious, that, through fear of the earl's approach, many of the besiegers at Oxford stole away, wherever they were able, and the rest remitted their vigilance, and kept not so good a look-out as before ; more anxious for their own safety, in case it came to a battle, than bent on the destruction of others.[1]

But these matters, with God's permission, shall be more largely treated in the following volume.

[1] Some MSS. (C. D. G. K. L 2.) after "others" read, "This circumstance being remarked by the townsmen, the empress, with only four soldiers, made her escape through a small postern, and passed the river. Afterwards, as necessity sometimes, and indeed almost always, discovers means and ministers courage, she went to Abingdon on foot, and thence reached Wallingford on horseback. But this I purpose describing more fully, if, by God's permission, I shall ever learn the truth of it from those who were present :"—and omit "But these matters, &c."